AND GLADLY TEACH

Bliss Perry

And
GLADLY TEACH

Reminiscences

BY

BLISS PERRY

And gladly wolde he lerne, and gladly teche.
Chaucer, *The Prologue*

Boston and New York

HOUGHTON MIFFLIN COMPANY
The Riverside Press Cambridge

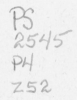

The Riverside Press
CAMBRIDGE · MASSACHUSETTS
PRINTED IN THE U.S.A.

TO

MY SISTER

GRACE PERRY

PREFACE

I HAVE had a long and exceptionally happy career as a teacher at Williams, Princeton, and Harvard. It began before I was twenty-one, and ended at seventy, for I did not wish to have it said of me, as was once remarked of a venerable Oxford don who refused to retire, that he had all the Christian virtues except resignation.

This term of service was occasionally broken: by two years of graduate study in Germany, one year of lecturing in various universities of France, and ten years devoted to editing the *Atlantic Monthly* — although in the first of these ten years, and the last two, I was carrying college work at the same time. I have never travelled very far from the beaten paths in America and Europe — except on an occasional fishing trip — but I have had the good fortune to know many interesting persons, in and out of my own profession. I have written many books. They might be better, but they were as good as I knew how to make them.

All this is pleasant enough in recollection in one's seventy-fifth year, and yet why write about it? Was not Sir Leslie Stephen mistaken in thinking that there never was a dull autobiography? It seems to me that I have read many such. Nevertheless I feel now like recording some memories, with or without excuse. One can always claim, of course, that he is writing reminiscences for the benefit of his grandchildren, but I fear that my grandchildren will be too busy earning a living to care whether Grandfather did or did not know Mark Hopkins and

Mark Twain and Woodrow Wilson. Indeed, as far as my observation has gone, the grandchildren of men of letters seldom read any of their grandfather's books.

A better audience than one's family may perhaps be found in the members of one's own profession. I once asked my colleague Edward Channing if he were conscious, in the moment of composition, of shaping his sentences for any particular group of readers. 'Certainly,' said the historian; 'I always write for my former graduate students.' We cannot know what Macaulay and Carlyle — who never had any graduate students — would have thought of Channing's answer. It might have amused them. Yet there is certainly something to be said for neglecting the 'general reader' and addressing your pages directly to the professional brethren who already understand you and your theme. I have taught thousands of students who seemed interested in what I had to say, but they may not be aware of the startling changes in the conditions of college teaching in the United States during the last half-century. The Williams, Princeton, and Harvard men of the present generation have little conception of the curious picture presented by those institutions when I first knew them; and it may conceivably amuse some of my old pupils to see how I turned from a collector of birds and butterflies, and from plans for the study of medicine, into a teacher of literature, and what accidents and odds of good and evil fortune befell me on the way.

Of one thing I am sure. I could never say, as President Eliot did when I used to beg him to write his autobiography: 'I am not interested in the past. I am interested in the future.' In his very latest years, it is true, and especially at the Saturday Club, Mr. Eliot often dropped into reminiscent talk to which I listened with delight; but when he was on his feet and facing a public audience, his favorite themes were the education and religion and society of the future. He was a serene and superb figure; a far greater man, I imagine, than Thackeray; but I wish he might have shared Thackeray's fondness for sitting on the rear seat of the stage-coach, facing backwards, so that he might watch the road over which he had come. In that case Mr. Eliot might have forgotten the future for a little while, and written that autobiography!

Fortunately enough, neither genius like Thackeray's nor greatness like Eliot's is an essential factor in this business of telling what has happened to oneself. But it is essential, surely, to feel the fascination of the past, to try to reconstruct in memory that infinitesimal portion of it which has affected one's own experience: and it is certainly advisable — though extraordinarily difficult in practice — that an autobiography should tell the truth. Not, thank Heaven, the whole truth or the whole of one's performances: that swift reversal of the revolving film of consciousness must be left to drowning men.

                                                    B. P.

CONTENTS

ILLUSTRATIONS

AND GLADLY TEACH

I

'THE BUTTERFLY BOY'

I will dare to say, that this Boy lives a merrier Life, and wears more of that Herb called Hearts-ease in his Bosom, than he that is clad in Silk and Velvet; but we will proceed in our Discourse.

JOHN BUNYAN, *The Pilgrim's Progress*

'MAY God forgive me,' wrote Sir Walter Scott in his *Journal*, 'for thinking that anything can be made out of a schoolmaster.' There is nevertheless a good deal of the schoolmaster in the Perry blood. My father was Arthur Latham Perry, of Williams College, who has been described so charmingly in his son Carroll's book, *A Professor of Life*.

Father was descended from the Reverend John Perry, of Farnborough, Essex, who died in 1621. His son and grandson, both named John, were weavers in London and emigrated to Watertown, Massachusetts, in 1666, shortly after the Great Fire. In 1718 the Perrys took up farms in Worcester, and it was from Worcester that my grandfather Baxter Perry went to Harvard College, like two of his brothers. He was graduated in 1817, and proceeded to Andover Theological Seminary. He married Lydia Gray, of those Scotch-Irish Grays who had come from Ulster to New England in 1718. Settled as a Congregational minister in Lyme, New Hampshire, just north of Hanover, Baxter Perry died there of brain fever a few months before my father was born. This was in 1830. The parish allowed the widow the use of the brick parsonage for a while, and gave her one hundred dollars in money. When she died, a half-century later, she still had that one hundred dollars in the savings bank. She was a tall, gaunt woman with severe blue eyes, and had been in her youth a school-teacher.

She had four children. Her two boys put themselves through Thetford Academy by working for neighboring farmers. Baxter went to Middlebury College and became a lawyer in Boston. Arthur, drawn by the fame of Mark Hopkins, came down the Connecticut River, over the Hoosac Mountain by stage-coach, and arrived at Williams — a powerfully built, black-haired, poorly dressed, and very serious-minded freshman — in 1848. Slowly he made his mark. He liked to relate, long afterward, how President Hopkins, hearing him debate in his junior year, picked him for a future professor at Williams. When he was graduated in 1852 he wore upon the Commencement stage a pair of badly patched shoes, but it may be hazarded that his Metaphysical Oration on 'The Ideal Theory' held the audience. He taught school one year in Washington, D.C., and then Dr. Hopkins called him back to Williams, at a salary which the great Doctor promised should soon be one thousand dollars. He was made a Professor in 1854. For a few years he taught German, in addition to the work of his chair in History and Political Economy, and at Williams he remained for the rest of his life.

In 1856 he married Mary Smedley, daughter of Dr. James Smedley, of Williamstown. The Smedleys had come from Colchester, Connecticut, as soon as the French and Indian wars were over, and had been among the first settlers of the town. Captain Nehemiah Smedley had led a company at the battle of Bennington, only twenty miles from his farm, in 1777. 'We will see who is going to *own* this farm,' said the Captain. His Colonel, who commanded the Berkshire troops on that hot August day, was Benjamin Simonds, who as a boy of twenty had been taken prisoner at the surrender of Fort Massachusetts to the French and Indians under Rigaud de Vaudreuil in 1746 and carried to Canada. The Colonel's daughter Rachel was the first white child born in Williamstown; and Colonel Simonds and Captain Nehemiah Smedley were the two great-grandfathers of my mother.

The Colonel's portrait, painted by W. Jennys in 1796, hangs in the Perry homestead. He had beautiful grave lips and a significantly square jaw. 'A firm supporter of his country's independence' is the modest inscription upon his tombstone; and the Hessians in the battle of Bennington may not have liked his looks. I have often thought of him when gazing at the portrait of Rigaud de Vaudreuil in the National Gallery at London: a slender, delicate, high-bred figure in blue velvet and gold braid. I was never quite sure that it was *our* Rigaud de Vaudreuil, but last summer I grew rather excited in comparing this portrait with the Colonel's, and exclaimed to the solitary attendant in the Gallery:

'Do you see that fellow in blue velvet? He was the man who commanded seven hundred French and Indians and captured my great-great-grandfather in a little log fort in Massachusetts and kept him prisoner in Canada for a year. Now in a fair fight Colonel Simonds could have taken that Frenchman and snapped him over his knee!'

'Really,' said the attendant.

By the middle of the nineteenth century the Smedleys had slipped back a little in prosperity and prominence in

town affairs. Deacon James, my grandfather, was a pillar
of the Congregational Church and a passionate lover of
Williams College; he attended seventy-five Commencements. He had had only his freshman year at Williams,
and then transferred to the Berkshire Medical School at
Pittsfield — then affiliated with the college — where he
was graduated in 1829. But he always loved the scraps of
Latin remembered from that one year. He would greet his
grandsons with a stentorian '*Quid habes te, hodie?*' to
which we would respond '*Bene, bene!*'

In a worldly sense, the Deacon never got on. He prac-
tised medicine for a few years, but suffered from dyspepsia
and from an inability to decide which of two patients he
ought to visit first on his morning round. Usually he
cracked and ate a quart of butternuts while trying to make
up his mind. His friend Dr. Sabin soon got most of the
local practice, and Dr. Smedley moved to a farm on South
Street, at the foot of Stone Hill, where he raised small
fruits for the market. The brick house and farm were
owned by his wife, Lucy Bridges, granddaughter of
Colonel Simonds. Three of their four sons served in the
Civil War, and there were two very pretty daughters, my
mother being the eldest of the children.

Grandfather had an uncanny skill in raising and grafting
fruit, but otherwise he had no scientific interests and he
never read anything except the Bible, the *Missionary
Herald*, the *New York Observer*, and the weekly *Springfield
Republican*. He was an eloquent and endless talker. The
happiest summer of his life had been spent as a 'colporteur'
for the Bible Society, riding with religious books in his
saddle-bags up and down Vermont, addressing churches
on Sundays and leading morning prayers at the farm-

houses where he was entertained. His facility and ingenuity in this exercise of devotion were extraordinary. His grandchildren, shifting their weary little knees on the kitchen floor and watching the tall clock, calculated that he usually prayed twenty-two minutes — except twice a year, on the day of the College Commencement and the day when he took us on the annual huckleberry party to East Mountain. On these occasions, by the skilful omission or merging of the more remote missionary stations, his petitions were concluded in precisely eleven minutes.

He was full of antique precepts for farming. When we boys assembled each year to help with the haying, he would direct us gravely to 'rake a raking two rakings wide' as we followed the wagon. Uncle Will, his bachelor son who had returned from the War a semi-invalid and lived with the old folks, used to resent his father's undeviating pattern of rules, and would whisper to us that it was just 'wheelbarrow and sheepskin.' This phrase, which passed into a family proverb, had its origin in Grandfather's ritual in feeding corn to the hens. He would invariably spread a sheepskin on the bottom boards of his wheelbarrow, and then, taking his seat with his back to the wheel and holding a shovel with blade upright between his knees, proceed to scrape the ears of corn against the blade of the shovel, while the chickens swarmed around him with tumultuous delight. For all I could see, it was an adroit and congenial method of feeding hens, but in the eyes of Uncle Will it was sheer pedantry.

Perhaps Grandmother Smedley had her rituals also, but they were never upon her tongue. I always picture her as sitting tranquilly in her rocking-chair by the northwest window of the sitting-room, looking out over her lovely flower-garden toward the road. Like most farmers' wives in the old days, she did all the domestic work of the household, but she gave the impression, not of being busy at it, but of having already performed it with light-footed efficiency. She was a tiny person, still wearing her grey hair in ringlets which did not detract in the least from her appearance of quiet dignity. She had brought up six children, had steadied her emotional husband in his recurrent moods of depression and failure, and now sat listening to his flow of talk with an inscrutable smile upon her face. She kept the family purse in a drawer of the old dark highboy in her bedroom, and there was always a little money in it, though where the money came from — except from small sales in the currant, plum, and grape seasons — no one ever knew. To her grandchildren she was an adorable person: gracious, hospitable, self-effacing, delicately reticent, and with a mysterious silent sweetness like that of the yellow rosebuds which she seemed always to be watching from her window.

Her daughter Mary, my mother, inherited her smile and her tranquillity of soul, though Mary was far more of a talker and a laugher. She was twenty-three when she was married — after a year or two of school-teaching — and unless the daguerreotypes are wrong she already possessed that serene beauty which she never lost. Her husband, the Professor, was twenty-six. He bought a story-and-a-half white house on the west side of Spring Street, where the Bank now stands. On the lot directly opposite was built in 1867 a big brick public school, but in the eighteen-fifties and sixties Spring Street was a quiet country lane with no shops and only a dozen very simple houses. There was no village water supply, and the street took its name from Bill Walden's famous spring, where many households drew their drinking-water. The Perry house was shaded by tall yellow locusts on the north and by cherry and maple trees in the front yard. There was a barn, and a big vegetable garden stretching westward up the hill. Father was without covetousness except for land, but in 1872, having bought several acres on the hilltop now called Grace Court, he moved the Spring Street house up the hill, and doubling its size, built the present Perry homestead. It stood then quite in the open fields, almost the only building on the beeline from West College to Stone Hill.

But all of us children except the youngest were born in the white house on Spring Street, first a son, Gray, who died in infancy, then sister Grace, followed by five boys: Bliss, Arthur, Walter, Carroll, and Lewis. To make good measure, two orphaned Smedley cousins, Perry and Mary, were added to this noisy and cheerful company. Father, in one of his analytical moments and to the intense amusement of his older children, once declared that Mother, like many of the Smedleys, lacked 'mercantile sagacity.' But somehow she managed to feed and clothe and entertain and comfort her big brood, and to steer the sometimes unruly Professor without letting him know whose hand was at the wheel. If this was not the 'mercantile' type of sagacity, it was something infinitely more rare and fine.

I was born on November 25, 1860. Thoreau's *Journal* for that day noted: 'Very cold and blustering. Winter weather has come suddenly this year.' Probably it was even worse in Williamstown than in Concord, and my life-long dread of winter may have dated from my first breath. I was named after Mr. and Mrs. F. R. Bliss, of New Haven.

They had come from Berkshire County and were intimate friends of Father and Mother.

None of the Perry children showed dangerous signs of precocity. I visited Boston on my third birthday, and remember standing on a cane-seated chair and weeping bitterly for Williamstown. We older children must have been vaguely aware of the War, for I recall a neighbor's son coming to the door with the news that his father had just died in Libby Prison. This was in 1864. But Mother rarely spoke of her brothers who were at the front. I have never met a man old enough to recall Lincoln's death who did not remember precisely where he was and what he was doing when the news reached him. I was playing with Mary Mole, aged eight, near her father's saddlery shop — where Morgan Hall now stands — when the church bell tolled. 'I think it's just as mean as it can be,' was Mary Mole's verdict upon the assassination. I was four and a half, and agreed with her. Grandmother Perry, who used to pay us long visits, taught me to read, and recorded that I had read the entire Bible before I was six. Yet this feat — which I do not remember — was nothing for those days, when we were all expected to 'beat the track of the alphabet with sluggish resolution.'

My sister and I attended at first the 'little white' schoolhouse below Consumption Hill. We had to carry footstools, for our legs were not long enough to reach the floor when we were seated. It was a great day for us when we watched the first work on the new schoolhouse opposite our home. Milo Nichols, a Negro who lived near us, dug the first trench for the foundation. He was just out of Pittsfield Jail, where he had been serving time for some transgression which Father compendiously described as 'wicked.' Milo was a barber by trade, and used to cut the hair of the Perry boys. He had a steel engraving of Charles Sumner in front of his chair, as did many of the Negro barbers in Massachusetts.

Race questions troubled us very little then. Billy Fortune, a former slave boy whom one of President Hopkins's sons had brought back from the War as a body-servant, went to school with us, and though he could never learn arithmetic, became the most romantic and popular of our school-fellows. A few French families had begun to drift down from Canada, drawn by the lure of the cotton mill, where some English and Welsh operatives were already employed. There were also Irish in town, many of them hard drinkers and lovers of a row. The state lines of Vermont and New York bounded Williamstown on the north and west, and there was a good deal of illegal liquor-selling. Our peaceful Sunday afternoons were sometimes broken by the shouts of drunken fighting on Water Street, around Welch's blacksmith shop. Probably Bill Meade! The only recourse in such emergencies was to summon the sheriff, Captain Hoxsey. The Captain was a heavy, slug-gish-looking fellow, but when called upon to break up an Irish fight, he went into action with joyful and devastating promptness. With one bull-like rush he would trip the ringleader and lock a pair of enormous hands around his throat. There the hands stayed until the victim's face turned the exact shade of purple which the sheriff deemed sufficient. Then Judge Bulkley, in the district court room over Charlie Mather's store, attended to the legal details, and the dignity of the Commonwealth of Massachusetts was vindicated.

Our Sundays, however, were ordinarily tranquil enough.

In the morning we attended the college chapel service and then the Sunday School of the Congregational Church. The afternoons dragged a little. Father never did any college work or book-writing on Sunday, though he often preached for congregations that were too poor to afford a settled minister. In the afternoons he read Milton — using the copy which his father had won as a *detur* at Harvard — or else Wordsworth or Whittier. Mother, glad of a day of comparative rest, preferred the *Youth's Companion* to Milton, and read the stories aloud to us. Father never cared for fiction. The only novel in his father's library at Lyme had been Miss Porter's *Thaddeus of Warsaw*. We missed Scott's novels entirely in childhood, although we read Dickens eagerly. Sister Grace used to lie on the floor, rocking the cradle of the latest baby with one hand, and turning the pages of Dickens with the other; and I remember how she sent us boys to sleep by reciting 'A soldier of the Legion lay dying in Algiers,' while the sickishly sweet odor of the locust blossoms drifted in through the bedroom window.

There were always plenty of books in our little house, and plenty of laughter. When we were not laughing at one another, we developed our powers of ridicule by describing our neighbors. Father would never allow us, however, to make fun of anyone who was poor or unlucky, and as most of the inhabitants of Williamstown came under one or both of these classes, our range was limited. 'God made the old man poor,' Father would quote from Whittier with tears in his eyes. As a political economist he knew well enough that the old man's poverty might have been due to liquor or laziness; but he remembered his own youthful penury, and in bitter weather rarely forgot in family

prayers to intercede for '*the poor, in this inclement season.*'
That solemn phrase increased my dread of winter.

As regularly as the September equinoctials came a domestic storm, more terrifying to us children than the gales
outside.   Once in a while Father lost his temper over a
refractory cow or horse, but rarely over a human being.
Stovepipes, however, were different. There were no fur-
naces in Williamstown in our childhood — and in fact only
two bathrooms and one lawnmower in town. Houses were
heated by stoves, and here lay one of Mother's peculiarities. On most matters she was the least fussy of persons,
but when it was a question of trimming and placing the
kerosene lamps, and of adjusting stove-dampers to the
ever-changing Williamstown climate, she had an amazing
pertinacity of opinion. Every autumn the hardware man
would set up the stoves for her, but he never succeeded in
getting the pipes at precisely the height and angle to suit
her. Then, in a very pleasant voice, she would summon
Father from his study to assist in the final adjustment.
He loved to work outdoors, but he had little manual
dexterity and was supremely indifferent to the exact angle
of a stovepipe. Mother was calm, but remorseless. 'Just a
little higher, Arthur.' 'Now a little more to the left.' And
so on. Father would begin to sigh and groan and then to
express himself in words. Though he never actually swore,
he could load the most ordinary language with profane
implications. '*Fush to Bungtown!*' was a favorite expletive
which he had brought from Lyme, and if those stovepipes
had had a sensitive ear, they would have blushed. The
more awkward and excited the Professor grew, the more
unperturbed was Mother. 'Now a little to the right,
Arthur.' '*Fush to Bungtown!*' And so it went, while the

children listened with awe and Mother continued to smile, until the annual storm had blown over and the stovepipes were exactly where they always had been.

We had few visitors from out of town. I remember that General Garfield, a favorite pupil of Father, visited us not long after the War. How handsome he looked with his brown beard, and how cheerfully he waved a big and redolent cigar as he explained, 'Now, Professor, about that battle of Chickamauga!' Long afterward I came to realize that Chickamauga did need a good deal of explanation. We missed another interesting visitor for a curious reason. Delegates from the New England colleges were to hold a meeting at Williams and were to be entertained in the homes of the faculty. The Harvard delegate was assigned to the Perrys. But Mother drew the line. She had just been reading about the ghastly murder of one Harvard professor by another, years before. I think we had a new baby in the house, and she was perhaps more apprehensive than usual, but at any rate she declared that she could not sleep at night if one of those Harvard professors was under her roof. The potential assassin from Cambridge was therefore quartered elsewhere. He proved to be James Russell Lowell.

Besides the *Republican* and the *New York Evening Post* — for both of which papers Father wrote occasional editorials — he read Mr. Godkin's *Nation*. He disliked religious journalism, though he had a high regard for one of its leaders, Henry Ward Beecher, whom he met frequently on the platform of free-trade meetings. My parents were much concerned over the Beecher Trial. I was scarcely old enough to know what it was all about, but I have never forgotten Father's characteristic remark on the day

after Mr. Beecher had taken the witness stand and declared his innocence: 'Well, Mary, that settles it. Mr.
Beecher has evidently been a *very foolish* man, but if he
says he is innocent of adultery he *is* innocent.' And thereafter he dismissed the whole matter from his mind.

What Father really needed, in his overstrenuous days
of our childhood, was a dog and a pipe. Unfortunately
both he and Mother disliked dogs and hated tobacco.
Father's favorite mode of expressing his disinclination for
tobacco and his preference that his sons should not use it
was as follows — and the language would be shocking to
one who did not understand how deeply the Professor enjoyed heightened rhetoric: 'I would rather see one of my
sons in his coffin than see him smoking a cigar!' One
Saturday noon, while we were eating dinner, he had just
delivered himself to this effect when the hired girl (there
were no 'maids' in those Arcadian days) came in from the
kitchen to say that Aaron Ballou wanted to see Mr. Perry.
Aaron was a cripple from the White Oaks who came to
the village once a week to sell packages of fine white sand
from Broad Brook. It was used to scour knives. Father
left the table, but when he returned he changed the topic
of conversation. After dinner I asked Mother why Aaron
Ballou had wished to see Father. Mother kept her face
very sober — except her eyes — as she explained: 'Poor
Aaron is a slave to the tobacco habit, and your father
gives him twenty-five cents every Saturday to keep him in
tobacco for another week.' It may be added that when
Father entertained his classmates at their fiftieth reunion,
he amused his sons — all of whom were by that time
smokers — by asking Walter to pick out a box of cigars
for the class of 1852: 'And see to it that those cigars are
good!'

As I look back upon it, the indoor pleasures of our child-hood, aside from books, were very limited. Games were few. Card-playing was not approved in most faculty families. None of my boy and girl friends knew how to dance. Our elders never gave 'dinners.' Until after I was twenty-one I never saw wine served at table, nor entered a theatre nor heard a symphony concert. There was no music in our Spring Street house, though Father later bought a piano for Arthur. We had a few good engravings, and Father had brought from Europe some excellent relief maps of Switzerland and other countries, which were a delight to children. Mother had good luck with flowers in winter, though they never matched the splendor of the bachelor Professor Gilson's hyacinths. In general, there was little artistic taste in the village homes.

On the other hand there was, at least in the faculty circle of a dozen families, a keen and cultivated enjoyment of the natural beauty of that northern Berkshire region. Professor Albert Hopkins, a depressing preacher at times but a mighty tramper, guided his Alpine Club of young men and women to every picturesque spot within a dozen miles of Williamstown. Professors Bascom, Dodd, and Perry knew every mountain peak and all the back roads and trails. Grandmother Smedley, when I was a tiny little fellow and was trudging 'across lots' with her one after-noon, stopped to look at the autumn colors on the hills. 'This is a beautiful world!' she exclaimed, and then stood silent. I believed her.

But we boys naturally followed the quest of excitement rather than pure beauty. We all put sports first: baseball and swimming in the summer, field hockey (which we called 'shinny') in the spring and fall, and skating and sliding in the winter. There were more hills in Williams-town than ever there were in Rome, and everybody except the aged coasted and went sleigh-riding. Yet my own real year began with the first robin, followed, after a couple of wretched months, by the first butterfly. My passion for birds and butterflies was not shared by any of my brothers, but a couple of other boys — Sanborn Tenney, son of the Professor of Natural History, and Rob Clark, son of the college carpenter — were fellow enthusiasts. Professor Tenney was infinitely kind in showing us how to collect and preserve our specimens, and it was a proud day when he accepted some of my best mounted butterflies for the college museum. In fact I won in the village the nickname of 'The Butterfly Boy,' not through any lightness and brightness of mood — for I believe I was preternaturally serious — but by reason of my tireless pursuit of speci-mens. We called birds and butterflies by their Latin names, and this added to the charm of the chase.

Small game was then plentiful. From Uncle Baxter in Boston I received on my twelfth birthday a double-bar-relled muzzle-loading shotgun. I took it to bed with me. Uncle Will provided me with a shot-flask and an ancient powder-horn which I was sure the Smedleys had used in the Revolution. With the Morehouse boys, natural no-mads from Virginia, I blazed away at hawks, crows, and red squirrels, and an occasional hare or partridge. We knew nothing about shooting birds on the wing. When we had no money for percussion caps — which was all too often — we could go fishing, or trap woodchucks in sum-mer and muskrats in winter. We roamed the hills for huckleberries and raspberries, chestnuts and butternuts. If we learned nothing else, we learned that a stream should be followed to its source, and that the higher the mountain the wider the view. I have had many Ph.D. students who never made that discovery.

To the Perry boys, Grandfather Smedley's farm was a Paradise. I think he liked Walter best, and used to call him his 'little four-year-old,' for at that age Walter had begun to ride the old mare when Grandfather was plough-ing, and had driven as straight a furrow as Uncle Will. In the fall, we helped bank the house for the winter, and were even allowed — though this was a delicate job — to caulk with cotton the window sashes of the sitting-room and bedrooms, so that no fresh air could enter between November and May. The sanitary and medical science of that era was a little queer. I remember having a sharp attack of croup and being tucked carefully between the soft flannel sheets in Grandmother's spare room, while I fought desperately for breath. Grandmother calmly sewed pieces of salt pork on a strip of red flannel, sprinkled red pepper on the pork, heated the whole contrivance red-hot over the stove and pinned it around my neck. Yet the present Dean of the Harvard Medical School assures me that she might have done much worse.

June was my own favorite month at the farm, for there was a great crested flycatcher's nest in the apple tree by the pond, red roses from Colchester, Connecticut, were in blossom by the old cellar hole where they had been planted a hundred years earlier, red-winged blackbirds nested in the rushes, red-fins darted in the tiny brook, and east of the Stone Hill road, in a grove where Williams students now hunt for golf balls sliced from the first tee, there was then a nest of the very rare yellow-billed cuckoo. There would be young partridges on Stone Hill by June, and al-ways the chance of seeing a fox.

All through the summer we boys devoured the Deacon's choicest fruit — plums and pears and then grapes and apples. For most of the varieties he had French names, marvellously mispronounced. *Fameuse* apples we called, after his example, 'Farmruse,' and why the *Doyen d'été* pear should have that name we never knew. Grandfather thought that hard cider was good for boys 'in moderation' — one of his favorite words. He let us open, though it cost us a shudder, the box of human bones, relics of his early medical studies, which he kept in the woodshed loft. He thrilled us by recounting how, in the dreadful influenza epidemic of the eighteen-twenties, each college student was told to cut fresh hemlock boughs and put them under his blankets, and to mix a gallon of rum with a gallon of molasses and drink all he could hold before going to bed: 'and by the blessing of God not a soul was lost!'

In one respect only did we have any fear of him. As befitted a Deacon in those days of personal exhortation, he had very clear views about what he called 'the plan of salvation,' and he was likely to ply his grandsons with highly embarrassing if not indelicate questions as to the state of their souls. Did we feel that we were still 'out of the Kingdom'? Luckily Grandfather had a tangential mind, and we developed great skill in dodging the main issue and directing his curiosity into other fields. But still he could scare us, particularly with his tale of Judge Bulkley — the village 'atheist,' reputed to be wealthy — who had in his youth, one dusky evening, met the Devil in the form of a Black Man. Grandfather could point out the very spot, in a corner of the rail fence near Doctor's Brook, where this drama had taken place. The Devil had offered John Bulkley riches in exchange for his soul; John had

agreed to the compact, and had never repented. We boys
all knew the Judge. We could see him every afternoon,
sitting on the upper porch of Charlie Mather's store,
smoking cigars in the sunshine. It was an awesome sight,
and I, for one, used to run past him rapidly whenever I
had birds' eggs hidden in my hat; for he represented the
majesty of the Law, and he had sold his soul to the Devil!

By the time I was thirteen, I could handle fairly well a
butterfly net and a baseball bat, a fish-pole (we had no
'rods' then), and the double-barrelled gun. We had
moved up the hill from Spring Street and Father now kept
two cows and a horse. A quaint little Irishman, 'Dusty'
Quinn, who lived in terror of his big red-haired wife, did
most of the outdoor work. We had an enormous garden
south of the house, where Father, with the assistance of
his sons and Dusty Quinn, raised prodigious crops of vegetables. He loved to load them into our lumber wagon
and drive off to bestow them upon his less fortunate colleagues and upon widows in general. He usually wore a
silk hat, and to my boyish sensitiveness the hat did not
suit the lumber wagon. I said so. 'It's the only hat for a
gentleman to wear,' he replied, with perfect simplicity.
But we boys thought there were too many vegetables in
the world. It seemed to me that I weeded miles of carrots
when I wanted to be chasing butterflies, and I dislike the
taste of that vegetable to this day.

And then Father was stung with the splendor of another
thought. He had planned to send his sons away to boarding-school when they were fifteen. Would it not be an
excellent discipline for each boy, at the age of thirteen, to
assume sole charge of the cows and horse? Dusty Quinn,
who disliked milking and really had enough to do with

digging ditches and helping Father to plant trees, thought
well of the Professor's proposal. Bliss was the oldest boy;
'and the lot fell upon Jonah.'

I did not enjoy it. The cows were not so bad, though
they were of a wild stubborn Ayrshire breed which Father
was then fancying. Milking was good training for one's
wrists and forearms, though I did not realize this until
later. But the Perry horse was to me a horror. We had in
due succession three of these 'equine beasts, half horse,
half devil,' as Carroll calls them: Cobden, Chevalier, and
Slim. They all ran at the slightest excuse. Father, a fear-
less and very reckless driver, did not mind; nor did my
brothers Arthur and Walter, both of whom were skilful
horsemen and seemed to like the excitement of a spill. But
I was terrified by it. I had to feed and groom the horse, of
course, and harness and unharness him; yet I feared and
hated the beast, and from that time on I have never
touched a horse's rein without apprehension; much as I
like to look at them in the ring or on the bridle path.

The ingenious Dr. Freud had not, in 1873, invented the
term 'inferiority complex,' but that was what ailed me,
and my vain struggles with that brute of a beast increased
the malady. There was no real reason for it, except in my
worrying mind. I was a tallish, pale, delicate-looking boy;
shy and sensitive, and I hope gentle-mannered; disliking
loud noises and violent words; hating the brutality and
cruelty of the big boys on the school-ground, and dreading
to see, at the Smedley farm, a calf or pig or even a chicken
killed. Of course I had killed butterflies with a drop of
benzine, and had shot birds and squirrels without re-
morse. A gun was somehow different! As one of the
younger boys in each successive grade of the public school

I had endured stoically the hair-pulling and arm-twisting propensities of my elders. Of course one must not cry or tell the teacher, for that would be breaking the unwritten code. The small boy had to keep back the tears, pretend to smile — and hope to God that some day he would be big enough to hit back!

In the woods and fields I was perfectly happy, and also when I was playing ball. Somehow I had been chosen captain of a nine, at twelve. Two of the players, Clarence and Frank Grant, were colored boys, sons of our 'hired girl.' Clarence became, in time, catcher and captain of the Cuban Giants, and Frank (whose portrait I drew later in a novel called *The Plated City*) was a famous second baseman for Buffalo before the color line was drawn. Rob Pettit, our left fielder, afterward played for Chicago and went around the world with Pop Anson's team. We called ourselves the 'Rough and Readys.'

I was also perfectly happy, in this period, with a book; any book. The school work went easily enough. In fact everything was well enough, except that I was unhappy about myself. Was I a born coward? Every day taught me that I was afraid of a horse. I was a timid swimmer, and after I had seen Clarence Grant break through the ice of the New Pond — to be rescued, just as his strength was gone, by Clarence Smith — I became a timid skater. Was I timid all through? Was it just because I was a Professor's son, and could call birds and butterflies by their Latin names, and hated quarrels, and wanted to be let alone, that a few bigger boys seemed bent upon making my life miserable? Was it perhaps my fault? Was I 'peculiar'? I worried about it every night and morning, as I pressed my forehead against the flanks of those wild

Ayrshires and milked desperately with aching wrists, believing, as did all boys in that epoch, that the cow would die by some strange death if I did not milk her dry.

It was a butcher from Hancock named Hadsell who let the first ray of light into my morbid mood. He was a tall, brown-faced and wrinkled fellow, who drove his cart to Williamstown twice a week, peddling meat. Sometimes he would reach our house so early that we were still at morning prayers, and when invited by Father to join us, Mr. Hadsell would sit down, in his blue smock, and listen reverently. He was, I believe, a Cornishman by birth; at any rate, he watched me wrestling one day with another boy, and called me, with great secrecy, to the back of his cart. 'Bliss, would you like to learn a side-holt that no one around here knows?' I was slow, and the old Cornishman as quick-footed as a cat, but after a little I mastered his 'side-holt.' Nearly fifty years later I demonstrated it to an amused Olympic wrestling champion. 'It's a kind of modified hip-lock,' he explained; 'but it wouldn't be allowed today'; and indeed it did involve some risk to the opponent's ankle. But in 1873 no one was squeamish, and I doubt if young Harry Esmond ever had more secret comfort from his *botte de Jésuite* than I had from Hadsell's 'side-holt.'

Then came the episode of the stolen hockey stick. I had cut it on the slope of the 'gully' — which our elders called 'Flora's Glen,' insisting that it was here that Bryant had written *Thanatopsis* when he was a sophomore. They were wrong about that. But the hockey stick was a beauty, and Mick Meade, son of the terrifying Bill Meade of Water Street and cock of the walk in our grammar grade, had stolen it. I reported this theft at home. Mother was pacific, as always: she thought that if I asked Mick 'very politely' for it, he would give it back. But I had tried that already. Father's advice was cryptic, but colored a little by his strain of Scotch-Irish blood: 'My boy, if you don't stand up for your own rights, no one else will!' I pondered that saying until the hour for the school recess. I had sparred once with Mick for a couple of minutes, and knew that I was no match for him. He was a year or two older, a head taller, and very quick with his hands. But I wanted my hockey stick, and when he came out at recess I grabbed at it. We were still wrestling furiously for it when Miss Carver rang the bell for the end of the recess. So perfect was her discipline that Mick and I broke away instantly, being more afraid of her than of each other. But I had the stick. As the procession of boys streamed back toward the schoolhouse, the dead silence was broken by Mick. 'Bliss Perry? I could lick a whole regiment of Bliss Perrys!' And then piped up another Celt, little Danny Collins, son of Pat the college janitor, and short-stop on my nine: 'I'm damned if I think you can lick *one* of them!' Sweeter words of praise I have never heard. Of course Danny had uttered an absurd opinion — and yet? And yet? But Mick Meade moved to Greenfield shortly thereafter — no doubt luckily for me. He became a prosperous saloon-keeper.

(God rest the soul of Danny Collins. When he died, as a policeman in Indianapolis, it was reported in Williamstown that the hacks at Danny's funeral covered four city blocks.)

Oddly enough, the three boys who most harassed me by petty persecutions were in my Sunday-School class. The teacher was the loquacious and warm-hearted Miss Abby

Mather. One day we ventured — for we were always thinking about fighting, though few of us had actually fought — to ask her about the Bible verse: 'As much as lieth in you, live peaceably with all men.' She expounded fluently the doctrine of non-resistance. 'But, Miss Abby,' said one of us, 'suppose the other fellow keeps pitching on you all the time?' 'Well,' replied Miss Abby gracefully, as if yielding a point, 'I suppose sometimes it *just doesn't lie in you.*'

A great light dawned upon me at that instant. If it didn't lie *in* me to put up with any more persecution, then the Bible did not say it was wrong to fight! I had already, with another boy, picked up somewhere a set of boxing-gloves, and had learned at least to give and take punishment cheerfully and to watch the other fellow's eyes. Within a week after Miss Abby had innocently let down the bars, and, as it happened, at an evening 'sociable' of Sunday-School pupils in the vestry of the Congregational Church, one of the three who had long made my life miserable said or did something which was the last straw. I hit him under the chin.

He was a solidly built lad, from a fighting family, and was game. He pointed to the door, and in a minute we were outside, quite alone. A little snow was falling, but there was plenty of light from the vestry windows. Neither of us spoke. He came in fast, with a furious right. I knew just enough to block it as I swung my left to his jaw. To my surprise, and certainly to his, it dropped him. He was up in a second, and rushed in, again leading with his right, and again I blocked and landed with my left in the same spot as before. He went down a second time, and it seemed to me that he got up rather slowly from the icy path. Once more he came on, but now with both arms whirling and with no guard at all. Curiously, I found myself liking him, but nevertheless I must have hit him very hard, for when he went down for the third time, the fight was over. I hope I helped him to his feet, but am not sure about it. At any rate, we shook hands with boyish solemnity, and went back into the vestry for the ice-cream. We were friends for the next thirty years. Neither of us ever mentioned the incident, as far as I know, but somehow a strange peace brooded thereafter upon Miss Abby's Sunday-School class.

I pass over a couple of other combats. They may be a blemish upon the career of a future officer of many Peace Societies, though they cleared the air at the time. Yet the Amos Jackson incident, which closed this 'storm and stress' period, was queer enough to deserve record. It happened in the spring of my fifteenth year. Amos was a broad-shouldered, bow-legged, long-armed Negro, who had no recognized father or mother, but lived in a hut by Phebe's Brook with an old woman named Phebe Jackson. He used to attend school occasionally, though we supposed him to be twenty, and he dominated the ball field. All of us feared him for his harsh and cruel ways, but no one questioned his invincibility. I remember talking with other boys about it, and that one of them said that the only spot on Amos where a blow would hurt him was the temple. How sanguinary boys can be! But no one ever fought Amos, except in imagination.

All this by way of prelude. One day Amos had tormented one of my younger brothers in a particularly nasty way. I arrived just as it was over. My brother was sobbing quietly, and Amos was standing unconcernedly over the home plate, bat in hand. Will Cooper still says, after nearly sixty years, that I went so white that Will was frightened. I was in a cold fury: I wanted nothing on earth, at that instant, except the chance for one clean blow, and then I expected to be killed. Amos saw me coming, but suspected nothing, and I could not have spoken had I wished. But for once in my life I 'let go,' driving every ounce of weight and all the speed and passion there was in me into a straight right to his temple. And then I was scared; for the bat fell out of his hand, his face turned ashy grey, his knees began to tremble horribly, and he crumpled down on the home plate and lay there. Minutes went by. Then he reached for his bat, rose groggily to his feet, and without even looking at me slouched home across the fields. We had been terrorized by a phantom. Amos was 'yellow,' though no one had ever known it. — But I have never hit anyone since then.

In September of that year, 1875, I went off to boarding-school.

II

GREYLOCK

And in the world, as in the school,
I'd say, how fate may change and shift;
The prize be sometimes with the fool,
The race not always to the swift.

THACKERAY, *The End of the Play*

I DID not go very far, for Greylock Institute in South Williamstown was a little less than five miles away. The 'South Part,' as we called it, was a purely farming section of the township, stretching along Green River and the hills on either side. Where the New Ashford and Hancock brooks joined to make the river, there was a tiny village: Sabin's Hotel, Bill Morey's store, a blacksmith shop, a church, and a dozen houses. Save for Ames's two-horse stage, which traversed daily the twenty miles from Williamstown to Pittsfield, returning in the afternoon, and bringing the mail and an occasional passenger, the isolation of the village was complete.

On the plateau above it stood the big new building of the Institute, erected after the fire of 1872. Mr. B. F. Mills, born on a farm a mile to the west, had started the school in 1842, and he had a gift for teaching boys. Now his sons were helping in the enterprise. The new building — with steam heat, bathtubs, and other modernities — was a gallant, but as it proved, a disastrous venture: for there was no endowment and a heavy mortgage, and by 1889 came bankruptcy and the end of the Institute. The building was used for a while as a summer hotel, but this project also failing, it was torn down in 1932.

But in 1875 'Mills's School,' as it was still called locally, was in its full glory. There were about a hundred boys, drawn largely from prosperous families in New York, Cleveland, Cincinnati, and Chicago. Most of them were preparing for Williams or Yale. The tuition was five hundred dollars a year, the instruction was excellent, and more beautiful and healthful surroundings for a boys' school were not then to be found in New England.

All this, however, did not help the loneliness of a new boy on his first evening. Mother had taken me down in the blue carry-all, Arthur driving. She looked serious, for Grace had already gone to the Westfield Normal School, and now her oldest boy was leaving her. Father was in Germany that summer, having gone over to escort my blind cousin Edward Baxter Perry — later a well-known concert pianist and the originator of the musical 'lecture recital' in America — who was to study the piano under Kullak and Clara Schumann and Liszt. At supper there was not a boy I knew: I got the impression of tailor-made clothes and vast sophistication. As I wandered out to the yard, after supper, the pariah of the school — though I did not know that at the time — invited me to 'pass ball' with him. His name was Smith, and he had an unpleasant nickname, based upon his lack of a handkerchief and his alleged habit, when fishing, of carrying worms, trout, and maple-sugar all in one pocket. But he had a good arm, and soon we were throwing long balls to each other across the yard.

It had happened in the preceding June that I had packed

the 'Rough and Readys' into our lumber wagon, and —
bribing another boy to drive Cobden — had come down,
like the wolf on the fold, to ravage the Institute's junior
team. We made forty-eight runs. I played second base,
and was lucky enough to make a jumping left-hand catch
of a fly to short centre field. It was really easy, but it had
pleased the crowd. And now, as Smith and I were passing
ball, a couple of house-painters, of the true lazy Williamstown breed that never missed a ball game, were leaning
against the fence, smoking their pipes and watching us.
Smith threw a ball very high and to my left. I had to jump
for it, but pulled it down. One of the painters took his
pipe out of his mouth and strolled over to me:

'Was you the fellow that played second base on the
Rough and Readys last spring?'

I nodded, and he turned back to his companion. '*That's
him*,' he said.

Only a few grey-haired athletes, I fear, can realize the
comfort which those two words poured into the lonely soul
of the new boy. I was somebody, to someone, though he
was merely a lazy house-painter; and I walked into the big
strange schoolroom for the evening study-hour with my
head up.

'Mr. B. F.,' father of 'Mr. George,' 'Mr. Charles,' 'Mr.
Silas,' 'Mr. Carl,' and 'Miss Blanche,' presided over the
study-hour. It closed with evening prayer. 'Mr. B. F.'
was a fine figure of a man in his late sixties. I can still hear
his rich voice in the solemn phrases with which he invariably concluded his evening petitions: 'Bless the sick
and *those appointed soon to die*.' (On an autumn night that
sounded as if any one of us might go before morning!)
'And finally, O Lord [brightening up], grant us an *abundant*

entrance into the Kingdom of Heaven!' That 'abundant entrance' suggested somehow a full-rigged ship coming into harbor with plenty of sea-room. I liked it — and if the kindly old 'Mr. B. F.' did not find an abundant entrance himself when his own turn came, there is something wrong with the chart.

When engaged in his favorite task of teaching mathematics, however, 'Mr. B. F.' was not in the least mystical. He was realistic and explosive. 'Kelligg, Kelligg,' he would roar at the unlucky Sam Kellogg, 'x^2 is no more equal to $2x$ than a thunderstorm to a pair of bars!' I disliked mathematics, but I could get 'Mr. B. F.'s' point of view.

Inasmuch as all of us were preparing for college, and the entrance requirements were practically identical everywhere, the school curriculum for the upper classes was simple. We studied Latin, Greek, and mathematics and nothing else, as far as I can remember; though we were expected to read a few essays by Addison and Macaulay, and to declaim at stated periods. 'Mr. George,' who had his father's erect carriage and orotund voice, taught Latin; he was later Professor of English and Dean of the Amherst Agricultural College. Greek was taught admirably by Mr. F. W. Fiske (Williams 1872), who was still teaching in 1934 in St. Paul Academy, Minnesota. 'Mr. Charles' was chiefly occupied with the commissary department — running the school farm and attending to the supplies which had to be hauled by wagon from Williamstown and Pittsfield. My most vivid recollection of him is his dashing up on horseback at the time of the disputed Hayes–Tilden election and announcing in the schoolyard that the Democrats were about to march on Washington, to seat Mr. Tilden as President. I doubted that. I knew that Father, a Republican since 1856, had become disgusted with Grant's second administration and had voted for Tilden; but I could not quite see Father marching on Washington, gun in hand! 'Mr. Silas' was noted chiefly for his magnificent bass voice. He studied grand opera, and might have been another Chaliapin, if he could only have kept on the key.

All in all, the teachers were competent and friendly. Now and then a tough boy, who had been dismissed from some other school, needed a little corporal punishment, and got it promptly from 'Mr. George.' But in general we were a happy family, well fed, well housed, and free from petty supervision. We all took, on our own initiative, plenty of exercise: football (then a new game to me) and baseball in season, with Indian clubs and dumbbells if the weather was too stormy. In the winter a squad of us, in moccasins and sweaters, ran every evening at dusk over the icy road to Big Rock and back. We measured an even mile on the level New Ashford highway, and held track meets. We tramped in all seasons up the southern Taconic summits or through the lonely, winding New Ashford and Hancock valleys. I did no 'collecting' at Greylock, but I had one roommate, C. Brown, of New Jersey, who showed me how twelve-inch trout could be taken on a worm in a deep meadow brook that was less than twelve inches wide; and another boy, whose name I have forgotten, gave me my first real glimpse of fly-fishing — as described in my *Pools and Ripples*.

I was allowed to spend one Sunday each month at home. Usually I walked, by the Stone Hill road, not having the money for stage-fare. On the other Sundays I listened to Father's preaching in the South Williamstown

Church, before a congregation consisting of Greylock boys and farmers. His salary was exactly equal to my school tuition. On pleasant Sundays he would drive down in the blue carriage or in our winter 'pung,' but in rough weather he rode horseback, arrayed in a sealskin cap, a huge beaver collar, and with a black valise, containing my laundry and some choice apples from the Smedley farm, flapping from the saddle. Bumping along in this fashion, he presented a strange appearance: a combination of Don Quixote and the Vicar of Wakefield. My schoolmates laughed at him, no doubt, though for the most part they were too well bred to do so when I was present. But the moment he divested himself of his uncouth wrappings and stood by the side of the pulpit to face his congregation, he was superbly master of the situation. My brother Carroll has pictured him in *A Professor of Life.*

'He was tall of stature, with an inborn dignity and grace of bearing. His head was noble, his eyes blue and full of light. The nose, almost invariably the index of mental power, was perfect in fullness, straightness and strength. He had a musical voice of great richness and beauty which he used with studious care; a voice of depth and range, an utterance precise without being finical, and an articulation that was a joy to ear and mind.... Logic, humor, scorn, humaneness, earnestness and satire all blended in the impulse to convince or convict.... His sermons always had a place for ideas. The text was likely to be out of the Old Testament, since this he dearly loved; it was so human, so picturesque, so full of noble poetry, so religious, so true. And the men in it! When they were wicked, they were so damnably wicked; and with what relentless enthusiasm he would show them up!'

It is not strange that I was proud of him, and sensitive when other boys made fun of his peculiarities. I wondered whether I was really accomplishing enough at Greylock to justify the sacrifices he was making. Of course, one ought to prepare the daily lessons; but there were other things that I now felt like trying. Butterflies and birds' eggs had been well enough. How about learning to write?

I began to make verses — very wretched ones of course — and as editor of the school paper made my initial venture into fiction with 'A Story of the Maine Coast.' In the first instalment, printed in March, I succeeded in placing the hero and heroine adrift in a dory, right under the bow of an oncoming ocean liner. This was a pleasing situation, and I stopped with a 'Continued in our Next.' Unluckily I lacked the inventiveness and the seamanship to extricate the unhappy pair from this predicament, and the April number announced that 'Owing to unforeseen emergencies, the "Story of the Maine Coast" will be omitted from this issue.' By the time the May number appeared, the baseball season had opened, and no one, including the editor, gave a thought to that girl who had been left in the dory since March.

Perhaps a streak of indolence inherited from the Smedleys was already at odds with the restless energy of the Perrys. I discovered long afterward that in both of the Greylock years and in the year following I had kept a diary; but each of the three diaries, begun so ambitiously on January 1, came to a feeble end on January 17. How much more dependable is a seventeen-year locust than a seventeen-day diarist! Nevertheless, one of those Greylock diaries contains a sentence which proves that a boy of sixteen can sometimes diagnose his own weakness: 'It

Kinsman

ARTHUR LATHAM PERRY

seems to me that I would give anything to lead my class — *except work for it.*'

Yet I must have worked more or less, for when the class was graduated in June, 1877, I served as valedictorian. During the preceding winter I had discovered Emerson's essays, and was intoxicated by them, as I still am. My valedictory oration, delivered in the little church on a hot night in a new black frock coat, was entitled 'Adaptation.' It was pure Emerson and water. I had been drilled on it by one of the teachers, Mr. Brodie, a graduate of Hamilton — a college then famous for its high-flown 'oratory.' With intense earnestness, in a shrill falsetto voice, and with the strangest emphasis upon unimportant prepositions, I declared to the amazed audience that 'The wing of a bird is as well adapted to motion in the air as the fin of a fish is to motion in the water, yet neither can do the work of the other.' My brother Arthur, who listened to this performance and is the best mimic in a family which contains even such artists as Carroll and Lewis, can still declaim the opening sentences of that speech. Bill Pratt, the half-witted 'Saw-Buck Philosopher' of Williamstown — an impassioned orator himself and no mean critic of the art — once complimented me in college upon my 'gloomy shine' upon the platform. But I wish Bill might have heard that Valedictory upon 'Adaptation.'

III

'THESE CRUDE YOUNG MEN'

Ah! that life that I have known! How hard it is to remember what is most memorable.
We remember how we itched, not how our hearts beat.

THOREAU, *Journal*

HALF the advantage of going to college lies in going away to college. Your mother packs your trunk, your father gives you his blessing and some money, and you are off, like the hero of a picaresque novel, to make your own way in the world. To my sister Grace, who left for Wellesley just as I was entering Williams, college was a romantic adventure. 'Pioneers, O Pioneers!'

For me it meant loading a little furniture into the lumber wagon and driving across the field where the Thompson Laboratories now stand to the south entry of West College, on whose fourth floor I was to room for the next four years, taking my meals at home. It was the only sensible thing to do, for an old law of Williams allowed free tuition to the sons of professors. Father, with five boys to educate, and Professor Safford, with four, were the most obvious beneficiaries of this ancient statute. I admired Father's pioneering energy in seeking out Mark Hopkins's college for himself, instead of following his own father's example and going to Harvard. I still like to meet men who tell me that they went to Amherst because Garman taught there, or to Bowdoin for Hyde, or to Yale for 'Billy' Sumner, or Stanford for David Starr Jordan. It makes education seem real. In my student days in Germany, men were constantly migrating from one university to another in order to get the benefit of some particular course offered that year by a famous scholar. For men mature enough to know what they want, all this is admirable; but it is fairly certain that not one out of ten American freshmen knows what he wants or where he can find it.

So all the Perry and Safford boys, aware that the paternal salary never exceeded twenty-five hundred dollars, went cheerfully to Williams; and there was one period of fourteen years when either a Safford or a Perry, or both, ornamented the college nine. But we could scarcely feel that romantic glamour about Williams which many of our classmates experienced. We had been born and bred in that briar bush. Still, we thought it as good as any other, and indeed it was, for most of us; though we were informed occasionally that a gifted and ambitious boy might be better off at Harvard, where the youthful President Eliot was introducing some very radical ideas.

In 1877, however, Williams was laboring in the trough of the seas. Mark Hopkins, weary of the executive duties which he had never really enjoyed, had resigned the presidency in 1872, though he continued to serve as Professor of Philosophy until his death in 1887. He had been succeeded by Paul A. Chadbourne, a former teacher of science at Williams, who had been President of the University of Wisconsin; a versatile, restless person, with great gifts as a naturalist, but somehow miscast in the rôle of a college president. John Bascom, one of the most powerful and original minds of his era, had left Williams to succeed Chadbourne at Madison, although he was to return to us later on. Remsen, a brilliant young chemist, had gone from Williams to Johns Hopkins in 1876. Sanborn Tenney, who had helped me so much with butterflies, died suddenly in the summer of 1877. If he had lived, my career might have been very different, for if I had any secret ambition stronger than another in 1877, it was to become some day a professor like Sanborn Tenney, with a museum of natural history to enrich and arrange!

This demoralization of the science courses in which Williams had once been eminent was not corrected until after our graduation in 1881. It did not affect, however, the studies of our freshman year. These were the immemorial Latin, Greek, and mathematics. The fifty or more boys in our class recited in each of these subjects every day. There were no sections; good, bad, and indifferent students had precisely the same assignments and were called up in turn. We were doing, literally, what our fathers had done before us. My first Latin lesson, in the preface to Livy, was, as I discovered later in Father's diary, exactly the same assignment which he had had in 1848; and it was also precisely what my son had at Williams as a freshman in 1916. For sixty-eight years at least, and probably much longer, it was the same squirrel in the same cage! One would think that some Professor of Latin, at some time, in an access of emotional insanity might have altered the assignment, even if he kept the dreadful secret to himself.

The theory was, of course, that what freshmen needed was grammatical drill, and that certain Latin and Greek texts were convenient, not to say hallowed implements for this purpose. The irony of the situation was that some of us actually liked Latin and Greek, loved to turn those splendid periods into the best English which we could command, and were ready to be interested in whatever the

Greeks and Romans had to say. But we fared less well in the classroom than some boy with an accurate verbal memory for the list of rules and exceptions as set down in the grammars of Goodwin and Allen and Greenough. I had been captivated in school by the poetry of Virgil. That meant to me the six books of the *Aeneid* that were then required, but I cannot recall that any teacher informed me that Virgil had ever written anything but those six books. What Virgil's real place was in Roman literature and in world literature was never mentioned. I liked to read Horace, and a knowledge of the scansion certainly increased my sense of his cleverness, but in the college classroom his wit and wisdom seemed to evaporate, and there was only the grammar and scansion left. The extracts which we read from Thucydides and Herodotus were interesting, but we were warned never to use 'ponies,' and no one hinted to us that we would do well to read in an English translation the entire work of these or any other Greek authors. Professor Fernald was an admirable drillmaster in the rudiments of the Greek language, but his conscientious interpretation of his duty as a teacher left him no time to initiate us into the wonders of Greek literature — even in an English dress.

I obeyed strictly that rule forbidding the use of translations. When we came to read Cicero's *Letters* — for which no 'pony' was available — many of my friends were in sore trouble. I have lived long enough to hear Cicero described today as a 'stuffed shirt,' but I found his *Letters* amusing and eloquent, and I wish that as an undergraduate I could have had Gaston Boissier's *Cicéron et ses Amis*, which I remember reading with my children one winter in Rome. But I had four classmates who could not read a sentence of the *Letters* without a translation, though they knew their Latin grammar well enough. We were then reciting to Professor E. H. Griffin at five in the afternoon. I used to come up from baseball practice about four, and having then a knack for fluent though somewhat inaccurate reading of Latin at sight, I would translate Cicero's *Letters* to my four grammatical classmates. I do not doubt that my Latinity was much like David Garrick's. 'He has not Latin enough,' declared Samuel Johnson, who had once taught 'Davy.' 'He finds out the Latin by the meaning rather than the meaning by the Latin.' At any rate, that was what Professor Griffin evidently thought of me, for at the end of the term all of my four friends received a better grade in Latin than I did.

Professor Griffin was in truth a delightful gentleman, as those who knew him as Dean at Johns Hopkins will remember. But we freshmen thought him singularly aloof; suave but unapproachable. He had great ingenuity in explaining the subjunctive mood, and he invented, I imagine, a variety which he called 'the subjunctive of softened statement.' That phrase seemed to fit Professor Griffin like a glove, and when we were at a loss to explain a subjunctive in any other way, we would try a shot with that 'softened statement.' Professor E. P. Morris, of Yale, who for a few years succeeded Griffin in the chair of Latin at Williams, once confided to me that there was no such thing as a 'subjunctive of softened statement,' and never had been! But it was a useful fiction in 1877 and 1878 — something like Santa Claus.

I have been associated with grammarians all of my professional life, and have toiled as hard as most men over the grammar of many languages. But a certain scepticism about the ultimate value of this labor was implanted in me, innocently enough, by my father. He had been chairman of the School Committee one year when I was in the graded school on Spring Street, and among his whimsicalities was an ancient grudge against the conventional teaching of English grammar. His own mother, he was wont to remark, had once lost a 'parsing match' because she refused to try to parse the phrase 'That yew-tree's shade' in Gray's *Elegy*. She declared that she could parse it well enough if she had ever seen a yew-tree! Father always defended her position, with roars of laughter at all pedants. It happened that during his term on the School Committee, my class had a grammar lesson every morning at nine. He excused me from attendance, with this injunction: 'My boy, put in all the time you can on Latin and Greek grammar, for those are inflected languages; but forget that there is such a thing as English grammar.' The result was, that not having to report at school until ten o'clock, I added greatly to my already excellent collection of birds' eggs, and am absurdly ignorant of the formal rules of English grammar to this day.

Father's theory, of course, was that one should learn to speak and write one's mother tongue by ear, and by ear alone; and it was easy for him to point out, as he was deeply interested in the nature and history of languages, that the great Greek poets and dramatists had written in that way, since the study of grammar had not then been invented. He would not have affirmed that the ear is not aided by constant practice in the translation of other tongues — the more of them the better. I still possess the big Latin and Greek lexicons which he bought at Thetford Academy and used in college. He paid for them by working for various farmers. He had the habit of leaving his Latin grammar at the end of a furrow, after glancing at the declensions and conjugations; repeating them aloud as he ploughed the long furrow down and back, then turning the page to a fresh task of memory, and ploughing on. He sent his sons to the best preparatory schools he could find: Arthur and me to Greylock Institute, Walter to Williston, Carroll to Andover, and Lewis to Andover and to Lawrenceville. But none of his children, except Sister Grace, ever learned Latin grammar as thoroughly as he did. He wrote as pure and lucid English as Cobbett or Tom Paine, but having once ploughed his Latin and Greek well into his system, he composed, like Cobbett and Paine and for that matter Lincoln, by ear alone.

Enough, however, of Greek and Latin! Our third subject was mathematics, in which we were instructed, in a gloomy basement room of the old gymnasium, by Professor Dodd. 'In his younger days,' as I have written elsewhere,[1] 'he had been a Latinist, until the loss, by fire, of his manuscript Latin grammar disheartened him, and he accepted a chair of elementary mathematics, which he kept till his death. He fulfilled his duties as instructor with perfect gravity and fidelity, but cared wholly for other things: for his collections of Phaedrus and black-letter Chaucers; for Scott's novels, which he used to read through once each year; for the elder dramatists; for Montaigne and Lamb. Weather permitting, he drove from twenty to forty miles a day in his rusty, mud-covered buggy; he knew every wild flower, every lovely or bold view, within reach of Williamstown. To be his companion upon one of these drives was to touch

[1] *The Amateur Spirit*, p. 98.

the very essence of fine, whimsical, irresponsible scholarship.'

But to us freshmen he appeared to be simply a taskmaster. The system by which, irrespective of our training and aptitudes, we were all herded together in one classroom, was not of his devising. He was himself performing an uncongenial duty, and he did not see why we should not perform ours. We had a few brilliant mathematicians who used to annoy him purposely by substituting original demonstrations in place of those given in Loomis. We had one man, at least, who had no conception whatever of the meaning of geometry, but whose verbal memory was so remarkable that he could recite every proposition by heart. Dodd gave him a high mark and he ultimately became a bishop.

Yet one adventure of my own in his classroom may serve to illustrate Professor Dodd's wisdom and patience in handling a sulky boy. I disliked mathematics intensely, and aimed to do just enough work to secure a passing grade. One day, in our study of trigonometry, he told us to be ready to box the compass. It did not involve ten minutes of work, but I balked at it, holding that boxing the compass was a sheer mechanical exercise, beneath the dignity of a college classroom. Dodd called us up by lot — or at least pretended to do so — for we were never certain that the name written on a piece of paper and drawn from his pasteboard box was the name which he actually announced. At any rate, 'Perry' was the first name called to box the compass. I rose decorously, shook my head firmly, and sat down. It meant a 'zero.' For six days running, this little ceremony was repeated, to the delight of the class. Then I consulted the oracle of the coal-closet, for on the inside of that closet door in No. 32 West College I kept a careful record of my 'zeros' and 'x's' under Dodd. Those six 'zeros' in a row looked as big as the national debt, and a very few minutes of applied mathematics proved to me that I could not afford to take another one if I wished to pass the course. Accordingly on the seventh day, when the Professor began the hour by inquiring mildly, in his queer throaty voice: 'Perry, are you ready to box the compass for us today?' I boxed it, amid great applause. Dodd twinkled, but said nothing; he knew all along that he held the winning card.

Our life in West College, as in the other dormitories of that period, was primitive enough to have satisfied Rousseau. In fact, we may almost be said to have lived like the beasts that perish. There was no water except what we carried up in pitchers from an outside pump. It may be imagined that we carried as little as possible. Even in the gymnasium, which I frequented for four winters to keep in training for baseball, there were only three or four hand-basins for washing. 'Showers' had not been invented, and there was neither water nor money for tubs. We had to provide ourselves with coal stoves, as no dormitory was heated. There was no service of any kind, except that ash-cans and slop-pails were placed in the hallway of each floor, to be emptied whenever the college janitor got around to it. If we chose to sweep our rooms occasionally and make up our beds, we did so; but this was a matter of individual taste rather than prescription. Carpets were a rare luxury: I had an oil-cloth to cover the middle of the room, a table with a kerosene 'student-lamp,' two or three chairs, a bookcase, and a few prints.

But happiness, as many an unwashed philosopher has pointed out, does not depend upon furnishings. We had youth and health and high spirits. I fear we kicked too many ash-cans and pails downstairs; and since our fathers were charged two dollars a term for any windows we might break and we considered this charge an economic outrage, we took pains to smash, each term, two dollars' worth of glass, very roughly calculated. Carpenter Clark, in deep gloom, described a student as 'a window-breaking animal.' That was also the opinion of Dr. Chadbourne, who lived in the beautiful President's House opposite West College. The favorite sport of the denizens of the north entry of West College was to smash a few panes of glass, start the ash-cans rolling, blow a tin horn, and yell 'Chad!' Instantly, at any hour of the day or night, the President would jump out of his front door like a 'jack-in-the-box,' gold-headed cane in hand, his eyes blazing behind his gold-rimmed glasses, and his beard and coat-tails flying all abroad. If he caught a student he would expel him on the spot, though he usually took him back, with the kindliest admonitions, the next morning. I used to wonder that it never seemed to occur to so bright a man that, if he simply stayed in his study, our whole game would be spoiled. He thought himself, however, a masterful disciplinarian, and that the secret of discipline was in threats. He was the first President of Williams to take any interest in the beauty of the college grounds, but his method of persuading undergraduates to share his desire for better lawns was simply to post notices: 'Keep off the Grass.' We had never heard of

such a thing, and those words became, alas, the unofficial
motto of his administration! Professors were expected
to act as policemen. A few years later, at Princeton,
when the same question arose of protecting the lawns
against the ball-playing and short-cut propensities of
undergraduates, I heard President Patton drawl out
indolently but with finality: 'Are not pleasant relations
between students and faculty more important than a
little grass?'

It was fortunate that most of our surplus energy went
into athletics rather than mischief. Williams had given
up intercollegiate rowing, and organized football was still
a thing of the future, but everyone played baseball after
a fashion, and it is impossible to convey to a present-day
undergraduate the enthusiasm which we felt for it. The
annual 'horn-game' between freshmen and sophomores,
when tin horns and monstrous 'devil's fiddles' were used
by each class to rattle the opposing team, was the chief
athletic event of the year — more important, in fact,
than the 'college' nine's games with Amherst. I happened
to be captain of our class team, and caught. The mask,
invented by Thayer of Harvard, was just coming into
use, but the first models had brittle wire and were likely
to be broken by a foul tip. Otherwise the catcher had no
protection whatever: neither chest pad nor shin-guards
nor even a regulation glove, though many catchers bought
a pair of farmers' buckskin gloves, cutting off the fingers
of the left-hand glove, and padding the palm with a
handkerchief. This helped a little, but not much. Fielders'
gloves were unknown, and most of us carried bone-bruises
from one end of the season to the other. Pitchers were
beginning to work the curve ball, though still compelled

to throw underhand, at a distance of only forty-five feet from the plate. There was no coaching except what the captain ventured to offer, and he had to be tactful about that; and there was no medical or other supervision. If we were hurt, we were hurt. I still carry the scar of a left finger badly broken by a foul tip; I remember pushing the bone back under the skin, wrapping a handkerchief around it and playing the game out, since we had no other catcher. It was boyish folly, of course, but any one of us would have preferred to lose a finger rather than lose a ball game.

We formed our own social groups with entire freedom. There was of course, among the freshmen, a 'West College crowd,' a 'South College crowd,' and so on; but these associations were spontaneous and flexible. The Greek letter fraternities, which since our time have assumed great prominence in the social life of Williams, were then a minor matter. There was no organized 'rushing season,' and though a few freshmen were pledged in advance, not more than a third of each class — and those mainly the wealthier men — joined the fraternities. The rest of us were called 'neutrals,' and though we indulged in occasional satire upon what we considered the snobbishness of awarding a claim for social distinction upon a cash basis, there was little heart-burning over it, and no apparent effect upon class politics or individual popularity. The question of remaining a 'neutral' was simplified for me by Father's attitude. As an undergraduate he had been a charter member of Alpha Delta Phi, but twenty-five years of observation had convinced him, rightly or wrongly, that the fraternities did more harm than good, and he directed his sons not to accept an invitation. By the time his youngest boy entered college, Father had retired from teaching and relaxed his rule; so that Lewis, who had already been excused from learning to milk (the only real blot upon his career, in the opinion of his older brothers!), was allowed the additional indulgence of joining a fraternity.

There were, however, two other undergraduate organizations (both of them now extinct) which I joined early and greatly enjoyed: the Lyceum of Natural History, and the Philologian Literary Society. The 'L. N. H.' had had an honorable history, had sent out the first scientific expedition ever attempted by an American college, and had helped to train many distinguished naturalists, like F. H. Snow ('62), W. K. Brooks ('70), and E. A. Birge ('73). As Professor Tenney's chair had not been filled, we were obliged to work without any supervision, but we had rooms in Jackson Hall, and free access to zoological collections. We organized our own field work, wrote reports, and tried our hand at dissections. I spent a good deal of time trying to learn to mount birds, but I had no real instruction in that art, and finally, after removing the skin from a great blue heron — a rank feeder on frogs and fish, and quite too 'high' when it was brought in — I abandoned the effort in disgust.

The rivalry between the Philologian and Philotechnian literary societies had once been intense, and freshmen had been pledged to one or the other before entering college. I 'went' Philologian, like my father. Each society had pleasant rooms in South College, with excellent libraries, which were then more used by undergraduates than the college library. At the weekly meetings there were essays, orations, and debates. We elected an undergraduate 'critic,' who was usually merciless. I debated with zeal throughout my college course, and was thought by my classmates to have uncanny luck in being on the winning side. As a matter of fact I had a 'system,' whose secret I guarded as closely as I had once guarded old Hadsell's 'side-holt.' It was very simple. In a small college you knew rather accurately the mental habits of each of your opponents in debate. If the other boy was likely to spend two hours in preparation, I spent four; if he spent ten, I would spend twenty. It worked. Not long ago, I explained this 'system' to a group of Harvard intercollegiate debaters, but it did not seem to impress them. They had hoped I would talk about the 'strategy' and 'tactics' of debating — which are indeed interesting enough; but if you have mastered a particular subject twice as well as the other fellow, you may not need any strategy in order to smash him. Alas, how fluent and cocksure I was in those old debating days, and when we Philologians man-handled the Philotechnians in joint debates — the smiling Mark Hopkins acting as judge, as he did in my father's time — how ineffably proud we were! It seemed almost as important, though perhaps not quite, as banging out a base-hit when a hit was needed.

At the end of freshman year, I was promoted to the 'college' or varsity nine, and usually played third base thereafter. Bowdoin, Union, and Amherst were about the only colleges we played, though some of our keenest games were with semi-professional teams from manufacturing towns near-by, like Hoosac Falls, Blackinton, North Adams, and Renfrew. We had both a spring and a fall season, and toward the end of my senior year I discovered

that baseball was taking a great deal of time. For four
years I had scarcely gone trout-fishing or mountain-
climbing except in vacations, and now I had developed a
sudden passion for archery. I explained this to Captain
Fred Fox at the close of a Saturday game, and resigned
from the team. The Amherst game was only two or three
weeks away. Fox was a taciturn fellow, and one of my
best friends, but when I mentioned the claims of archery,
he found plenty of words for once, and on Monday I
was the first man to report for practice. I think I have
wanted few things in life more ardently than to make a
hit the last time I came to bat in college. I got it — and
then an extra game was scheduled, and I had to get it
all over again. Even now, after more than half a century,
I have vivid dreams of those old strains and chances and
mischances of the game. When the Boston Symphony
Orchestra played *Til Eulenspiegel* for the first time in
Cambridge, a very musical lady declared that there were
only two men in Sanders Theatre who smiled at the right
moments, Professor Münsterberg and myself. I did not
dare to confess to her that I was really one hundred and
forty miles distant from the music, playing over again
a ball game against Renfrew, where I came in very fast
from third base to field a bunt and missed it altogether!
What Münsterberg may have been thinking of, I cannot
say.

Our classroom work in the sophomore and junior years
gained somewhat in interest and variety. The elective
system had not then been introduced, except that a few
choices were offered, as for instance between French and
German. The science courses were still in confusion, and

the financial depression of the eighteen-seventies had made it impossible for President Chadbourne to raise money for the vacant professorships. We had lectures in physics and chemistry, but no laboratory work, and we learned very little of these subjects. But we were fortunate in having Dr. Chadbourne in botany and mineralogy. He had taught those classes, as well as chemistry, for fifteen years at Williams before going to Wisconsin; he had made mineralogical surveys in the Rocky Mountains, had led Williams scientific expeditions to Newfoundland, Florida, Greenland, and Iceland, and made researches in Norway, Sweden, and Denmark. Professor W. E. Hocking, of Harvard, tells me that Chadbourne's Lowell Institute lectures on 'Instinct in Animals and Men,' published in 1872, were fifty years in advance of the theories then current. No doubt he had a touch of the foible of omniscience; he once boasted to President Eliot that he could go into any classroom at Williams and conduct the recitation. Eliot was shocked.

But the fact remains that Dr. Chadbourne was a remarkable teacher of outline courses in the field of natural history. We forgot all of his petty vanities and egotisms, all of his shortcomings as an executive. These superficial matters fell from him like an official robe; we saw nothing but the born teacher who should never have forsaken his vocation. He made the dullest boy, for that hour at least, fascinated by crystals and stamens. He dictated terse and brilliant summaries of the main principles of botany and mineralogy; he made us draw illustrations and bring in specimens. We 'L. N. H.' men were delighted, although we were disgruntled to discover later that the prizes in natural history went to the professional prizewinners of our class, who might not know one bird, rock, or flower from another, but who could memorize every word that fell from 'Chad's' lips and pass them back to him in neat notebooks and bluebooks.

I chose German rather than French. Professor Gilson, a lame man with a dark, silky beard, was a Romantic by temperament and had been confirmed in it by long sojourns in Germany. He was an intimate in our household, and had given me as a small boy Kingsley's *Water Babies*, a book full of the strangest natural history, and containing what I thought was a wonderful sentence spoken by Mother Carey ('natura naturans') in her Peacepool: 'I am not going to trouble myself to make things. I sit here and make them make themselves.' That seemed to me to explain Darwinism. I tried hard to please Gilson now, and he was a patient and enthusiastic teacher. I can never read the wonderful quatrain of the Harper's song in *Wilhelm Meister*, beginning

'Wer nie sein Brod mit Thränen ass'

— lines that reveal the very essence of Gilson's own personality — without remembering how he asked us once to bring an English translation of that quatrain to the next recitation. I toiled all the evening over a metrical translation, quite unaware that thousands of men had attempted that task without much success. As we were going into the classroom the next day, I was accosted by 'Fatty' Smith, the best poker-player in our class, but notably weak in German. 'Bliss,' he said, 'lend me your translation. Gilson called you up yesterday, and he won't call you today; but he is sure to call me!' It seemed priggish to refuse, for 'Fatty' was in a tight place; and I parted with my carefully wrought jewel. Smith was the first man called, and obediently wrote that translation upon the blackboard. Gilson read it, looked quizzically at 'Fatty' Smith, and then his eye roamed over the class and rested upon me. 'Perry,' he said blandly, 'will you write *your* translation upon the blackboard?' I had to think fast, but by dint of using phrases which I had rejected the night before, I managed to produce a second version. Gilson shook his head as if in deep depression. 'Bliss,' he remarked sadly, addressing me by my first name, 'your poetical style reminds me of Ossian.' I suppose none of us knew who Ossian was, but I found Macpherson's poems in the college library that afternoon, and decided that Professor Gilson had not intended to compliment me. Charming, lonely, sorrow-stricken Gilson, with his inner life so completely hidden from that group of happy-go-lucky boys!

> *'Wer nie sein Brod mit Thränen ass,*
> *Wer nie die Kummervollen Nächte*
> *Auf seinem Bette weinend sass,*
> *Der Kennt euch nicht, ihr himmlischen Mächte!'*

Under the system of required courses then in vogue, we all studied three subjects under my father: the Constitution of the United States, English history, and political economy. His public reputation, then at its height, had been won in the latter field,[1] but it often happens that a teacher with wide-ranging intellectual interests is known to the academic public mainly by one of his courses, while his best teaching may actually be done in courses that

---

[1] See Carroll Perry, *A Professor of Life* (1923), and the sketch by Broadus Mitchell in the *Dictionary of American Biography*.

do not catch the public eye. I think that my father's lectures on the Constitution were admirable, although we were not mature enough to grasp all of their implications. We could not appreciate, for instance, the significance of many of those Supreme Court decisions which he analyzed with such zest. As Grandfather Smedley once said of John Bascom's sermons in a little church in Pownal, 'He put the fodder too high for the calves.' On the other hand, his course in the history of England has been criticized as being too elementary — 'practically a memoriter exercise.' I cannot agree with this verdict. It is true that we were required to familiarize ourselves, for each recitation, with a few pages of J. R. Green's *Short History of the English People*, then a new and — to me at least — a fascinating book. But this was only the beginning: we had to rise and state the substance of each of Green's paragraphs in our own words, and then discuss the facts and judgments involved, amid constant questioning and illustrations offered by the Professor and the class. To me it was an immensely stimulating course, and in view of my subsequent studies, quite the most valuable one which I had at Williams, although there were some moments in Mark Hopkins's recitation room which made a deeper impression upon me at the time.

In the famous course on political economy I was self-conscious, and often alarmed lest Father, in the intensity of his convictions, should become too excited. He had just turned fifty in our junior year, and seemed in robust health and splendid vitality; but he had toiled and thought and felt too passionately, and ten years later he was a broken man. On many aspects of his subject he was content with clear and dispassionate exposition.

Production and exchange, labor and capital, land and currency and credit, he could discuss with scientific precision and poise. But when he came to foreign trade and American tariffs, he smelled the battle like a war-horse. His very bones cried out against 'Protection, falsely so called.' I had heard all this at home since I had heard anything, and I had no doubt that Father, like his friends W. G. Sumner and David A. Wells, was on the right side of the tariff reform argument. I think so still. But I hated to have my classmates egg him on, by their questions, to more and more dogmatic and extravagant utterance. There was no help for it. His absolute frankness, his devotion to truth as he saw it, his ethical conviction that tariffs drawn in favor of privileged groups were simply a question of Right and Wrong, made him a formidable advocate, and his wit and humor were weapons that often made the class howl with delight, even though these weapons were turned against their own arguments. 'Peri's' classroom was alive — everyone admitted that; but I wondered whether it were not too controversial, too much of a spectacle. A generation later, at Harvard, one might have seen much the same intermittent intolerance in a very different man, Irving Babbitt. Babbitt had naturally a finely critical intelligence, but when he touched Rousseau and Romanticism he threw dispassionate criticism to the winds and became a stark, uncompromising dogmatist, a Peter the Hermit, leading a Crusade. A delightful passage in Logan Pearsall Smith's *More Trivia* may serve to illustrate the point:

'I expressed my conviction briefly; but the time-honoured word I made use of seemed unfamiliar to [these youngsters]; — they looked at each other and began whispering together. Then one of them asked in a hushed voice, "It's *what*, did you say?"

'I repeated my monosyllable loudly. Again they whispered together, and again their spokesman came forward.

'"Do you mind telling us how you spell it?"

'"I spell it, I spell it with a *W!*" I shouted. "W–R–O–N–G — *Wrong!*"'

Arthur Latham Perry and Irving Babbitt had scarcely a trait in common except this: they respected the unfashionable word 'Wrong' and were not afraid to shout it.

In view of my undergraduate interest in speaking, writing, and miscellaneous reading, it is curious that I can recall so little about our class work in English. I remember that we studied D. J. Hill's *Rhetoric* and were informed that the distinction between 'synecdoche' and 'metonymy' was important. We had a *Manual of English Literature*, and must, I suppose, have recited from it. My brother Carroll, whose class also used a *Manual*, avers that he learned just one thing about English literature in college, namely, that 'The lyrics of Edmund Waller can never die.' I did not carry away from the classroom even as much as that.

We were obliged to write and deliver 'orations' once or twice a year under the supervision of the Professor of Rhetoric, Llewellyn Pratt. He was a courteous, cultivated gentleman, and a master of public speech; and no doubt he gave our productions as much attention as they deserved. It was very little. We had also, during part of each year, the services of a friendly and enthusiastic Professor of Oratory, George L. Raymond, author of many volumes of verse and a series of books on Aesthetics. We used his *Orator's Manual*, containing an ingenious and elaborate system of voice-production, stress, gesticulation, posture, etc. We called him 'Bulldozer,' because he was nervous in the classroom and easily overawed; his nickname when he taught at Princeton was 'Mary' — for the same reason. But no one could be kinder to me, or more encouraging. Up to my senior year, the 'gloomy shine' of my oratorical efforts had not impressed the judges of our contests, but now, under 'Bulldozer's' direction, I toiled away, in the big empty Museum room of Jackson Hall, at his 'vocal exercises,' and learned the trick of deep-breathing and the proper 'placing' of the voice. Even the moth-eaten stuffed moose behind the glass cases must have thought the performances of this young Demosthenes absurd, and I let no one, except Raymond, know what I was doing. But I was bent, grimly and ferociously, upon mastering every secret of *The Orator's Manual*, in order to win the Graves Prize speaking contest at Commencement. And there was really more than that at stake, though I did not then suspect it.

Whatever the defects of the curriculum were in our day, we had the inestimable advantage of plenty of time to ourselves. In our senior year, for example, we recited in ethics or philosophy, at nine in the morning and five in the afternoon. Dr. Chadbourne and Dr. Hopkins were supposed to divide these courses, but Dr. Chadbourne spent the fall term stumping the country for Garfield, and as he was retiring from office at the end of the year (and was also trying to run two cotton mills!) he left most of the senior instruction to Dr. Hopkins. We had textbook assignments, but a half-hour of preparation was all that most of us gave. The theory was that seniors should have ample time for reading, writing, and general reflection upon man's place in the universe! This suited me exactly and the winter nights in Williamstown were long.

I had been elected an editor of the college paper, *The Athenaeum*, in my sophomore year, and was greatly flattered until I discovered that the youngest editor was expected to read all the proof and write whatever verses were needed for 'fillers.' I kept at it, however, and learned to write my share of those smart and caustic editorials which long have been the curse of Williams journalism. I wrote about new books, hailing Swinburne's latest volume, for instance, with all the rapture with which undergraduates of today have welcomed D. H. Lawrence and Ernest Hemingway. Robert Louis Stevenson was just beginning to print short stories. Any day might bring a new book by Browning or Tennyson, Darwin or Huxley, Hardy or Arnold. Emerson and Carlyle were living, though they had ceased to write. But Whitman, Whittier, Holmes, Longfellow, and Lowell were still productive. Melville was alive, though we did not know it, and Mark Twain was very much alive indeed. And so were Victor Hugo and Ibsen, Turgeniev and Tolstoi and Karl Marx.

'Here is God's plenty,' and enough to turn any boy's head. No one was aware of the deep and subtle change about to take place in the spirit of English literature. We had already had the best that the Victorians could offer, and after 1880 there was to be less of that 'quality of nobleness' which had been the distinctive trait of English writing since 1830. But we boys in a rural New England college knew nothing about literary tendencies or literary labels: it never occurred to us that we were 'Victorians' or 'Puritans' or even New Englanders. There were the books if we wanted to read them, and whether the authors were American or English, Romantics or Realists, mattered little to us.

I read without any plan or purpose except to gratify an appetite for books. Unluckily, none of us, I think, read in college any Latin and Greek except what was required. That was the tragedy of the system: we broke with the classics just when they might have served us most. I read no French as an undergraduate and only a little more German than was demanded. I was still reading Emerson, and began now to dip into some of the authors whom he praised, like Montaigne and Rabelais and old Burton of the *Anatomy of Melancholy*. I had read Milton and Wordsworth and Whittier since childhood, and can no more recall my first reading of *The Scarlet Letter* than my first reading of *Hamlet*. But now I began to make some discoveries: Keats and Byron (though neither Shelley nor Coleridge as yet), Carlyle (to whom I was introduced by a 'village atheist,' a Welsh cobbler who trained his dog to bark whenever the Methodist Church bell rang!) and Browning and Walt Whitman. What happiness in picking such 'finds' as these from the upper shelves of the college library, and carrying them off to 32 West College! I was warned that Mark Hopkins had declared that *he* could not understand Browning, but secretly I believed that the old gentleman had not made much of an effort. I was sure that there was 'gold in them hills,' and I mined them for a score of years. There was no one to share my enthusiasm for Browning and Whitman, but Fred Bard and I used to wander over the hills spouting

Swinburne and *The Earthly Paradise* and *Sigurd the Volsung* to each other, and when Fred reported that his barber in New York (or it may have been a barkeeper) could declaim more pages of *Sigurd the Volsung* than either of us, our cup of delight was full.

Yet I think that for the majority of our class the chief intellectual adventure of the senior year was the morning or evening hour with Mark Hopkins. He was then seventy-eight, but his powerful frame and noble features showed little or no trace of the burden of years, and there was never, up to the time of his death at eighty-five, any apparent diminution of his mental vigor. This exceptional endowment played its part in the spell which he cast upon his contemporaries. No one can furnish an adequate definition of greatness, but Mark Hopkins, like Gladstone and Bismarck, gave the beholder the instant impression of being in the presence of a great man. He had already become in his lifetime a legend, a symbol of teaching power: 'Mark Hopkins on one end of a log, and a student on the other.' ¹

Four of his pupils and colleagues, Professors Bascom, A. L. Perry, Carter, and Spring, have made painstaking analyses of the Doctor's personality and methods. They all agree that he was not, in the strict academic sense, a 'scholar'; the source of his power was not in his knowledge of books. But that is an old story in the history of the world: 'He taught them as one having authority, and

---

¹ As a matter of fact, this famous phrase, as originally uttered by General Garfield at a Williams dinner at Delmonico's in 1872, did not contain the word 'log.' Washington Gladden, who heard the speech, reported that Garfield's actual words were: 'A pine bench with Mark Hopkins at one end of it and me at the other is a good enough college for me.' *Life and Letters of James Abram Garfield*, by Theodore C. Smith, New York, 1925, vol. II, p. 812.

not as the scribes.' Any teacher can study books, but books do not necessarily bring wisdom, nor that human insight essential to consummate teaching skill. I think that the peculiar gift of Mark Hopkins has rarely been better described than by a single phrase from my old friend Professor Dodd. I was driving with him over Mason's Hill, a year or two after my graduation, and I was telling him about attending the brilliant lectures on the history of philosophy which Stanley Hall was then giving to Williams seniors.

'After all,' I said — captivated by the new horizons which Stanley Hall was opening for us — 'Dr. Hopkins taught us nothing about the history of philosophy.' 'No,' said Dodd slowly, 'he taught you nothing *about* philosophy, but he taught you *to philosophize*.' This is essentially what my father wrote, in pointing out that the Doctor's favorite question — 'What do *you* think about it?' — was the key to his success as a teacher. After beginning by asking the pupil what the textbook stated upon this and that topic, the Doctor would almost invariably inquire: '*What do you think about it?*' 'It stole the hearts of crude young men to hear such a man as he was plumping down upon them from his desk, as if it were a matter of much importance, such a question as that! It suddenly increased their own self-respect.'

To discover that you had a mind — narrow, commonplace, or ill-trained, perhaps, but a mind of your own, was a thrilling experience. You rose when your name was called, and sometimes the Doctor's initial questions, like those of Socrates, seemed remote from the matter in hand. The fascination lay partly in the effort to guess what the

Doctor was driving at. He knew, and we did not, but the game gradually revealed itself as one bland question succeeded another. He always had an objective and sometimes the class perceived it more quickly than the boy who was on his feet, trying to keep his wits and to avoid foolish answers. But often the objective was remote: we were like a party of mountain-climbers, conscious that we were well above the timber-line, but ignorant of the particular peak for which the guide was headed. We were having a good climb and were made to feel that we could keep up the pace and get some grand views, even though the Doctor did not seem to care whether we reached any particular hut by nightfall. To some men in each class, no doubt, he seemed a philosopher without a system, a moralist indifferent to definitions. He was in truth a builder of character who could lay a stone wall without ever looking at a blue-print.

All of us recognized his immense latent power. 'Half his strength he put not forth.' Yet this apparently indolent wrestler with ideas — never dogmatic, never over-earnest, never seeming to desire converts to any creed or platform — was ceaselessly active in studying the members of each class and in directing, however subtly, the questions by which he sought to develop and test their individual capacity. 'Also he knew men at once,' it was said of Cosimo de' Medici, 'when he looked into their eyes.'

I must limit myself to a single illustration of this wise handling of one of his 'crude young men.' In our senior year the mutterings of the famous Andover controversy in theology began to be heard throughout New England. Was 'everlasting' punishment the same thing as 'eternal' punishment? What was really at issue was not the exact meaning of some Greek words, but the whole Calvinistic conception of the actuality of a fire and brimstone hell. I had been brought up in a very liberal and deeply religious household, and I knew that on this question of a material hell my father and his friend John Bascom thought very differently from Grandfather Smedley. Being now twenty and fond of debating, I was wholly on the side of the 'new theology,' as it was then called. Nobody knew where Dr. Hopkins really stood, although he was supposed to be a pillar of Orthodoxy. He was an old man and a wise one, and refused to be drawn into controversy.

One Saturday morning, in reviewing some passage from a textbook, he called me up and put this question: 'Perry, do you think that the fear of future punishment is a proper motive for human action?' I fear the light of battle gleamed in my eyes, for I saw the whole of the New Theology at stake in the Doctor's apparently abstract and innocent inquiry. And the textbook had said 'Yes'; which was only an additional reason why a self-confident youth should take the other side. So I straightened my shoulders and answered 'No, sir.'

The Doctor looked me over. 'I will repeat the question,' he said slowly. 'Do you think that the fear of future punishment is a proper motive for human action?'

'No, sir, I do not.' I was ready to debate against a whole Bench of Bishops; *Athanasius contra mundum*; Luther at the Diet of Worms, etc., etc.

To my disappointment, the Doctor straightway called up 'Turk' Parsons, a missionary's son, who recited the textbook position with fluent precision. But by that time the Doctor seemed to have lost all interest in the question, and went on to something else. The fight was evidently off, and I sulked for the rest of the hour. When the class was dismissed, I had to pass directly in front of the Doctor's desk. He leaned over toward me, bowing his magnificent shoulders and superb head. It was as if an old lion had turned in his cage to look at you, only that all the bars were magically down.

'Bliss,' he said gravely, 'did I understand you to say that you thought the fear of future punishment was not a proper motive for human action?'

I was still obstinate. 'Yes, sir, that is what I think.'

The leonine features relaxed into a captivating smile. 'Well, now, Bliss,' he remarked confidentially, as if to a very intimate friend; '*a great many young men have felt about that question exactly as you do.*'

All the anger and conceit went out of me. I saw myself, not as a lonely rebel, but as one of the great company of the immature. With one sentence Mark Hopkins had put me in my place, and had nevertheless managed to let me feel that he liked me. I hope I had manners enough to thank him, for no teacher had ever rendered me a greater service.

The class of 1881 was the last to be graduated under President Chadbourne. We represented, although we were not aware of it, the end of an era. President Carter's administration was to bring in new professors, new methods of instruction, new buildings and endowments, and a large increase in the number of undergraduates. The rural isolation of Williamstown began to be less marked, though it was still to be a score of years before telephones and motor cars began to herald vaster changes still. I do not pretend to hold a brief for the old order of things, either at Williams or at the other Eastern colleges of our time, but before the old order is quite forgotten, it is fair to say that with all of its obvious defects, it bred some very good men. William Howard Taft (Yale, 1878), Woodrow Wilson (Princeton, 1879), and Theodore Roosevelt (Harvard, 1880) all belonged to our undergraduate generation. Their children, and now their grandchildren, have enjoyed far richer academic opportunities than those three men. Whether the second and third generations have worked as hard or felt as keen a prompting of ambition for leadership is perhaps an idle question; but the educational conditions that obtained in the late eighteen-seventies were not quite so unfruitful as they may easily be made to appear.

At Williams, at least, it must be admitted that during the eighteen-seventies there were more teachers of national reputation, in proportion to the total number of the faculty, than there have been in any subsequent period. The multiplication of courses and instructors, made necessary by the sudden increase of students, has resulted, as probably in all American colleges, in a lowering of the proportion of teachers of exceptional ability. There is less extreme poverty, and no physical hardships whatever, for Williams undergraduates today; but whether luxurious surroundings are really any stimulus to scholarship — even in the 'houses' of Harvard and the 'colleges' of Yale — remains to be proved.

Our social life, like our aesthetic life, was undeniably barren. We had practically no contact with our professors outside of the classroom, and it did not occur to us that this might be desirable. When one thinks of the tutors and preceptors and advisers and deans of today, it is curious to remember that we had no one to 'hold our hand' in time of trouble, and that — precisely like the university students of France and Germany both then and now — we had not the slightest desire to have our hands held. We wanted to be let alone. We chafed very little over the rigid requirements of attendance: chapel twice a day, and no allowance whatever of classroom 'cuts' except for illness. Discipline, swift and simple, was administered by the professors who served as 'class officers,' for deans had not been invented.

About half the men in our class confessed to taking an occasional drink, although I do not remember seeing a single drunken undergraduate in the four years. Nevertheless, of the ten men who were photographed for the varsity nine in our senior year, four were hopelessly ruined by drink before they reached middle life. My own impression is that at Williams, Princeton, and Harvard — the colleges that I have known best — there has been a fairly steady improvement in undergraduate morals for the past fifty years. (My son says that I know nothing about it!) There is certainly less attention given to formal religious exercises, such as the class and college prayer meetings of half a century ago, and the rôle of religious leadership of the college, once taken by such professors as Albert Hopkins, is now left to chaplains and pastors. It is probably true that the informal and inevitable ethical discussions by undergraduates avoid just now the unfashionable words 'right' and 'wrong.' The boys use other synonyms in their restless search for originality in expression. But to affirm that they are no longer interested in what was once called right and wrong seems to me a complete misunderstanding of the undergraduate mind. 'Not interested in right and wrong?' said one of my ablest colleagues once, as we were walking home from a lecture on Goethe's *Faust*; 'why, at bottom, young fellows aren't interested in anything else!'

Whatever the gains or losses which the subsequent years have brought to American colleges, our undergraduate days were now over. Trained or untrained, wise or foolish, we had had our chance. Our Commencement was saddened by the assassination of President Garfield, just as he was leaving Washington on the way to his twenty-fifth reunion at Williamstown. He was one of the most popular of the alumni, and his election to the Presidency had been one of the excitements of our senior year. Only a few hours after the tragic news reached us (Saturday, July 2) came the first of the Commencement festivities: the Graves Prize contest in the public delivery of the six best essays written by seniors. No one pays much attention to such contests now, but in our day crowds attended them. I remember how 'Bulldozer' Raymond rushed up to us six boys — who were quite excited enough already — to tell us that all subsequent Commencement exercises would probably be cancelled, as Garfield's death was momentarily expected; and that we must do our best before the great audience that had gathered. My speech was on Russian Nihilism, and I had toiled as hard over it as the Boy Orator of the Platte did upon his 'cross of gold' masterpiece. And I doubt if even Bryan ever declaimed with a fiercer conviction that he was right! For once my 'gloomy shine' seemed to dazzle the eyes of the judges, and I had my reward for all of the lonely months of practice in the cold and empty Jackson Hall.[1]

On Sunday President Chadbourne preached his last Baccalaureate. The news from Washington seemed more encouraging. On Monday we beat Amherst in baseball. In the evening we listened to Senator J. J. Ingalls's oration before the Adelphic Union of the literary societies. I had to preside, but recall the orator's eloquence less vividly than my own struggle to decide whether I ought to wear my new (and first) swallow-tail or a blue suit. Luckily I put on the latter, for the famous Senator from Kansas strolled down to the church ten minutes late, smoking a long cigar, and clad in a checked suit of very loud pattern. He explained that the trunk containing his evening clothes had been lost in New York. Privately I believed that that trunk was, as the Senator once said of purity in politics, 'an iridescent dream.' On Tuesday I read a long and solemn Class Poem inspired by George Eliot; Mr. T. B. Aldrich showed me a great kindness in rejecting it for the *Atlantic Monthly*. In the blazing noonday of Wednesday, clad now like most of my classmates in a swallow-tail, I delivered a graduating oration on 'The People's Poet'; probably a plea for more men like Burns. But I remember nothing whatever about it except

[1] Nihilism was very much on the American mind in 1881, following the assassination of the Czar. Wendell Phillips had just delivered his famous oration on this subject before the Harvard chapter of Phi Beta Kappa, leaning gracefully upon the desk and talking for one hour and fifty minutes as if he were extemporizing. So perfectly, in fact, did he create the illusion of spontaneity that President Eliot told me that his own classmate, Professor A. S. Hill, who was sitting in the audience next to Eliot, and who had often heard Phillips, felt certain that the orator was not delivering a prepared address. But Dr. Eliot had the galley proofs in his pocket at that very moment; and declared that Phillips did not alter by a syllable the carefully written and memorized text!

Professor Pratt's candid remark upon the manuscript: 'Page after page, Bliss, you seem just on the point of saying something, but you never quite reach that point!' However, I forgave this undoubtedly just criticism, for I collected the Van Vechten Prize for extemporaneous speaking, and had more money in my pocket than I had ever had in my life.

Of course, in those final days I was trying to do too many things. Even now, and many times each year, I have a recurrent dream that I am about to be summoned to the platform to deliver a graduating speech; but alas, it is unwritten, and there are only a few minutes left. Oddly enough, there is always a double consciousness about this dream, for I invariably say to myself, in my distress: 'You have been making all kinds of addresses, for half a century. You could easily make a better speech than these youthful classmates of yours, if only there were five minutes in which to collect your thoughts.' But there are no five minutes: — that is the agony of this hallucination. There is not even one minute! And then I wake up, roll over, and thank Heaven that I have retired and need never make another speech.

IV

FINDING A JOB

Let down your bucket where you are!
BOOKER T. WASHINGTON

HERE, then, was one of those 'crude young men';
five months short of twenty-one, just under six
feet two, just over one hundred and eighty; with
a vigorous appetite for three meals a day and for nine
hours of sleep; with no very brilliant record in scholarship (I had barely scraped into Phi Beta Kappa) and
certainly with no visible means of support. What next?

I had seen almost nothing of the world outside of
Williamstown. In 1873, with my boyhood and lifelong
friend Charles Bliss, of New Haven, I had visited Saratoga
to see an intercollegiate boat-race, and we had gone back
to New Haven by way of New York. In 1876 our fathers
had given us the choice between going to the Centennial
Exposition in Philadelphia and taking a walking trip in
the White Mountains. We chose the latter, and there were
more trout in those mountain streams than there ever will
be again. In one vacation I had spent a month with
half a dozen college friends in cruising from Portland to
Bar Harbor and back again in a twenty-two-foot cat-
boat, camping on shore every night. We did our own
cooking and our own navigation — mostly without charts
— and lived on fifty cents apiece per day. Blue flannel
shirts, old black trousers, and not a razor on board! But

Kinsman

'THE JUSTIFIED MOTHER OF MEN'

Mrs. Arthur Latham Perry with her daughter, her five sons,
and her nephew, Perry Smedley.

in most of the summer vacations my sister had brought some of her Wellesley friends home with her, and we camped for two or three weeks, with other young people from Williamstown, on the Bald Mountain clearing, a mile and a half from the top of Greylock. One may drive to the summit now in a motor car; but I prefer to remember how we used to start up the wet and blind little trail with lanterns at two o'clock in the morning, so as to hear the first thrushes in the hemlocks near the summit heralding the dawn. Those few weeks in the woods were the happiest of the whole year. I learned to love an axe and a camp-fire, and to all of us, for many a year, 'a good camper' was the highest word of praise which any boy or girl could win.

Yet obviously one could not make a living by it. A college graduate, in the year 1881, was supposed to be headed for some profession. To become an expert in natural history required years of training; so did the ministry (for which, in any case, I felt little 'vocation'); and so did medicine, though I thought very seriously of following that profession and indeed went so far as to plan, with my classmate Amadon, to enter a medical school in Philadelphia. But the stubborn fact was that I could not fairly ask Father for any more help; Arthur was in college now, and Walter was leaving for Williston Seminary. Was there anything that I could teach, with-out further preparation?

Once, lying on the bluffs of Bald Mountain, I had ven-tured to confess to a friend that if I could have what I really wanted, I should like sometime to teach English literature! What a dream it seemed then! It was like a boy about to take his first violin lesson, and saying that he would like to be a Kreisler. But just before graduation I received two offers to teach English; one in Robert College, Constantinople, and the other in the American College at Beirut, Syria. I talked it over with Father, and decided in favor of Beirut, though it meant a contract for two or three years. I looked up the steamer routes, and was on the point of promising to go, when the incoming President of Williams, Dr. Franklin Carter, made me a proposal which took me utterly by surprise.

It appeared that Professor Raymond, who was leaving Williams for Princeton, had recommended that I should be asked to take over his work. (Perhaps I had been his only pupil who took *The Orator's Manual* seriously!) Professor Pratt, of the chair of Rhetoric, was also leaving, and it seemed that Professor Griffin, who was to be transferred from Latin in order to succeed him, wished to be relieved of the freshman and sophomore work in Rhetoric. Would I take the position of Instructor in Elocution and English, on a one-year appointment with leave of absence for four months in the winter for special study? The salary was microscopic, but would be increased in case I were reappointed.

I told Dr. Carter about Beirut. 'You could learn Arabic!' he exclaimed, with a true scholar's enthusiasm for the chance of acquiring a new language. But I was not so keen about Arabic; and if one must choose between teaching Arab boys the rudiments of the English language and teaching Williams students the rudiments of public speaking and of writing, I was inclined to vote for Williams. It looked to me like the first round of a ladder. I declined the call to Beirut, and became overnight, to the intense delight of my father and mother, but, I imagine, to the wonder and amusement of Williamstown, a member of the faculty.

The title 'Instructor' had not been used at Williams for years. All of the twelve teachers listed in the catalogue for 1880-'81 bore the rank of Professor; the theory being that instruction should be in the hands of experienced men. My appointment broke this tradition, and I became the pioneer of a long line of young fellows who had to learn their job by doing it. Perhaps it is not the worst way to learn, though one's pupils may suffer in the process.

Two events of the opening year are still vivid to me. One was the surrender of my soiled varsity baseball suit to the '84 man who was to take my place upon the team. Only three months since I had worn it for the last time, but already I was in the 'old grad.' state of mind: I considered my successor an inferior player, and that the athletic standards of Williams were suffering a decline! The other event was my first faculty meeting, in President Carter's library. Four or five new professors had been brought from other colleges; all the others were my former teachers, men with grey beards and black frock coats. Never, at any subsequent faculty meetings at Princeton and Harvard have I had anything like the sense of dignity which I felt then: I was really a member of the society of gentlemen and scholars. Idealists all! The top of the ladder reached even unto Heaven, and though I was perched insecurely on the very lowest round, I was already seeing visions and dreaming dreams.

I was brought back to earth sharply. The first item of business had to do with undergraduate journalism, and as I had been an editor of the college paper, President

Carter began by asking my opinion upon the point at issue. I stated it as clearly as I could. Then — perhaps mischievously — the President called upon my father as the senior professor. 'What my boy has just said,' remarked Father cheerfully, 'doesn't mean *anything*.' Everyone laughed, Father, as usual, loudest of all; and it was thus that I was initiated into the faculty circle.

I remember but little about meeting my first classes. The freshmen had individual drill in declamation; for the sophomores, I think I used Bascom's *Rhetoric* and Earle's *Philology of the English Tongue*. Brother Arthur was in that first class; later I had Walter and Carroll and (in a graduate course at Princeton) Lewis. I was an intensely earnest instructor. Arthur still makes fun of my zeal in that period for the divisions of the Indo-European family of languages and for the profound distinction between metaphor and simile. In the matter of discipline there was never any trouble except once, and that was a plain case of disobedience. I may have been merciless, for I was still under twenty-one; but it was clear that either I or the other boy had to go, and I preferred to stay. On this whole matter of discipline, over which so many sensitive young teachers have agonized, I think my father's advice to me then was the word of final wisdom: 'Remember that your classroom is, for the time being, your own house. Treat the men as your personal guests, and you will have no trouble.' I must at times during the next fifty years have seemed an anxious and worried host, but the guests — and what thousands of them there have been! — were uniformly considerate.

I worked feverishly during that autumn term. I lived at home, but otherwise my position was solitary. As

one of the faculty I was already infinitely removed —
by the tradition of that day — from any real companion-
ship among the boys with whom I had played the year
before, and the new professors were much older men.
I took no recreation except walks across the fields to the
Smedley farm. Most of the daylight hours were spent
in the old chapel, coaching declamations and orations.
The evenings were devoted to the correction of essays,
and to preparation for the morning classes; there was
sometimes a little Browning or Walt Whitman or Montaigne before I went to bed. I like to remember that on
my twenty-first birthday Father presented me with his
own gold watch (which I still carry) and wore a silver time-
piece himself until the class of 1884, somehow getting
wind of this transaction, presented the Professor with a
gorgeous gold one. When winter set in, I left for Andover,
to take special work in public speaking under Professor
J. W. Churchill.

Andover Hill, crowned by the ancient brick buildings of
the Seminary and Academy and by a few lovely dwelling-
houses of the Colonial type, had altered very little since
my grandfather Baxter Perry had gone thither to study
theology, half a century before. But the once famous
Seminary has long since migrated, first to Cambridge and
then to Newton; and the invasion of motor traffic and
the grandiose new buildings of Phillips Academy have
destroyed the charm of the once quiet hilltop. During that
winter of 1881–'82 I boarded in the stone 'Harriet Beecher
Stowe' house with a queer collection of 'theologues.' I
hope I profited by their conversation; at any rate, they
furnished me with the material for a couple of short stories
for my *Salem Kittredge* volume.

Professor Churchill held the chair of Homiletics in the Seminary and also gave instruction in elocution in the Academy. He was an excellent preacher and writer, and one of the editors of the *Andover Review*, but his popular reputation throughout New England was due to his 'readings.' He had a singularly rich voice and features that expressed every color of emotion. His reading desk, lighted with lamps fitted with reflectors, was modelled after that of Charles Dickens. He invariably closed his programs with a humorous selection — 'to send them home happy,' as he told me — and his interpretations of Dickens, Mark Twain, and Bret Harte were masterly. Privately, I think he preferred to read *Hamlet* or *The Ancient Mariner* or Rossetti's *Sister Helen*. He never read in public from the Bible except when he was preaching, and I remember his saying to me that 'a clergyman should always read the Bible as if he were himself listening to its message as well as conveying it to the congregation'; a counsel of perfection which is violated every Sunday.

He was extremely kind to me, discovered that we were distant kinsmen, and would let me pay him nothing for attendance upon his 'vocal exercises' for the theologues and for the private lessons which he gave me twice a week. He knew that I had no desire to become an 'elocutionist,' but he wished to stimulate my interest in every form of public address. Once when I was reading to him an assigned passage from *Hamlet* he stopped me. 'Do you really understand the difference between suggestion and imitation, in interpreting a character? Have you read Lessing?' I said that I knew Lessing's plays, but nothing else. 'Well, you must read his *Laocoön* — here is my copy — and then read the *Hamburgische Dramaturgie*.' I did it; I would have read *The Book of Mormon* if Churchill had recommended it.

He soon discovered that though I knew a little about Greek drama, I had never had the opportunity of attending a theatre, and he made me go to Boston twice a week for the matinees. I used to get a 'New England boiled dinner' for thirty cents at Marston's restaurant on Brattle Street, and then stepped straight into fairyland. Imagine the transport of entering a theatre for the first time, with senses unspoiled by familiarity, and seeing Booth play Hamlet! I have seen Hamlets enough since then, in many countries, and most of the famous actors and actresses of my time, but I still think that there were magical moments in Booth's rendering of Hamlet that are unmatched in my experience of the stage; although Forbes-Robertson's Hamlet, either with or without the Elizabethan stage-setting, was perhaps a better balanced work of art.

What I craved in that first winter of playgoing, however, was not so much balanced art as hypnotic illusion. I sat one day in the gallery of the Boston Theatre watching John McCullough play Othello. As he was smothering Desdemona an Irishman near me leaped to his feet in uncontrollable excitement, crying: 'That's right, Othello! If she was my wife instead of yours, I'd break her damned back!' An unfeeling usher ejected the Irishman, who had no doubt been drinking, but I suspect that when *Othello* first delighted the pit of the Globe Theatre in London, Master Shakespeare, who understood his patrons, would have allowed that Irishman to stay.

For comedy, in that winter, we always had William Warren at the Boston Museum, supported by Mrs. Vincent, Annie Clark, Jack Mason, and other sterling actors.

D'Oyly Carte's company was singing *Patience*. I heard
Patti in a farewell performance, Mary Anderson as Juliet,
W. J. Florence in *The Ticket-of-Leave Man*, and Janauschek
in *Bleak House*. How those names 'date'! Major Henry L.
Higginson was financing the first season's concerts of the
Symphony Orchestra. I watched George Henschel conduct, and heard him in a song recital give *The Two
Grenadiers* so splendidly that when he returned to Boston
for the fiftieth anniversary of that first season, I could not
help telling him that I had never heard the song rendered
with such passion. Just before returning to Williamstown
in March, I made my first pilgrimage to Cambridge, going
out by the horse-cars from Boston, and standing a few
moments, reverently, in the falling snow, before the gate
of Craigie House. Longfellow was dying, though I did
not know it, and a month later Emerson was to follow him.

Professor Churchill generously gave me permission to
use at Williams his 'vocal exercises' and printed charts for
the criticism of speakers, and we corresponded for many
years. He amused me by his gay letters describing his ad-
ventures with Matthew Arnold during the latter's American lecture tour of 1883–'84. Arnold had had no experience
in public speaking, and when he read his lecture in Sanders
Theatre, Cambridge, he was so inaudible that many Harvard students walked out. President Eliot, at whose home
Arnold was staying, told me afterward how bitterly Arnold was troubled by his inability to hold the audience.
'What shall I do?' he exclaimed to Eliot, as they were
walking back to Quincy Street. 'I cannot make myself
heard, and yet I must deliver these lectures. I need the
money!' Whereupon he stopped, took off his hat, hung it
on the top of one of the stone fence-posts in the 'Delta,'

and, in Eliot's words, 'clutched his hair in the immemorial Jewish gesture of despair.' President Eliot, practical and helpful as always, replied that he would send for Professor Churchill in the morning. He did so, and Churchill, posing the famous critic on the platform of Sanders Theatre and taking his own position under the back gallery, diagnosed the trouble at once. Arnold knew nothing about 'speaking to the back of the hall' and invariably dropped his voice — instead of raising the pitch a trifle — on the final word of each sentence. A half-hour of expert coaching relieved Arnold's despair, and when he visited Andover the Churchills gave him an elaborate 'breakfast,' which is described, in terms that gave Churchill much annoyance, in Arnold's *Letters*. 'The Apostle of Sweetness and Light,' Churchill wrote me, 'was not an Apostle of Truth. Never, in the utter *abandon* of household freedom on washing-days, ironing-days, sudden departures of irate cooks, etc., etc., did my wife ever place before me such a *mess* as the Apostle Matthew declares he ate at our house.'

I slipped back, in the spring of 1882, into the groove at Williamstown. I was responsible, naturally, for the train-ing of the Commencement speakers, and it was by this that my usefulness to the college was most likely to be judged. There were no Daniel Websters in the class of 1882, but I gave them a dozen rehearsals apiece, instead of the tradi-tional two. After the Graves Prize speaking, the faculty, who were the judges of the contest, assembled at the President's to vote. Richard A. Rice, one of the new professors and afterward a great friend of mine, blurted out his opinion that all the contestants had spoken 'like dolls stuffed with sawdust.' As I had obviously furnished what-ever stuffing there was, I was hurt; not having yet learned that any critical dictum uttered by Rice immediately moved his auditors to take the other side of the question. At any rate, President Carter reappointed me as Instructor for a five-year term. The salary, if I remember rightly, was twelve hundred dollars; two thousand dollars being then the usual salary of a Professor.

'Dr. Carter thinks very highly of you, Bliss,' said Father one day at table. Then he went off into a brown study, and quite forgetting what he had just said, added, to the huge delight of my younger brothers, '*He is a poor judge of men.*' As a matter of fact, Dr. Carter's judgment of teachers was, in general, excellent; but it was impossible that he and Father should see eye to eye on any question of college policy. Father affirmed stoutly that he was the best friend that Dr. Carter had, and he could not understand why his sons always smiled at this assertion. The two men — each of them devoted to the college, and associates in teaching for many years before Carter had been called to Yale and then back to the Presidency of Williams — were naturally antipathetic. One was an aristocrat, the other a democrat; one was a pessimist, and the other an optimist. These congenital differences would have counted for little if the two had not been thrown constantly together in the faculty of a small college, where, like Arctic fellow voyagers, or as in Browning's 'Soliloquy in a Cloister,' men get on each other's nerves.

Personally I owe Dr. Carter much — and not merely because he offered me my first chance to earn a living. He was a man of admirable scholarship, perfected in Europe; and of discriminating literary taste. After he had resigned the nerve-racking burden of the Presidency and had learned to play golf and to smoke cigars without fear of setting a bad example to undergraduates, he was a delightful and stimulating talker, a mellow and charming person. But in the eighteen-eighties, and especially to a young fellow who was working for him, he was undeniably 'difficult,' and often the prey of black moods and morbid, overconscientious fancies. His health in those years was delicate, but he spared neither himself nor any of his staff. He created a new Williams, and if a college president has the imagination and the energy for such a task as that, the mere matter of his personal popularity among teachers and undergraduates may be overlooked. I was never wholly at ease with Dr. Carter as long as I was teaching under him, but a New England college of that day was a stern school at best, and a teacher's chair was not supposed to be cushioned with any intimacies.

He watched us, with those glittering eyes, incessantly. We were expected to attend chapel regularly and to take our turn in conducting the service unless incapacitated by sheer physical terror, or by immovable obstinacy, as was the case with Dodd. The service was simple, and so far as a required service can be, was devout. You announced a hymn, read a brief passage of Scripture, and offered prayer. To read in public from the Bible is no hardship if one has any ear for rhythm and any sense of that 'glory of words' which Tennyson so foolishly denied to Browning. Later I always took my turn in leading chapel at both Princeton and Harvard, but at Williams I was very young and extremely self-conscious; and the obligation of offering an extempore prayer in public was one that should not have been thrust upon any layman. Henry Lefavour, afterward destined to a distinguished academic career, was, I believe, the first instructor at Williams with enough sense and courage to use the Prayer Book in chapel. But I had been bred as an extemporising Congregationalist, and blundered through as best I could, although always in terror of the ordeal. Even now I have recurrent dreams about it: I am in the pulpit and cannot find the hymn, or else I am searching frantically for the chosen chapter, while the congregation waits. 'I was looking for Ephesians,' says one of Thomas Hardy's rustics, 'and says I to myself " 'Tis nothing but Corinthians and Thessalonians in this danged Testament."'

In the classroom, however, we were left free to do our work in our own way. I began to try experiments in teaching what the later textbooks called 'Description' and 'Narration.' I labored ceaselessly with budding orators, quite unaware that the drift of undergraduate interest was already beginning to set against oratory and debate. Perhaps I was too rigid in holding every man to such work in my field as the college required, for I remember my surprise when Elbert Baldwin, '84, after I had been teaching two or three years, said 'Thank you!' when I had finished one of his rehearsals. It may not have been literally the first 'Thank you' that I received from a Williams undergraduate, but it was the first that I recall. The accepted convention was that I did my job and saw to it that students did theirs; and then we were quits. We were living in Calvin Coolidge's New England, and the social climate was austere.

In the evenings I worked steadily at French and German, read Chaucer through, and re-read Shakespeare and other Elizabethan dramatists. It was obvious that I could never teach the history of the English language thoroughly without a knowledge of Anglo-Saxon. No one in Williamstown knew a word of it, but I sent for March's Anglo-Saxon grammar and reader, and mastered them as well as I could. I went in one vacation to Dr. Sauveur's summer school at Burlington, Vermont, to improve my Anglo-Saxon under a tall, sandy-haired Texan named Primer, and also took a German course with H. C. G. von Jagemann, then of the University of Indiana. Later we were colleagues at Harvard. Von Jagemann told me, with the enthusiasm of a true philologist, that Anglo-Saxon would not be enough: I ought to study Gothic, and Old and Middle High German. He gave me a list of textbooks and I ordered them from Germany. Again there was no one in Williamstown to help me, but I had faith in Von Jagemann, and ploughed on by myself. I hoped sometime to get leave of absence for work in a German university. Beyond that goal, in those days, the imagination of a young fellow anxious for scholarly training could not go! It seems to me now that in my early twenties I had intellectual curiosity, energy, and patience, but whether these qualities were sufficient for the making of a true scholar, I could not tell.

My distaste for all the formal ceremonies of college Commencement seasons must date from that period, when I had to preside at so many contests, and arrange for programmes and ushers and for the comfort and glory of distinguished guests. Of these latter, one of the most amusing was that cheerful demagogue Governor B. F. Butler, who in 1883 had been refused the conventional honorary degree hitherto bestowed upon Governors of Massachusetts by Harvard. However, he turned up at Williams, having already received there the degree of LL.D. in 1864. Whether the Trustees had really studied his military record, no one can say. He was full of anger against Harvard now, and knowing that any hit against that institution is sure to raise a laugh at any other college, he made the most of his opportunity. I can still see him at the Commencement dinner, shouting: 'Young gentlemen, whenever you are attacked by *an institution which denies the divinity of our Lord*, I say to you, on the word of an old soldier' — here he paused, and after wiping his brow with a torn and not overclean handkerchief, waved the handkerchief like a flag and thundered: '*stand by your guns!*' Of course we cheered him delightedly, but I noticed at the President's reception that evening that there were some guests who refused to be presented to the Governor.

I took far too little recreation in that period. The tension was too great. Still, I played a little tennis — a game which had just reached Williamstown. I recall a few delightful tramps with Father, who took no recreation at all except in connection with his studies of local history. We climbed Mount Williams together, and between the top of East Mountain and the Dome we discovered a boulder on which General Hazen must have stood, we thought, when he was running the north line of Massachusetts and made that 'blessed error of the compass,' as Father always termed it, by which the three miles of Williamstown which later became the seat of the college was given to Massachusetts instead of to its rightful owner, the State of Vermont. We tramped along the top of Hoosac Mountain in search of traces of that 'old Mohawk Trail' which Father had discussed so often with his classes that it was already immortalized in an undergraduate song, long before the present motor road over the mountain received the name of the Mohawk Trail. I much prefer my memories of pok-

ing around in the wild azalea bushes on the summit with
Father to the sight of the hot-dog stands and advertising
signs which defile the Trail today.

We studied again the site of Fort Massachusetts, a mile
or so west of North Adams on the road to Williamstown.
Father, while still an undergraduate, had verified the lines
of the old stockade and planted an elm tree to mark the
spot. The first tree died, but in 1859 he planted what is
now known as the 'Perry elm,' which has recently been
enclosed by an exact reproduction of the original stockade.
I had the pleasure in 1908 of pointing out this elm to James
Bryce. He was on his way to Williams to attend the in-
auguration of President Harry A. Garfield. There was no
smoking compartment in the Pullman from Boston, and
Mr. Bryce had come into the day-coach smoker, with
Lawrence Lowell, for a pipe. With his dusty frock coat,
black skull cap, and very black short pipe, he looked more
like a scholar than an ambassador. I had met Mr. Bryce
occasionally, and asked him to share my seat. I was reading in a new *Atlantic* an article on Horace's student life in
Athens. 'I have been wondering for years,' exclaimed
Bryce, 'how Horace's father ever managed to send him to
Athens!' I remember thinking that Bryce was probably
the only man in Washington who knew that Horace had
ever been in Athens. Just then we were passing the Perry
elm, and I told him in a few words about the chain of British forts that had once protected the frontier against the
French and Indians. He seemed not to have heard of
them, but the next day, in the Ambassador's speech, there
was an eloquent passage about 'the memories of those
terrible conflicts which gave North America to the British
race, one of which is commemorated in that flag-pole and

elm tree which stand on the site of the old fort of Western Massachusetts.' I wondered whether he had learned from his old chief Mr. Gladstone the art of 'saying something which he had learned the night before with the air of having known it from all eternity.'

For some years I had done no fishing, but between 1881 and 1886 the Reverend Jonathan Wadhams, who had married my mother's sister and was settled in Ashfield, occasionally asked me over in July to go trout-fishing with him. He had a steady little black mare, and we drove over the hills of Franklin and Hampshire counties and brought back heavy baskets of small trout. On one of these visits my uncle asked me to give a public 'reading' to raise money for a new stove for the parish-house. I could not refuse a kinsman who had given me such good fishing, and the reading took place. (Brother Arthur affirms that I rang the church bell for it myself!) Among the audience were the two most distinguished summer residents of Ashfield, Charles Eliot Norton and George William Curtis. All went well until I announced that my next selection would be the grave-diggers' scene from *Hamlet*. Whereupon either Norton or Curtis — I was too much embarrassed to notice which one it was — rose politely but firmly from the front pew, and walked out. I could not blame him, for I would have liked to walk out myself! But we raised enough money to pay for the stove.

Once in a while I gave public lectures on Browning, with illustrative readings, venturing as far from home as Pittsfield and Albany, and on one occasion, greatly daring, as far as Smith College. I published one or two short stories, and wrote some verse which I showed to the kindly Professor Dodd. His verdict upon the poetry was character-

istically cautious: 'I don't know whether you are on the
right road, but you are on *a* road.' I did not try to get
those verses printed.

In 1885 I was called to the University of Indiana, then
under a new and vigorous President, David Starr Jordan. I
had never been west of the Hudson River, and had no desire to go to Indiana. The technique of using a call to a
larger institution in order to boost one's salary at home had
not been developed, and I said nothing to anyone about
the call. In fact, I had forgotten the incident completely
when many years later at a college dinner in San Francisco
President Jordan, then of Leland Stanford, amused the
audience by relating how he had once called three young
fellows to the University of Indiana without knowing any
of them personally. They had all declined. One was a
Norwegian named Nansen, who had published something
about fishes. Another was a recent graduate of Johns
Hopkins named Wilson, whose book on *Congressional
Government* struck Jordan as original and well written.
The third (and, it must be admitted, a bad third in that
company!) was the former instructor at Williams whom
Jordan then proceeded to introduce. The young President
had gambled in 1885 and lost; but the other young men
had gambled too, and whether they won or lost by declin-
ing to go to Indiana, who can tell?

Eighteen-eighty-six was a red-letter year. It opened
with the greatest happiness that could possibly come to
me, my engagement to Annie L. Bliss, of New Haven,
daughter of those old friends of Father and Mother after
whom I had been named. We had known each other since
childhood. She was now a student at Smith, but was
planning, with her room-mate, to spend the winter of 1886-

'87 in Berlin, studying literature and music. It became
necessary to count upon a long engagement, for in the
spring of 1886 I was promoted to a professorship, with a
two years' leave of absence for graduate study. The college
granted me part salary for this period, and as I had saved
a little money and could borrow a little more, the travelling
expenses could be met; but we decided to postpone our
marriage until my return from Europe. Naturally I discovered plenty of reasons for preferring Berlin, for the coming winter, above all other German universities.

That one should go to Germany in order to study the
language and literature of England seemed in the eighteen-
eighties far more natural than it would today. For seventy
years the more ambitious young scholars of America had
gone to Germany for their training; slowly until 1850, but
rapidly thereafter. It scarcely occurred to them that they
could go anywhere else. At Oxford and Cambridge there
was then no provision whatever — save a single course in
Anglo-Saxon offered by Oxford — for the study of 'English.' The remarkable development of English scholarship
in France, headed by such pioneers as Jusserand, Legouis,
and Angellier, and continued brilliantly to the present day,
had not yet begun. At Harvard, it is true, Professor Child,
in 1886, was offering courses in Anglo-Saxon and Chaucer
in alternate years, and Professor J. W. Bright was beginning to teach the history of the English language at Johns
Hopkins. But the very few graduate courses offered in
my field in American universities were chiefly modelled
upon German methods and given by men who had received their own training abroad. That Germany possessed the sole secret of scholarship was no more doubted
by us young fellows in the eighteen-eighties than it had

been doubted by George Ticknor and Edward Everett when they sailed from Boston, bound for Göttingen, in 1814. When my classmate Starr Cutting and I sailed on the *Pennland*, New York to Antwerp, in July, 1886, we were very certain that we were no Ticknor and Everett, but at least we had something of their sense of the boundless intellectual horizons awaiting young Americans in Germany.

V

BERLIN AND STRASSBURG

Ihr bringt mit euch die Bilder froher Tage,
Und manche liebe Schatten steigen auf;
Gleich einer alten, halbverklungnen Sage,
Kommt erste Lieb' und Freundschaft mit herauf.

GOETHE, *Faust*

THE *Pennland* was an old, slow boat of three thousand tons, not free from cockroaches, but staunch in heavy weather. Cutting had in charge a little French-Canadian girl from Brattleboro, who was bound for Leipzig to study grand opera. I shared in the escort duties, and the situation was one that would have amused Henry James or Howells. Among the passengers were two young men with whom I struck enduring friendships: John C. Perkins, afterward the minister of King's Chapel, Boston, who was bound for Marburg to hear Harnack, and William Roscoe Thayer, then a journalist in Philadelphia who already had half-a-dozen books in the back of his head, though his *Life of Cavour* was to come later, in his Cambridge years.

The hotel authorities at Antwerp and Cologne were puzzled by our solicitude for the comfort of the pretty little singer, but Cutting delivered her safely at Leipzig, while I went up the Rhine. Its beauty had not then been marred by industrialism. My fiancée, who had come over in May with a party of friends, was making a tour of Europe before settling down in Berlin in October, and I planned to

spend the intervening weeks at Heidelberg, where Father
had studied twenty-five years before. Heidelberg was to
me an entrancing place. I discovered Father's bookseller,
and called upon some of his old friends, simple pietistic
Baden folk, who brought out their best bottle of claret and
asked after Professor Gilson of Williams and President
Seelye of Smith, who had boarded there in their student
days. 'Ah, the dear Gilson! He played the flute, not by
note, but with his soul!' Father had told me that two
years in Germany would not be wasted if I could only
learn what the Germans meant by *Innigkeit*, and in talking
with those kindly and pious old souls, I got some inkling of
the meaning of that mysterious word. I took daily lessons
from a school-teacher in writing and speaking German,
climbed up to the Castle and the Königstuhl, boated upon
the Neckar, read *Der Trompeter von Seckingen*, and
watched with amazement the antics of the corps students
of the University, with their colored caps and big dogs and
jolly song. It was not in the least like Williamstown.

One day I followed a crowd of them into a 'public' lecture by the famous Professor Kuno Fischer. It was entering a different world from anything I had known. The
hundreds of young men ceased their chattering as the
Professor entered, at precisely a quarter past the hour, and
they stamped their applause. He was a slender, erect,
ascetic person with a shock of tousled white hair and
across his pale face a long scar from a student duel. For
forty-five minutes, without notes, he poured forth a tor-
rential stream of eloquence about the character development of Shakespeare's *Richard Third*. I must have missed
a good deal of it, for he spoke as rapidly as Phillips Brooks,
but the lecture was printed afterward and I still think it a

masterly piece of Shakespearean criticism. He stopped in
the middle of a sentence, as the hour struck, and stalked
out amid a tumult of cheering. Such was 'Kuno,' among
his idolaters.

The great event of those summer weeks at Heidelberg
was the three-day celebration of the five-hundredth
anniversary of the founding of the University. Harvard
was then precisely half as old. Delegates from all the
universities of Europe (except France!) were in attendance, and I saw for the first time the blaze of color in
academic gowns and hoods. They had not yet been adopted
in the United States. Flags of all nations (France again
excepted) fluttered over the narrow streets of the little
town. There was music each day at the Castle and from its
ample cellars a bottle of Rhine wine was passed through
the window to each guest. One had to show a ticket to be
admitted, and as only thirty tickets were allotted to American students from other German universities and more
than one hundred were in attendance, one of our brilliant
countrymen devised a simple plan for outwitting the
authorities. He marched a squad of thirty Americans into
the Castle grounds, each man exhibiting his ticket, 'good
for bearer.' Then our ingenious friend collected the thirty
tickets, walked out again and reappeared with another
squad, until we were all lined up before the hospitable
cellar window of the Castle.

There was one ironic note in the gifts presented to the
University Library by the universities and great cities of
Europe. The Vatican Library, instead of sending actual
books, presented a beautifully bound catalogue of some
hundreds of priceless manuscripts and first editions, originally plundered from the Heidelberg Library when the

city was captured by Tilly during the Thirty Years' War. These treasures had somehow found their way to Rome, and the Vatican, thoughtfully if not generously, now sent this catalogue for the information of German scholars! Book collectors, even the most exalted, have their own code of morals.

A glimpse of the attitude of South Germans toward the Prussians — which I was to see often enough during the next two years — was revealed at that celebration. The Prussian Crown Prince Frederick — soon to become the German Emperor in a tragically brief reign — came to Heidelberg to represent his father, the aged William First. As he rode on horseback through the streets, escorted by the Crown Prince of Baden and a troop of cavalry, there was little or no applause. I saw an aide-de-camp of the Crown Prince of Baden gallop along the silent, thronged sidewalks, shouting, 'Damn you, why don't you cheer?' But that crowd was not cheering any Prussians.

In September I migrated to Berlin by way of Frankfort and Leipzig. Cutting, later a noted professor of German at the University of Chicago, was making rapid progress, but the little French-Canadian girl, though she sang like a bird, proved not to be of grand opera calibre. Perkins joined me in Berlin, and we secured an immense room, with board, at one hundred marks apiece per month in a *pension* in the Taubenstrasse, not far from the University. Our landlady was the widow of a Protestant clergyman, and had a kind heart and a sense of humor. There were a dozen or fifteen at her table, and only German was spoken. I sat between a young Norwegian actor and a Jewish actress, both of them temporarily out of a job. The actress, perhaps thinking that I was too friendly, informed me that she had seven chambers in her heart: 'six of them are open to the general public, but the seventh is engaged.' I pointed to the engagement ring on my own finger, and thereafter we got along very pleasantly. Opposite us sat a medical student from Chile, who one day in a mood of despair announced to the whole table that 'every woman is a serpent.' The landlady looked at him with a motherly smile: 'My dear fellow, you are standing merely on the brink of psychology!'

Miss Bliss, with her college room-mate, Miss Bancroft, had been received into the family of an architect named Von Holst, a brother of Professor Von Holst of the University of Chicago. The Von Holsts lived in the fashionable Thiergarten quarter, had musical and literary tastes, and kept open house on Sunday evenings, where we met many artists from the Philharmonic Orchestra and many Prussian officers who came to dance with the three Von Holst daughters. It was a jolly and agreeable household.

I was duly matriculated at the University as a *vir juvenis ornatissimus Americanus, studiosus philosophiae*, my special branch of philosophy being philology. I registered for two courses under Professor Zupitza: a *privatim* on English Vowel Sounds and a *privatissime* Seminar of exercises in Gothic and Anglo-Saxon. I also chose Hoffory in General Phonetics, Rödiger in Middle High German, and Deussen in the History of Philosophy — a course in philosophy being required from each student enrolled under that faculty. The total fees for these courses amounted to only sixty marks for the semester.

The first real difficulty arose in gaining admission to Zupitza's Seminar. I had been told that one learned far

more in the Seminars than in the lectures, but I had not
been informed that there were really two classes of students admitted to a Seminar: namely, 'members,' and
'attendants' who took no part in the discussions. I presented myself at Zupitza's house and asked permission, in
German still far from fluent, to join his Seminar. Zupitza
was a brusque, red-headed Pole, of about forty. He pulled
down a copy of Ulfilas's Gothic version of the Gospels, and
asked me to translate. I did so. It was the first test of
those solitary winter nights in Williamstown, spent over
the grammars recommended by Von Jagemann. 'Very
well,' said Zupitza; 'now translate it into Anglo-Saxon.' I
explained in alarm that while I could read Anglo-Saxon,
I had never tried to use it as a living language. Zupitza
looked dubious. 'Begin, then, with this Gothic sentence,
and explain the vowel and consonantal shifts through the
various Germanic dialects until you reach the West Saxon.'
Since then I have heard droves of Harvard Ph.D. candidates execute this feat, but I had had no practice in it
and was terrorized. The consonantal shifts were easy
enough, but the vowels were perplexing. I soon found myself guessing, and of course guessed wrong. Zupitza rose,
and for the first time spoke in English — and his English
was all too plain. 'You don't know enough,' he said
roughly, and I bowed myself out.

I had a bitter half-hour. All the dreams of a life of
scholarship seemed tumbling. Fortunately, I had agreed
to meet my fiancée at the Jubilee Art Exhibition, held that
year in honor of the centenary of the death of Frederick the
Great. I arrived too early, and stood looking gloomily at
some of the paintings. All at once, in a picture of a
cavalry charge, I noticed something peculiar in the way the

sunlight was reflected from the convex surface of a horse's hoof. I glanced at the signature upon the canvas, and remembered that I had seen a painting of a galloping horse, by the same artist, in an exposition at Frankfort six weeks before. And oddly enough, my depression vanished. I said to myself: 'I have a good pair of eyes and a good memory for things seen, and I can write decent prose. If I fail as a scholar, I can at least get a job as reporter on some newspaper at home.' In fact I had already begun to send thumb-nail sketches of Berlin — mostly restaurant and street scenes — to the *Springfield Republican,* and the *Republican* was calling for more. The next morning came a polite note from Zupitza, saying that if I wished to come into his Seminar as an 'attendant,' he would be happy to have me do so.

I accepted the invitation, for that was all I had ever wanted. I knew that I could not as yet command enough German to take part in technical discussions, and in the very first Seminar that I attended I learned how infinitely superior was its standard of philological discipline to anything I had known. Two black-haired Jewish students fell into an argument with Zupitza over some matter involving Greek and Latin etymology, and one could not but be aware that the German training made our college Greek and Latin seem like child's play. Zupitza's lectures on English vowels occupied four hours a week from October to March. The history of each vowel was laboriously traced from the primitive Aryan down to the present. I took faithful notes, and still preserve them, carefully copied and indexed and bound, as a monument of youthful docility; but aside from the discipline involved in such tireless searching of sources, those lectures have never been of the slightest use to me. To tell the truth, Zupitza could make any subject dull; and so could Hoffory, a Dane who must have been related to Rosencrantz and Guildenstern. Rödiger was a little better, and I liked the *Nibelungen Lied*, but the air in those crowded Berlin lecture rooms was notorious for its foulness, and having luckily one free hour in the middle of each forenoon, I formed the habit of stepping over to the Old Museum, which was almost deserted in the mornings, and saving my soul alive by looking at Greek sculpture.

Deussen, in the History of Philosophy, was an admirable lecturer, covering his immense field with skill and enthusiasm. I was overwhelmed at first by the range of his knowledge, but one incident, trivial enough in itself, comforted me quite out of proportion to its importance. Deussen happened to make a remark about Saint Paul which made me look up from my laborious note-taking. I had read in the previous year some of the most recent studies of Saint Paul, and I saw that Deussen's statement — though it would have passed muster at Tübingen or Heidelberg in my father's time — was now out of date. And one lonely and depressed American student knew it! There was a joint, after all, in that shining armor of German omniscience; and for the next forty years, when some shy boy in my own classes came up to the desk and ventured to set me right on some mistaken date or rash generalization, I hoped that the detection of a professorial blunder would do as much for that boy's self-respect as Deussen's blunder had done for me.

It must be remembered that in such courses as were then offered by the Philosophical Faculty there were no tests whatever of a student's progress — save for the discussions and reports of a few advanced students in the Seminars — until the final oral examination and thesis for the Ph.D. We did not have to attend lectures unless we wished: the professor signed each student's registration book at the beginning of a course and again at the end, and that was presumptive evidence of his attendance. He might actually be at some other university for that semester, taking a particular course which he coveted. The system was excellent for the strong man who knew what he wanted, but fatal to many a weakling. The professor ordinarily gave a formal bibliography of his subject in his opening lecture, but whether we ever read any of the books recommended was no concern of his. There was then no card-catalogue for the library; only a set of huge folios in which were pasted the titles of the accessions of each year. We had, of course, no access to the shelves, and it sometimes took an hour for the attendant to find a book. As a matter of fact, it was easier to order a necessary volume from London than to attempt to draw it from the University Library.

Many of us American students found our chief intellectual stimulus — aside from our own private work — in occasional attendance at the lectures of some world-famous scholar upon subjects of which we knew little but which seemed to open wide doors. I can never forget Mommsen on Roman history — lectures given at eight o'clock on the dark Berlin winter mornings; or Zeller on Greek philosophy, du Bois-Reymond on physiology, or Hermann Grimm — who had first introduced Emerson's *Essays* into Germany — on the art of the Italian Renaissance. Most picturesque of all was the great Von Treitschke, orating in his always crowded lecture hall

on the glories of Prussian history and the future destiny
of the German race. He was stone deaf, and could not
hear the tones of his own immensely resonant voice;
there was something the matter with his tear-ducts, and
the moment he grew excited he began to weep involun-
tarily, wiping the stream of tears with his handkerchief
as he mounted from one climax to another. All of us
cheered him vociferously, not knowing that there would
one day be a World War and that Von Treitschke's teaching as to the military leadership of Germany in Europe
and the world would be reckoned by historians as one
of the causes of that catastrophe.

Dr. Carter had given me a letter of introduction to
Professor Ernst Curtius, a Greek scholar then at the
height of his fame owing to his archaeological discoveries
at Olympia. I was asked often to their Sunday evening
suppers. Mommsen was a frequent guest. One Sunday,
just as we were sitting down to an elaborate supper, a
messenger from the old Kaiser appeared, to bid Mommsen
to sup at the Palace. Mommsen grumbled. 'I shall have
to drive home first and put on my decorations; and I
know exactly what the Old Fellow will give me to eat.
It will be boiled fish and potatoes!' Frau Curtius assured
him, however, that she would keep the coffee hot for
him, and in an hour or so he was back, adorned with his
decorations, but still hungry and thirsty. I had a long
talk with him. He attacked President Cleveland for
recalling the American Minister at Athens just after the
Minister had shown some real interest in archaeology:
'If that be Democracy, I wish none of it!' Then he dropped
from German into French, giving a long quotation from
Racine which I fortunately recognized. 'Do you know

French?' he asked. I replied that I could read it a little.
'Read it a little!' he repeated scornfully. 'Unless a man
knows French thoroughly, he is ignorant of modern
history!' One evening he and Curtius were talking about
health and habits of work. Mommsen was then in his
seventieth year, and Curtius was seventy-two. It appeared that both men rose at five, took dumb-bell exercises, a cold sponge bath and a cup of coffee, and were at
their desks before six. In fact, Mommsen's regular lecture
hour, although at eight in the winter, was at seven in the
summer semester. I have had colleagues at Harvard who
rose just in time for their ten o'clock lecture, but I fear
that they gave men like Mommsen and Curtius too long
a start in the race.

That winter in Berlin was the gayest we have ever
known, save for much later winters in Rome and Paris.
Frau Von Holst relaxed her strict notions of Berlin etiquette sufficiently to allow me to escort my fiancée without
a chaperon to concerts, theatres, the opera, and art mu-
seums — although not to restaurants! Joachim was conducting the Philharmonic Orchestra. Frau Sachse-Hof-
meister was the soprano at the Royal Opera — a wooden
actress, but gifted with a lovely voice. Josef Kainz was
the leading actor at the Deutsches Theatre: the finest
Romeo I have ever seen, and a superb Don Carlos. The
Meiningen company came also, with the most perfect *en-
semble* acting then to be seen in Europe outside of Paris.
They played Shakespeare marvellously; in fact, there was
scarcely a week when some play of Shakespeare was not
running in Berlin. Ibsen's *Ghosts* was forbidden by the
police, after a single private performance at the Residenz
Theatre, and I remember the hushed, awe-stricken voices

in which my landlady, the Norwegian actor, the Jewish actress and I discussed till long after midnight the terrible and until then unmentionable dramatic theme which Ibsen had chosen. How the world of the theatre has changed since then! When I last saw Weimar, they were playing *Salome* to a matinee audience of schoolgirls in the old theatre which is faced by the bronze statues of Schiller and Goethe.

The eye of the most casual sight-seer in Berlin, in 1886–'87, was caught by the deliberate glorification of the Franco-Prussian War of 1870 and the worship awarded to the leading figures of the victorious side. It was heightened by new rumors of war with France, in the early months of 1887. We touched our hats to Von Moltke, Bismarck, and the Crown Prince as they rode daily in the Thiergarten. The old Emperor sat each noon at the open window of his palace on Unter den Linden and returned the salute of the soldiers as they changed guard. The son of the Crown Prince and the Princess Victoria of England, soon to become Crown Prince himself and then the Emperor William Second, was a constant attendant at the opera, theatre, and skating rink. Student gossip had it that he was a bad son and a bad husband, but Berlin gossip has always been malicious, and no one suspected how near he was to the throne. Politics were bitter. I heard Bismarck debate one day in the Reichstag against his waspish and merciless opponent Windthorst, and though Bismarck carried the vote as usual, I thought that the radical Windthorst had the better of the argument. This was only three years before the young German Emperor dropped the veteran pilot and laid his own course for ultimate exile in Doorn.

I was leaving Berlin in March for a spring vacation in

Munich and Vienna before settling down at Strassburg for the summer semester. I took some roses to Frau Curtius and bade her good-bye. 'Why are you going to Vienna?' she asked. 'I want to see the paintings in the Vienna galleries,' was the answer. 'I thought you were a philologist!' she said drily. I ruminated upon that remark for a long time. Was I a philologist, and could I ever become one? Zupitza, I fear, would have answered that question in the negative.

Nevertheless, after some picture-hunting weeks in Munich and Vienna, I was enrolled, late in April, at the University of Strassburg. I was still described as a *vir juvenis ornatissimus Americanus, studiosus philosophiae*, and after three semesters in that pleasant city the Rector certified: '*Es ist gegen denselben Nachtheiliges nicht vorgekommen*' — that is to say, 'Nothing detrimental to his character has come to light.' Thank you, Sir!

I had been drawn to Strassburg by the fame of that great scholar and delightful teacher, Bernhard ten Brink. He was of Dutch origin, and although only in his forties had written a brilliant *History of Early English Literature* and was unquestionably the foremost Chaucerian upon the Continent. In the first semester I took his *Beowulf* course and his Seminar on Middle English Romances; in the second, his English Metres and the Shakespeare Seminar; in the third, his *Canterbury Tales* and a Shakespeare Seminar again. In Philosophy I had Ziegler, first on Pessimism and then on Problems of Aesthetics; though I 'sat in' from time to time on Windelband's lectures on Psychology and Ziegler's on Schiller's theory of Aesthetics. These, save for one course given in French, Röhrig's *Le Théâtre Comique*, were my entire lecture programme, but constant participation in Ten Brink's Seminars involved the preparation of many written reports. There was an excellent library in the English Seminar room, and as Ten Brink had few students, one could work there undisturbed. I recall that this library had a first edition of Crashaw's poems, an excessively rare little volume which I greatly desired to steal — improper as such an act would have been for a *juvenis ornatissimus.*

A handful of Americans attended one or more of Ten Brink's courses: George Hemple, afterward a distinguished Chaucerian at Leland Stanford; W. D. Arms, a versatile teacher at the University of California; W. E. Simonds, now Dean Emeritus of Knox College; F. R. Butler, later of Goucher College and Boston University; and W. C. Dreher, a huge North Carolinian who drifted from theology to literature and then to economics, becoming finally a consul in Germany and financial correspondent of London and New York papers. During my editorship of the *Atlantic* he contributed regular 'Letters from Germany,' which were informing and entertaining. We used to tramp together, on holidays, in the Black Forest and the Vosges, and I remember how we spouted Wordsworth's 'Solitary Reaper' to each other as we walked over the battlefield of Wörth. Of all these men, of whom Simonds and I are now the sole survivors, Butler had by far the most brilliant mind. But he was lost, like Coleridge, in a huge scheme for a 'Methodology of Literature' and died before he could bring it into effective form.

We all found Strassburg a fascinating city. Except for the new German quarter around the University and the Palace, the ancient buildings and narrow streets along the river Ill had scarcely been altered since the student days

of Herder and Goethe. The Cathedral had been restored
after the bombardment of 1870, but the lovely façade
by Erwin von Steinbach was fortunately untouched.
New fortifications had been constructed, and immense
barracks for quartering the Fifteenth Army Corps, which
was made up from North German regiments. Alsatian
troops were not to be trusted. These provinces which
had been 'restored to Germany' by the Versailles treaty
of 1871 were treated frankly as a conquered territory.
French professors in the University had been expelled,
just as the German professors were in turn expelled in
1919. There were, of course, towns in Alsace that had been
almost purely French, as there were towns in Lorraine
that had been almost purely German. But Strassburg
had for centuries represented a blend of the two races.
It still remained in 1887-'88 a sort of 'buffer city,' administered by Prussians but with a political consciousness
of its own. More illuminating than many of the books
written about Alsace and Lorraine, both before and since
the World War, was a remark made to me by a small
girl who was playing with her baby brother in front of
the Saint Thomas Kirche. 'Are you French or German?'
I asked. 'Neither the one nor the other,' she answered;
'I am a Strassburger.' A peasant who owned a farm on
the battlefield of Wörth described to Dreher and me the
burning of his barn by the Prussian cavalry. 'I suppose
you are a good enough German now,' I hazarded. 'Why
not?' he replied shrewdly; 'they paid me for my barn.'
Throughout the city, however, though most persons
spoke both French and German indiscriminately, it was
noticeable that each shop or beer-garden had a *clientèle*
that was predominately either German or French, At

the theatre, there were usually two French performances each week, and Simonds, who had a good eye for such matters, used to point out to me that on the French evenings the ladies wore their shabby gowns with an air of distinction impossible for the German ladies to attain.

I lunched and dined, as it happened, with an Alsatian family on the Schiffleutstaden, where only French was spoken, and roomed in the Viehgasse with an old French soldier and his wife. My landlord was one of the irreconcilables. A branch post-office was near-by, and whenever the Imperial mail-cart, adorned with the Black Eagle, drove past his door, he would whistle the tune of a mocking French song, '*Avez vous vu Monsieur Bismarck?*' which was popular in Paris during the siege of 1870. It was a deep relief to his feelings to insult the Prussians thus, and sometimes the driver of the mail-cart, entering into the spirit of the comedy, would whistle back the same tune.

The landlady, a stout, motherly person, felt very sorry for me because I slept with the window open, took a cold sponge bath, drank very little wine, and had to speak and write German at the University. One morning, after bringing up the usual chocolate and rolls, she reappeared with a dozen fat volumes of Balzac, and deposited them upon the table. 'Read that for half an hour each morning before going to your lecture, and it will do you good.' It did. I read Balzac through, and Daudet and Gautier and Zola — whose theory and practice of the 'Experimental Novel' was so violently discussed. In fact Zola's books were then banned in Germany on account of their 'immorality,' but I patronized a French bookshop where they kept, under the counter, copies of each Zola novel as soon as it appeared, and produced them with a smirk. I had now begun to read *Le Temps* and *Figaro*, and followed with zest the literary and dramatic criticism of Francisque Sarcey and Anatole France. One day Billy Arms showed me a letter from his friend Edward Rowland Sill, the poet, in which Sill advised him to 'stay in Germany long enough to get the German point of view, and then enough longer to overlook the German point of view from the universal point of view.' 'Now just what does Sill mean?' asked Billy. But we had to find that out for ourselves.

On Sunday mornings I used to attend a tiny old French Protestant Church, near the Ill. There were never more than thirty or forty worshippers, and the service in its austerity and simplicity still breathed the spirit of Geneva in the great days. The preacher was a young dark-haired Frenchman with a haunting beauty of voice and phrase. I did not learn his name at the time, but some years later, when Paul Sabatier's *Life of Saint Francis of Assisi* was widely read in Europe and America, I noticed that one of the countless editions was dedicated to that little congregation in Strassburg of which he had been the pastor. I had seen his name once on the register of a hotel in one of the hill towns of Italy, and under it the signatures of Paul Bourget and of Henry James.

In July, 1887, came the long vacation. Dreher gave me a tiny edition of La Bruyère's *Caractères* to slip in my side pocket, and I went up to Antwerp to meet Sister Grace, who was coming over for the summer. We took a look at the Low Countries and a few German cities, and then went to Switzerland to meet Miss Bliss, who had been visiting Italy and was now living in the family of a French painter near Interlaken. Here other friends joined us, and we made up a jolly party for Paris, London, the Lake country and Scotland. In September I saw them all sail for Home from Liverpool. I am not sure that there was a Liverpool rain that day, but I felt as if there were. Still, I was going Home myself the next July, and meantime I wanted some hard work.

I knew no one in London except a couple of hotel porters, but the kindly Ten Brink had given me a letter to his fellow Chaucerian F. J. Furnivall, and with Furnivall's backing I secured a desk in the British Museum. I needed access to any books on Aristotle's theory of tragedy which were not in the Strassburg Library. One day I noticed a bunch of seals on the watch-fob of a fellow worker in the Reading Room, and knew that I had seen them somewhere. The owner of these ornaments proved to be Charles Gross, a brilliant Jew who had led the senior class at Williams when I was a freshman. He told me that he had taken his degree in Göttingen in 1883, with a thesis on the history of Merchant Guilds in the Middle Ages. He had now been continuing his researches for four years, mainly in England, but had been unable to find an opening in any American college. 'I am absolutely discouraged,' he said. 'If I hear of nothing in the next six weeks, I shall go back to my father's clothing store in Troy, New York, and abandon the life of a scholar.' But Gross did not have to go back to Troy. Before the six weeks were up, President Eliot, who had never seen him, offered him a position at Harvard, where he became one of the most distinguished of American historical students.

One other remark made to me during that stay in London sticks in my memory. I noticed in the window of Quaritch's bookshop in Piccadilly a rare edition of some Anglo-Saxon text, and stepped in to ask the price. The elder Quaritch came forward; a fine old fellow with a big black beard. The book was priced at eight guineas, and I shook my head sorrowfully. 'Are you interested in Anglo-Saxon?' asked Quaritch, and I told him that I was studying it in Germany. 'Well, young man,' he said with a paternal smile, 'you will find as you go on how small a portion of the world's literature is represented by Anglo-Saxon!' Of course he was right, but I was not yet ready for what the poet Sill had called 'the universal point of view.'

I lingered again in Paris on my way back to Strassburg. I had no letters of introduction and lacked the courage to present myself to any of the scholars and men of letters whom I should have liked to meet. But I learned the chief streets on the 'left bank,' picked up some books along the *quais*, and discovered that my Alsatian accent left much to be desired.

By October I was back in the old quarters at Strassburg. After London and Paris, which always appear to be civilian cities, Strassburg seemed more than ever a military camp. Its narrow sidewalks were thronged with arrogant officers, and as they were forbidden by military etiquette to give way to any civilian, ladies were often obliged to take to the gutter. I was willing to give officers half of the sidewalk and a little more — as it was their country and not mine — but I fear I took a boyish pleasure in bumping into some of the biggest lieutenants as if by accident, and then apologizing in French for my awkwardness. Probably my French gave them more mental anguish than the bump! Those gentlemen had the unpleasant habit of drawing their swords when angered. I saw one workman,

badly cut across the face in a petty restaurant quarrel
with an officer, put under arrest and escorted by a squad
of infantry to the nearest barracks, followed by a mob of
several hundred Alsatians who were jeering and cursing
at the soldiers. As soon as the iron gate of the barracks
was locked against the mob, another officer brutally struck
and kicked the bleeding prisoner. 'That officer will be
degraded for this,' said one of my German friends, and
no doubt he was; but it was not a pretty sight.

Once outside the embittered city, however, everything
was peaceful and charming. The countryside was for the
most part level, and richly wooded and watered. The
blue peaks of the Black Forest and the Vosges were not
far away, and we could walk to the Rhine in forty minutes.
Everywhere the meadow paths led to tiny open-air restaurants, frequented by students. One could sit there
with a book and mug of beer and listen, in the spring
season, to the nightingales. I made a pilgrimage to
Sesenheim and wrote a story around Goethe's idyl which
Mr. Aldrich accepted for the *Atlantic*. The Meiningen
players whom I had admired in Berlin and Dresden came
for a guest-season in Strassburg, and I wrote an article
about them for the New York *Nation*, which Mr. Garrison
was then editing. I also wrote some short stories, using
Berlin and Strassburg as a background, and sold them to
Scribner's Magazine after my return. 'I thought you
were a philologist,' Frau Curtius had remarked, but the
fact was that I felt restless and dissatisfied unless I was
trying, in my free hours, to write something.

The German stock company in Strassburg celebrated
Byron's centenary in January, 1888, by a fine performance
of *Manfred*. The universal interest in Byron shown in

Germany was in striking contrast to British indifference, for the only recognition of Byron's anniversary in London, as far as one could learn, was a memorial service in the shabby Greek church in Soho. I asked Ten Brink one evening, at our weekly *Kneipe* in the Germania Restaurant, who of all the English Romantic poets would be most likely to be read by future generations. Would it be Wordsworth? Coleridge? Shelley? Keats? Ten Brink took a sip from the single glass of Rhine wine which he allowed himself. 'Byron, of course,' he answered. This was as final as another deliverance of his, in response to my question: 'Who are the greatest German poets since Heine?' Another long sip of Rhine wine: 'There aren't any!'

These literary judgments delivered in 1888 by a great scholar remind me of an interesting American visitor to Strassburg in February. I saw him first on the high platform of the Cathedral, above its unfinished tower, where the young Goethe had been wont to stand in order to train himself against dizziness. The American, a middle-aged, black-coated, black-bearded fellow whom I took for a clergyman, was having difficulty with a professional guide who spoke little English, and as the stranger knew no French or German, he was obviously getting nowhere. I told him to dismiss the guide and that I would show him over the Cathedral. I began, as the guides always did, by pointing out the shell-holes made in the great spire during the siege of 1870.

'A church steeple does make a good mark,' said the American quietly.

'How do you know?' I asked.

A softly reminiscent smile crept over his face. 'I had

charge of one of Sherman's batteries outside of Atlanta. I got a Methodist church.'

I decided that he was worth knowing, and after we had finished with the Cathedral I took him over to the University. The ornate German architecture did not impress him, but when we entered the library of the English Seminar, he ran an approving eye along the shelves and I saw that he was a booklover.

'There,' he said, pointing to the works of an English poet then utterly unknown to me, 'is a man who will be read when Byron and Shelley are forgotten.' His poet was George Crabbe.

I bade him good-bye in front of the University, but six weeks later I ran across him in Florence, where I was making an arduous and belated effort to learn Italian.

'What have you been doing since you left Strassburg?' I asked.

His face became beatific in its happiness. 'Do you know,' he answered, 'I've been puzzled all my life to know how the Romans stretched those big curtains over their amphitheatres. I've been in Arles and Nîmes, crawling on my hands and knees around those amphitheatres, and studying the sockets where they fastened the poles. I believe I know just how they did it.'

'Look here,' I exclaimed; 'I'd like to know who you are.'

'Me? I'm a boot and shoe man from Fort Wayne, Indiana.'

I should have liked to tell Ten Brink about my friend from Fort Wayne, but no European professional scholar could have understood the intellectual curiosity of that untrained American amateur.

Ten Brink's courses in that final year afforded excellent drill in linguistics, and sometimes much more than that. His lectures on the *Canterbury Tales*, like his lectures on *Beowulf*, showed the imaginative insight of a born man of letters as well as consummate technical scholarship. His analysis of English metres was keen for that period, but much of it has been superseded by the work of other investigators. The Seminars on Shakespeare were devoted mainly to a minute comparison of the Quarto and Folio texts of *Othello* and *Lear*; and as we had to translate the variant tests into German and carry on all the discussions in that language, I think we Americans wasted a good deal of time over mere mixing of mortar and sorting of bricks. We never really saw the palace of Shakespeare's mind from those Seminar windows. I spent many weeks, in the wonderful spring weather of 1888, in writing a laborious German report for Ten Brink on the Scottish dialects of the fifteenth century, but I have never glanced at the report since then, nor re-read *The King's Quair* on which it was based. To tell the truth, even *King Horn* and *The Pearl* were spoiled forever for me by our remorseless methods in the Seminar, and it was many years before I could recapture my first passion for *Othello* and *Lear*. We murdered to dissect; and yet without training in dissection, how could we ever learn the anatomy of literature? We might have found one answer to this old puzzle in Ten Brink's magical comments on *Beowulf* and Chaucer, for though he could dissect with the best of the anatomists, he was also endowed with a creative imagination which could on occasion make every dry bone live again. But how were we young fellows to know whether we, in turn, would ever be dowered with that gift of imagination? We could not know; but in the meantime we tried to handle the literary microscope and scalpel with Germanic thoroughness.

Simonds, Butler, and I spent long hours, like graduate students of today, in discussing the professional value of the Ph.D. degree. We had taken courses enough for it, and the requirements for a dissertation and oral examination were not, in that period, particularly severe. I think that Ten Brink wished that all of us should become candidates. He proposed to me as a dissertation subject a comparison of the texts of *The Taming of the Shrew* and *The Taming of a Shrew* (1594) — a task which was performed later by another of his pupils. But I was more interested in continuing my own work on theories of tragedy, and in hard reading for Ziegler's courses in Aesthetics. I wanted just then to grapple with ideas rather than with any more textual criticism. So it fell out that Simonds was the only one of our trio to present himself as a candidate — coming gallantly through with a dissertation on Sir Thomas Wyatt. Butler decided to take his chances for promotion without a Doctor's degree, and went on with his scheme for a Methodology. As for me, I was lucky enough to have a professorship already, at a college where I expected to spend my life; and though I knew that a 'Ph.D.' was a pleasant ornament to one's name in a college catalogue, I wanted other things very much more. None of us dreamed, of course, that within the next thirty years American colleges would insist upon a Ph.D. degree as a requisite for promotion, that its commercial value would consequently be reckoned with the precision of an actuarial table, and that all the academic 'go-getters' would take it in their stride.

Those spring months of 1888 were ominous for Germany. I was in Venice, Florence, and Rome during the Easter vacation, and missed whatever mourning there was in Strassburg when the Emperor, aged ninety-one, died on the 9th of March. His son Frederick, the Crown Prince whom I had seen so often in Berlin, now reigned in his stead; but Frederick died of cancer in the throat on June 15, and the young William Second succeeded him. I saw flags enough flying in Strassburg then, and my German friends hoped that all might be well as long as Bismarck remained in office. But Bismarck's days of power were numbered.

One hot morning in July I bought a silk hat, put on evening clothes, and paid my formal farewell call upon Ten Brink. He autographed his *Chaucer Studies* for me, and wished me all good fortune. I never saw him again. With a huge hamper of French and German books — and the silk hat — I sailed Home from Antwerp; but when I reached Williamstown I presented the hat to Abe Bunter, a locally famous Negro who wore it on Commencement Days for many a year. Abe, like the poet Sill, was ready to overlook the German point of view from the universal point of view.

VI

WILLIAMS AGAIN

Life consists in what a man is thinking of all day.
EMERSON, *Journal*

WE WERE married early in August, and by
September were settled in a boarding-house
in Williamstown, awaiting the opening of
the fall term. We planned to build a house of our own
in the spring, and I bought from Father on credit the
southeast corner of the Grace Court property. Neither
my wife nor I had any money; in fact, I was seven hundred
dollars in debt for my stay in Europe; but we had the fun
of paying that off in the first year, out of the professorial
salary of two thousand dollars. As a political economist,
Father held the cheerful theory that it was a good thing
for a young man to be in debt, provided he was anxious
to get out of debt; and he endorsed my note for the
seven thousand dollars which we put into the new house.
Of course it was a gamble, but we were in perfect health
and were used to counting the pennies. And after all, as
Walter H. Page said to me later, 'A man who won't bet
on himself isn't worth a damn.'

Aside from our own radiant happiness and the excitement of our financial ventures, I fear it was a dull winter
for the bride, though she will never admit it. No more
Wagner and Bach and Brahms, except what she played
on the piano; no more operas nor theatres, for vacation

trips to Boston or New York were too expensive to be thought of; no more pictures, except the few prints and photographs that hung in our two little rooms. We played whist for half an hour each day after the midday dinner with a couple of young instructors, and on Saturday nights there were two tables of whist in one of the faculty homes, with chocolate and crackers before we broke up at ten o'clock. There were no evening parties and very few 'dinners,' though we were invited occasionally to 'supper,' where we partook of escalloped oysters and fried chicken, and talked about college affairs. We saw nothing of any undergraduates except those whom I met in the classroom. It was not 'done.' In fact, during the four years as an undergraduate at Williams and ten years as a teacher, I was invited to a fraternity house precisely twice: once to a tea, which I was too shy to attend, and once to a funeral.

Williamstown had changed somewhat since I had chased butterflies and trapped muskrats as a boy. The outlying farms were growing less profitable. A few 'summer people' were beginning to buy desirable building sites, and the Yankee population was yielding increasingly to alien immigration. New buildings adorned the college campus and there were a few more people on Main Street and Spring Street. Fortunately, the mountains were unchangeable, although reckless and wasteful lumbering had denuded some of the summits and left ugly gashes in the timber of the Greylock range. The primeval pines were gone, but the second growth of hardwood came in fast, and the marvellous light on the hills made one forget Main Street and the college and all the signs of change.

Of course we were always made at home in the Perry

GREYLOCK FROM WILLIAMSTOWN

house, which was called in the family the 'Old Sod.'
Mother had had but one daughter, who was now teaching
Latin in Albany, and the new daughter by marriage was
the child of Mother's oldest friends. There were not so
many boys in the 'Old Sod' now: Arthur and Walter had
left college and were in business, Carroll was a junior in
the lazy, brilliant class of 1890, Perry and Mary Smedley
were growing up, and Lewis, the baby of the family, aged
eleven, was already making a reputation as a tennis
player. Mother was outwardly as serene and smiling as
ever, but she was worried about Father's health. He was
only fifty-eight, but he had aged perceptibly during my
absence and was unable to reconcile himself to some of
the changes introduced into the college by President
Carter. Accustomed to the old ways, he was violently
prejudiced against the elective system, which was then
gaining ground rapidly everywhere. Dr. Hopkins had
died in 1887, and Father, as the oldest professor in point
of service, felt isolated. Many of the new professors were
admirable men, but they were of a different generation,
and naturally supported the President in his reconstruction of the curriculum and his general policies. Father's
frank criticism of these changes was respected but outvoted, and he began to feel alienated from some of his
old associates and out of touch with the new men. It
was one of the inevitable academic tragedies, and it came
at a time when his nerves no longer had the former buoy-
ancy and resiliency. For the first time, we had to avoid
topics that were likely to excite him. His classes were
larger than ever, and the strain of enthusiastic teaching
left him exhausted.

There was no diminution, however, of his mental vigor.

He was spending long hours at his desk in writing a new textbook in Economics (the *Principles of Political Economy*, 1891), and was searching the archives in Boston and elsewhere for documents bearing upon the voluminous historical books which he was slowly preparing: *Origins in Williamstown* (1894) and *Williamstown and Williams College* (1899). Nor was there any lessening of his power of offhand phrase. I have printed somewhere his remark as we were walking together to morning chapel in the autumn of 1888. I was saying with some irritation — for Dr. Carter insisted that all professors should attend chapel regularly — that a rigidly required service involved a costly expenditure of time, and that scholars like Mommsen and Curtius were drawing ahead of their American rivals because, for one reason, they saved that half-hour a day. Father's reply was very fine: 'If you are turning a grindstone, every moment is precious; but if you are doing a man's work, the inspired moments are precious.'

Some of my own work, like that of every teacher, was of the grindstone variety; but by no means all. Oratory was still required, though the debating societies were growing less vigorous. Dr. Carter was excessively cordial upon my return from Germany, and talked of giving me *carte blanche* as to courses and hours. But when I submitted a schedule increasing the number of hours allotted to freshman and sophomore English I encountered the departmental jealousies which I ought to have anticipated. Both the mathematical and classical professors objected to any infringement of their traditional rights, and it took a year of diplomacy to adjust the matter. My associate in teaching English was a much older man who took no interest in the language and literature before Shakespeare, but ultimately I had the luck — which still surprises me — of arranging a required course for sophomores in Anglo-Saxon and Chaucer. Of course it had to be made very simple, but they learned to read easy Anglo-Saxon prose, then some *Canterbury Tales* and finally *Troilus and Criseyde*. In the next year I gave an advanced course in Anglo-Saxon to a small elective, using a German textbook, so that they picked up some German incidentally.

I revived my old course in Descriptive Writing, and had great fun with it. We were all reading Stevenson and Kipling then, and I was studying by myself the methods of Flaubert and De Maupassant. It was the epoch of the *mot juste*. I craved for myself as well as for my pupils a greater mastery of exact terms, and we worked away (for I took each assignment with them) on the precise rendering of observed form, color, sound, and motion. I assured the class that when they could describe a gold-finch singing in its billowy flight they could write English! They began by describing simple objects placed upon the desk; a lamp, a cast from Greek sculpture, a stuffed bird, a photograph, a colored lithograph (exposed for five minutes), and even the janitor, who was asked to walk once across the platform. Color troubled us a great deal. In a division of sixteen selected sophomores whom I asked to describe a certain landscape painting — a sunset off the rocks at Newport — a clear streak of color upon the horizon was named 'vermilion,' 'decided red,' 'orange,' 'angry red,' 'light red,' 'flame-colored,' 'dark crimson,' 'reddish-yellow,' and 'golden.' Obviously it could not have been all of these colors, and we then used the Milton Bradley Company's printed color charts to correct our findings.

None of us, naturally, learned to write like 'R. L. S.,' whom we worshipped, but all of us, I think, gained something from that training in acute observation and accuracy of phrase; and we went on from the transcription of visible fact to other and more purely intellectual tasks of composition. I published in the *Andover Review* a long essay on 'Christianity and Tragedy,' a difficult subject on which I had worked in Strassburg and London. I began to print short stories in the *Youth's Companion* and *Scribner's*, and remember vividly how we used the first cheque from *Scribner's*, after we had moved into our new house, to pay the winter's coal bill! I had been from boyhood a lover of Hawthorne, and now, re-reading his *American Note-Books*, I tried to verify as many as possible of the references to odd characters whom he met in North Adams and Williamstown during his visit of 1838. There were still a few old men who recalled the habitués of the Whig Tavern, fifty years before, and I found the very lime-kiln which Hawthorne noted then and used years afterward in his story of *Ethan Brand*. My essay on 'Hawthorne at North Adams' was accepted by the *Atlantic*, whose editor had already printed my sketch of Goethe's idyl at Sesenheim.

With these small feathers in my cap, I longed like many a young fellow to try my hand at a novel. I had only the college vacations for it, but in 1890 the Scribners published *The Broughton House*. I suspect that my proud and generous father, whose own books were issued by the Scribners, had guaranteed the publishers against loss. The galley proofs were decorated with comments in the beautiful handwriting of W. C. Brownell, thus beginning a friendship which lasted until his death. I remember only one of these comments now: 'I hope that your next novel will be ampler and more adulterous.' The scene of the story was Ashfield, which I knew well through fishing trips with my uncle, and the picture upon the cover (there were no 'jackets' then) was drawn from a photograph of the old Nehemiah Smedley house in Williamstown. *The Broughton House* has been out of print for many a year and is long since forgotten, but the critics in 1890 were somewhat extravagant in its praise, and I drank this in with a thirsty soul. I have never re-read the novel, though it meant so much to me at the time. I prefer to think that it was well written, though I admit that it might easily have been 'ampler and more adulterous.'

The following year, 1891, brought us the happiness of the birth of our first child, a daughter, and the sorrow of Father's increasing ill-health. He was evidently on the edge of a nervous breakdown, and upon the advice of his doctor resigned his professorship, after thirty-eight years of active service. He was pensioned as an emeritus professor, and, freed from the long strain of teaching, recovered slowly a fair measure of health. There were other changes in the family circle. Grandfather Smedley died in 1892, in his eighty-eighth year. Grandmother survived him half-a-dozen years, in a tranquil and reticent old age. After her death the farm was sold to a summer resident, and the old brick house and barn were pulled down and replaced by a modern 'mansion.' 'Magic-built to last a season' had been that Paradise of our boyhood, and now it was gone.

In the autumn of 1892 came a surprising letter from Professor George L. Raymond, of Princeton, whom I had succeeded at Williams. It appeared that he now wished to retire in order to devote himself to purely literary work, and that he had recommended me as his successor in the Princeton chair of 'Oratory and Aesthetic Criticism.' The latter half of this portentous title meant that he gave lectures on poetry and its relations to the other fine arts. There would be an assistant in the oratorical work, and the salary would be three thousand dollars in place of the two thousand dollars at Williams.

My first impulse was to decline. I was happily settled in Williamstown and expected to end my days there; in fact, I confided to my wife that I should never leave my own college except for a call to Yale or Harvard, and that such a call was obviously out of the question. We were gradually paying for the new house, and I could sell all the stories that I found time to write. Neither of us had seen Princeton, which was then little known in New England; and besides Raymond I knew no one there except Professor Henry W. Smith, of the Theological Seminary — a former Williamstown boy, a notable half-back and an expert fly-fisherman. Smith wrote us that Princeton was a delightful place and that chickens and sweet potatoes were cheap; while Raymond informed me that many Princeton professors were really 'men of the world' and belonged to clubs in New York. These arguments, however, did not seem wholly conclusive.

Nevertheless, out of courtesy to Raymond, I went down to Princeton during the Thanksgiving recess, and took a look at that straggling New Jersey village. We walked around the college campus. In front of Nassau Hall a half-dozen undergraduates, big fellows in corduroy trousers and turtle-neck sweaters, were kicking football; and through this group, with his head bowed as if in profound thought and totally oblivious of a football that whizzed past his ear, strolled a professor who did not look in the least like 'a man of the world.' It was 'Wick' Scott, the paleontologist. Princeton struck me as rather casual. We called on President Patton, a keen-faced man of fifty, about whom I then knew nothing except that he had led the successful heresy-hunt against Professor David A. Swing, of Chicago, whose liberal sermons had been the delight of Father and Mother. In fact, a little later, I heard Patton in the Princeton Chapel describe Christian truth as a securely locked safe with the burglar Matthew Arnold trying in vain to pick the lock! But the heresy-hunter received me most kindly, with witty, indolent talk about things in general. He was charmingly vague as to specific commitments and courses, and gave the impression of not taking either 'Oratory' or 'Aesthetic Criticism' very seriously. Still, he urged me to accept the call.

Some weeks of indecision passed before I summoned courage to consult with Dr. Carter. We were all afraid of him, but it seemed only fair to lay the Princeton matter before him. It was not, however, one of his most tactful days. If he had uttered one word of appreciation of the work I was trying to do at Williams or expressed any regret at the thought of my leaving, I believe that I would have stayed. But with a dispassionate wisdom for which I am now grateful, he advised me to make the change. 'That tore it' — as Mr. P. G. Wodehouse would say — and I sent in my resignation to take effect in June.

Father had enough venturesome optimism to approve this decision. Mother, like a true Smedley, could not see why anyone could leave Williamstown — and her oldest son least of all. Our family doctor, who was a professor

in the college, was amazed and troubled. 'You *can't*
go to Princeton,' he declared; 'you have just been elected
Deacon of the Congregational Church to succeed your
Grandfather Smedley!' But we were going. Our closest
friends in the faculty circle, Professor and Mrs. E. P.
Morris, had already left for Yale; and Mrs. Morris wrote
that she thought it good for the human plant to be re-
potted from time to time. The spring of 1893 went
swiftly, full as it was of plans for migration. I brushed
up enough Greek to coach a performance of the *Antigone*
at Vassar, and completed my college courses as well as I
could, taking some grim satisfaction in the discovery that
Dr. Carter was obliged to engage for the following year
two men to do the work that I had been doing. That was
eulogy, of a sort.

We were lucky enough to rent our house for the summer
and the following year, and as there were special reasons
for a very quiet vacation, we passed it in a farmhouse in
Dummerston, Vermont, near Brattleboro. Having agreed
to give a course in Poetics at Princeton, I worked in the
mornings on the history of aesthetic theories, a subject
on which I had had good courses in Germany. In the
afternoons I wrote one or two short stories and went
trout-fishing. One afternoon I had my first glimpse of
Rudyard Kipling, who was then living a few miles away
in his new house 'The Naulahka.' I was driving up a
long hill to fish a trout-brook, and overtook the alert,
eager little figure already so famous. Mr. Kipling was
marching along, arrayed in a Vermont farmer's wide-
brimmed, flopping straw hat, a black seersucker coat, and
linen trousers far too short. On his shoulder, as he peered
rapidly and cautiously over the fields from left to right,

was the biggest rifle I had ever seen. He was evidently out for a woodchuck, but if it had been a rhinoceros he could not have been more earnest about it. I could not help smiling at him, and if he had known that I was in pursuit, with equal fervor, of a few eight-inch trout, he might have smiled at me. But neither of us spoke, being Anglo-Saxons, and when I next met Mr. Kipling, some years later, it was at a big dinner party in New York, and I quite forgot to ask him whether he had killed his Vermont woodchuck.

VII

PRINCETON IN THE NINETIES

The old days were fine days,
Oh, fine days were they!
Fine days were the old days,
'Tis that that I do say.
Oh, do you mind those fine days
From June right round to May?
Fine days and fine days and fine days all the way!

Old Irish Song

THE first fortnight in the college town where we spent the seven happiest years of our life was distinctly domestic rather than academic. I had left my wife and two-year-old daughter, with a Vermont maid, in the Bliss home at New Haven, while I went on to Princeton to take possession of the unfurnished house which we had rented. It was a quaint old affair on lower Nassau Street, about a mile from the college, and had been built by a Dutch consul-general to New York in the eighteenth century. The grounds and garden were ample, but had been sadly neglected, and the Negro caretaker had thoughtfully removed most of the grapes and apricots on the day before my arrival. Our furniture was still in Williamstown, in use by the summer tenants, and no one knew whether the furniture or a new baby would reach Princeton first.

The Professor of Aesthetic Criticism, in a pouring

'freshman rain,' bought a cot-bed, discharged the Negro caretaker and moved in. Then I called upon the kindly Raymond for advice about tradesmen and a doctor. He was grandly adequate: 'Dr. Wikoff is the leading physician. You had better buy your coal from Captain Rowland, and tinware from Mr. Vandewater. Lyons is a good grocer, and I should strongly advise you to take a pew in the *First* Presbyterian Church.' Dr. Wikoff, who looked like Edwin Booth, gave me the address of a nurse in Philadelphia, fifty miles away. There were then no discoverable telephones in Princeton and no hospital. I took the next train to Philadelphia and engaged the nurse. It was raining harder than ever when I returned, but I had camped in wet woods often enough, and as soon as I had persuaded Captain Rowland and Mr. Vandewater and Mr. Lyons to deliver some coal, wood, kitchen utensils, and groceries, I felt sure that this camp was at least dry and warm and bound to be a success. And a success it proved: for the family arrived safely from New Haven, the freight car of furniture appeared miraculously from Williamstown, and the baby — a dark-haired and delightfully self-willed daughter — came into the world as a born Princetonian. But, as the Duke of Wellington said of the battle of Waterloo: 'It was the nearest run thing I ever saw in my life.' There was not even time to rent that pew in the *First* Presbyterian Church.

Next came the arranging of my college courses. The senior professor of English Literature was Dean J. O. Murray, who held much the same place in the hearts of Princeton men as Dean Briggs was afterward to hold at Harvard. He was a lover of old books and of trout-fishing, and taught Shakespeare well. The Anglo-Saxon and Chaucer electives were conducted by 'Granny' Hunt, who was then under sixty, but was already desirous of lightening his teaching load. And here came one of those curious forks in the road which have decided the destiny of so many teachers. Hunt offered to turn over to me the Anglo-Saxon and Chaucer courses; but I felt that he did not really wish to give them up, and our polite exchange of courtesies ended by my promise to take off his hands a sophomore course in Rhetoric in the School of Science, which, as I soon discovered, had the reputation of being the most unruly aggregation in Princeton. That interview ended my career as a teacher of Anglo-Saxon and Chaucer, subjects to which so large a part of my graduate studies had been devoted. 'In the place where the tree falls, there shall it lie.'

So I gave a senior elective in Poetics, to be followed by one in Prose Fiction, since I had already taught at Williams a course in the English Novel. Courses in fiction were then new and were naturally regarded as of doubtful value; but 'Poetics' was more safely vague, and had at least the prestige of the name of Aristotle. In the freshman and sophomore work in English and Oratory I had a delightful assistant in Harry F. Covington, who used to send us oysters and terrapin from his native 'eastern shore' of Maryland, and who knew, being an irretrievable procrastinator himself, exactly how far the Princeton lower-classmen could be driven by the stern methods of an imported Yankee. He saved me from many errors in judgment, though I never dared to entrust him with the turbulent School of Science sophomores. They were perfectly friendly, but sublimely indifferent to the rhetorical niceties discussed in the dull textbook which I had inherited; and I had to watch their eyes like a lion-tamer. The seniors crowded into the elective in Poetics, but after the first written examination — in which I conditioned the baseball captain, the football captain, and the son of the President — the numbers fell off a little and the grades improved.

The first faculty meeting struck me as very formal and conducted in accordance with the strictest parliamentary procedure. Its solemnity was a bit lightened at the start by a tall Princetonian who crossed the room and held out his hand. 'Are you the Perry who used to play on the Williams nine?' I admitted the fact. 'Well, I shall never forget that catch you made in left field when you played Princeton!' Those words sounded very loud in the hushed silence, for President Patton had already called us to order to listen to Dr. Duffield's opening prayer; and it was not until after the meeting that I could explain that the glory of that catch in left field belonged to my brother Walter and not to me. My seat that day and for the next seven years was next to the chair of a long-jawed, homely, fascinatingly alert man who was addressed by the President as 'Professor Wilson.' I had read some of his essays, but knew little about him. It was clear at once that he was a debater. I am not sure that it was at that first faculty meeting that Dr. Duffield had prayed that we might be 'endued with holy skill' in our deliberations. But the 'old guard' of professors, many of them trained in the tactics of Presbyterian General Assemblies, had quite enough skill already to delay or circumvent many policies of the 'young faculty,' who in 1893, for the first time, had the numerical majority. The floor leader of the 'young faculty' was Woodrow Wilson, ably seconded

by W. M. Daniels, Fine, Magie, and others. Dr. Patton
was an adroit presiding officer, whose keen enjoyment of
an academic debate was commonly unspoiled by any passionate adherence to either side. Any convictions that he
really had were conservative, but he delighted to watch
Wilson and Daniels cross swords with their elders.

Once, in that first year, he took the floor himself to
oppose Wilson, who was defending a verbal phrase used
in the administration of the Honor System: 'I pledge my
honor as a gentleman that during this examination I
have neither given nor received assistance.' The principle
of the Honor System, which Wilson had seen in successful
operation at the University of Virginia and desired to
introduce at Princeton, had been agreed upon by both
undergraduates and faculty in January, 1893, but some
of the details had still to be worked out. Dr. Patton had
never believed in it, and he now proceeded, from the floor,
to attack caustically that romantic conception of 'a gentleman's honor' which, as he declared, had once allowed a
'gentleman' to seduce a woman or kill a friend in a duel,
but would not allow him to cheat at cards! Now Wilson,
although he had not a drop of Southern blood in his veins,
liked to think of himself as a Virginian born. He was fond
of phrases and knew their power over the student mind,
and he resented Patton's ridicule of 'chivalry' as if it
were directed against Virginia and himself. He grew
white and very quiet, and it was then that he was most
dangerous. In his reply, he was scrupulously courteous
to the President, who had for personal reasons retained
his British citizenship, but Wilson understood the sen-
timental side of American undergraduates far better than
a foreigner, and he managed to convey that impression

with unmistakable clearness and with a passion that swept the faculty off their feet. They voted to retain the phrase 'my honor as a gentleman,' and it has remained in force to this hour.

The system works, of course, only in those colleges which have sufficient social solidarity to ensure that any offender will promptly be 'sent to Coventry' by undergraduate sentiment. One of the two violations of the code which occurred during my years at Princeton was in an examination in one of my own courses. I had left the room as soon as the papers were distributed, and there were no longer any 'proctors.' But a boy was seen to cheat, was reported by his classmates to the undergraduate 'honor committee,' and told to leave Princeton forever that afternoon. I knew nothing about it until Dean Murray announced at the next faculty meeting that Mr. X, on the recommendation of the student committee, had severed his connection with the college. Only those professors who have taught under the humiliating police system and then under the honor system can understand the happy difference made in the relations between professors and students. Yet without the requisite social solidarity the system is doomed to failure. It has worked admirably at Williams, for example, and at many other of the smaller institutions. Some of us made a futile effort, many years ago, to persuade the Harvard authorities to try it, but even Dean Briggs, generous and idealistic as he was, was not to be convinced that the scheme was workable at Cambridge. There are, alas, too many 'Untouchables' in every great university, as Briggs knew sadly well, and you cannot send a boy to Coventry if he lives in Coventry already.

We found both the physical climate and the social atmosphere of Princeton congenial. At first we missed the
mountains, and only gradually came to feel the charm of
the unbroken sweep of the New Jersey farmland and the
level skyline. The climate was relaxing and soothing after
the tonic sternness of New England. It was like living in
Strassburg after Berlin, or in Italy after Switzerland. I
had a curious sense of freedom. All small college towns are
more or less alike, and Princeton was then scarcely bigger
than Williamstown, but I had far less sense of being incessantly watched and judged. Perhaps I had taken too
seriously the responsibility of being an eldest son and the
youngest member of the faculty. At any rate I became less
self-conscious. One could smoke a pipe on Nassau Street
without losing caste. I had four mornings a week for
unbroken work in my quiet third-floor study, and there
was no official scrutiny of what I taught or wrote. The
watchful Dr. Carter seemed a million miles away.

Of course we kept in constant touch with the 'Old Sod.'
Father and Mother came down to visit us, as did my
sister in her vacations at Albany. My brothers were not
far away: Arthur was in business in New York and Walter
in Connecticut; Carroll was a curate in Grace Church in
New York, and then went to a parish of his own at Garrison. Lewis was still, in 1893–'94, a schoolboy at Lawrenceville, only five miles distant from us. There was much
visiting back and forth with the Bliss family in New
Haven, and many other old friends discovered that Princeton was an accessible and hospitable place.

The Southern influence had been strong there until the
Civil War, and though the college had never regained quite
its former quota of Southern students, there were still

enough of them to color the mood of undergraduates, and the community preserved many of the traditions of Southern hospitality. The college remained a small and compact social group. The influx of wealthy alumni as residents did not begin until about the time of the Sesquicentennial celebration of 1896, when the 'College of New Jersey' changed its name to 'Princeton University.' In our first years there an 'all-Princeton tea' — and there were many of them — meant sending out only one hundred and eighty cards. Everyone seemed eager to be on friendly terms with everyone else, and as newcomers from Yankee-land we were amazed at the number of 'first callers' whom we received. Even the venerable ex-President, James McCosh, came promptly with his beautiful wife, who was known affectionately as 'Isabella.' The old Doctor chatted gaily about his once famous theological debate with Mark Hopkins, and was still sure that he had had the better of the argument. Privately, I was a little shocked to discover that he had never heard of his fellow Scot, Robert Louis Stevenson.

It is pleasant to remember now that our first dinner invitation came from the ever hospitable Wilsons, and that they, with Wilson's classmate Robert Bridges of *Scribner's* and Professor George M. Harper, were the guests at the first dinner party that we gave. Our tiny dining-room, filled mainly with a huge Dutch oven and fireplace, could seat exactly six persons; but when we had the right six we thought it a charming room, though the food and wine and service were simple enough. All that the Wilsons asked was good talk, and it was chiefly about books. Wilson was the only colleague I ever had who could be trusted instantly to cap any quotation from

Burke. Mrs. Wilson, who became an intimate friend of my wife, told her with pride that they were spending each year more money on books than on clothes. But money counted for nothing socially in those days at Princeton, and we all lived very plainly. A professor's salary was only three thousand dollars, and we thought Wilson very lucky in getting a month's leave each winter for a course of lectures at Johns Hopkins, for which he was paid precisely five hundred dollars. Before long, however, he was getting much more than that for single magazine articles, and they could afford to build a house — for which Mrs. Wilson, who sketched and painted, made a clay model for the architect's guidance. We were all living in Arcadia then.

I grew very fond of those careless, warm-hearted undergraduates, in their black sweaters and corduroy trousers. This garb was of course a convention, a symbol of a democratic ideal. Luxury had not yet become the fashion. The dormitories, like those at Williams, had no running water, and the gymnasium had but three tin-lined shower baths for a thousand students. Most of them ate in boarding-houses, for not more than five dollars a week. Fraternities had long since been abolished; but there were half-a-dozen upper-class eating clubs, to which about a quarter of the juniors and seniors belonged. 'The rest of us,' writes A. C. Imbrie, secretary of the class of 1895, 'were barely conscious that there were such clubs. We could thumb our noses at them with complete self-respect. We suffered no crucifixion of spirit in sophomore year while candidates were being looked over. There was no excitement, no Bicker Week, and no heart-burnings that anybody was aware of.'

The 'young faculty,' most of them still in their thirties, numbered some brilliant investigators and teachers, and there was more substantial work done at Princeton in that epoch of 'the golden nineties' than is generally supposed. There was distinct literary ambition among many undergraduates. They tried to emulate Booth Tarkington and Jesse Lynch Williams, who had recently begun their careers by writing stories for the *Nassau Lit.* The prize essays printed in the *Lit.* seemed to me more mature than those written at Williams. Clio and Whig Halls, the literary societies then rejoicing in their new marble buildings, held meetings three times a week, and most of the faculty members assisted in the criticism of orations, essays, and debates. I journeyed to New Haven and Cambridge to help organize the first intercollegiate debates between Yale, Harvard, and Princeton, and for some years they excited great interest. Faculty coaching was then allowed, and Wilson, Daniels, and I matched our wits against teachers like Hadley of Yale and George P. Baker of Harvard. Ultimately the audiences discovered that while boys of twenty-one or twenty-two are at their physical best in intercollegiate athletic contests, they are nevertheless not quite so interesting in contests of the mind; and the intercollegiate debates now draw only a handful of spectators. Oratory was beginning in the eighteen-nineties to lose vogue in all the Eastern colleges, and the best I could do at Princeton in that field was to prop up for a while a building that was doomed to fall.

On the other hand, undergraduate interest in more purely literary courses was genuine. I offered to freshmen an optional survey course in English Literature and had forty men; there were from eighty to one hundred in the senior electives in Poetics and Prose Fiction. There were few graduate students in English at Princeton then, and these were largely from the Theological Seminary. When the new library was built we managed to secure a room for an English Seminar — to which Charles Scribner gave a generous gift of reference books — and here I gave graduate courses in Browning and in the influence of the French Revolution upon English poetry. 'Aesthetic Criticism' was fortunately a very flexible phrase, and under it I could offer practically any course in which I felt interested.

I think I can honestly claim that throughout my teaching experience I had enough 'New England conscience' to keep me from neglecting the college work for which I was paid, in order to indulge myself in outside lecturing or writing. But the writing impulse was very strong, and whenever the college work was fairly out of the way, I wanted to be producing something. Magazine editors kept asking for fiction and essays. Publishers suggested textbooks. In 1894 the Scribners published my *Salem Kittredge and Other Stories*, most of which had appeared in their magazine; and in 1895, encouraged by Burlingame, Brownell, and Bridges, who had liked *The Broughton House*, they issued my second novel, *The Plated City*. It had been written in the spare time of three months. 'Bartonvale,' the imaginary Connecticut manufacturing city, was a blend of Waterbury and Ansonia. The theme of the story was the color line in the North, and Mr. Howells, who had once handled that subject himself, warned me that it was distasteful to the general public. A few days ago I read *The Plated City* for the first time since its publication, and to my surprise I found its style and its mingling of romance and realism, of sentiment and irony, very much to my liking. Of course the book 'dates,' as do most of the now forgotten novels of the eighteen-nineties. The press-notices were flattering and the story had its day; even now a few old fellows speak of the picture of a professional ball game with which the book opens.

From 1895 to 1900 I did a good deal of editorial work for publishers: annotated school editions of *Woodstock* and *Ivanhoe*, a volume of *Selections from Burke*, and under the persuasion of F. N. Doubleday a series of *Little Masterpieces* of English and American authors, which grew to eighteen small volumes. The first issues, in sets of three slender booklets, bound in green cloth and manufactured to be sold at thirty cents a volume, were an attractive and daring venture in bookmaking on a very slender margin of profit. The later volumes were in less pleasing *format* and the price was raised to fifty cents. Doubleday and I had great dreams of improving the standard of literary taste in the United States by placing some of the best work of the greatest writers within reach of everybody; and in fact the sales in the first years reached nearly a million copies. But the profits were small, and ultimately the *Little Masterpieces* went out of print. Out of print also, now, is my final adventure in fiction, *The Powers at Play*, a collection of short stories which I had originally printed in *Scribner's*, *Harper's*, *The Century*, and *McClure's*, and which were published by the Scribners in 1899. The title was chosen from Browning's line: 'We caught for a moment the powers at play.' But the public could not be expected to know its Browning, and most of the stories, although I hope delicately written, dealt with a New England atmosphere that was already vanishing at the turn of the century.

The contact with authors and publishers during those years at Princeton was stimulating to a young fellow after the relative isolation of Williamstown. New York and Philadelphia were near at hand. How delicious was the terrapin at 'literary' dinners in Philadelphia, and how agreeably did their lions like Dr. Weir Mitchell, Talcott Williams, Owen Wister, and Miss Agnes Repplier fill the evening with talk! It was flattering to a beginner to be asked by Henry van Dyke to dine with 'some other writing men' at his house in New York and to find oneself seated between Stedman and Frank Stockton, with the chance for long talks after dinner with Cable and Howells. Charles Scribner used to invite each winter the staff of the magazine to dine with some of the contributors. I enjoyed particularly meeting A. B. Frost, who illustrated some of my stories, and H. C. Bunner of *Puck*, of whom Burlingame said once that he was the only man in New York who could judge one of his own stories as objectively as if it had been written by another author. I recall with delight one of these dinners when Barrie — not yet 'Sir James' or a dramatist — was the guest of honor and seemed to know something about the work of each of us. At the time of Stevenson's death Mr. Scribner said to me with some pride that his firm had sold as many as three thousand copies of each of Stevenson's recent books; and then he picked up a newly published book by Henry van Dyke and remarked: 'There is another man, any of whose books will also reach the three thousand mark!' That was in 1894, and I read the other day that one of Van Dyke's books — and by no means one of his best — had sold a million copies. But mass production and distribution was little known in the nineties, and even artists like

Conrad and Henry James found their books praised and unsold.

There was one exception to this rule: Rudyard Kipling's fame and sales kept pace with each other. Mr. and Mrs. Doubleday gave him a dinner one Sunday evening in the spring of 1899. The Doubleday children and some other little folks were brought in beforehand to greet him, and when they asked the myth-maker how the elephant *really* got his trunk, Mr. Kipling dropped down on the floor and kept the dinner waiting while he told them. I never admired his story-telling genius more. After dinner he entertained us by reciting cleverly an ironical and then unpublished poem about the United States. The guest who seemed to interest him most was Booth Tarkington, and he asked me what Tarkington had done. I replied that he was the only Princeton man who had ever been known to play poker (with his left hand), write a story for the *Nassau Lit.* (with his right hand), and lead the singing in a crowded room, performing these three acts simultaneously; and that we all felt that he was a coming writer! Knowing that Mr. Kipling had never seen Princeton, I ventured to ask him where he picked up the Princeton college yell which he used in *A Matter of Fact*; and the prince of reporters told me that on his earliest visit to the United States he had seen a college football game in Buffalo, and had heard for the first time an American college yell. A man who sat next him on the bleachers had said: 'You seem interested in these yells. I'll give you some more'; and among them was the 'Siss-boom-bah' of Princeton, which Mr. Kipling at once 'filed for reference' for some future story.

I walked away from that dinner with Booth Tarkington,

and he may remember how we stood a long time on the empty pavement at Madison Square, talking about the good luck that had just come to him. Mr. McClure was to accept both *Monsieur Beaucaire* and *A Gentleman from Indiana* and had brought him on to New York to complete the revision of both novels. 'Out in Indianapolis,' said Tarkington, 'I have been making bricks without straw.' But I felt then, as I feel now, that Indiana laid the foundation of Tarkington's great and deserved success in fiction. On the Tuesday after that Sunday evening, Mr. Kipling was struggling for life in an attack of typhoid fever.

I had been elected to the Authors' Club of New York in 1894. Through the generosity of Andrew Carnegie, who was a member, the Club was housed on the top floor of Music Hall on Fifty-Sixth Street. The fortnightly meetings were jolly enough. We smoked 'churchwarden' clay pipes, which were very hard to keep going, consumed more or less beer, and tried to be friendly. Frank Stockton explained one evening that friendliness ought to be easier for us than for actors, painters, or musicians, since these artists were compelled occasionally to see the other fellow's plays or pictures or to hear his music, whereas no writer in New York was ever expected to read any of his friends' books. I could not afford to attend the Club regularly, but I made acquaintance with many interesting men: literary veterans like Edward Eggleston of *The Hoosier Schoolmaster*, R. H. Stoddard the poet, and Mark Twain — with his stubborn shock of grey hair, fierce eyebrows, and drawling voice. He told me once, after his wife's death, that he had no one now to tell him whether one of his manuscripts was fit for publication — 'for I don't know, myself.' Those pathetic words were the clearest proof of the unconscious quality of his genius. Mark's old friend W. D. Howells was often at the Club, and was always charming though never really gay. For gayety, however, we could count upon the garrulous 'Andy' Carnegie and the stories of F. Hopkinson Smith and Dr. Weir Mitchell. At the formal annual dinners of the Club, Hamilton Mabie of *The Outlook* often presided; he was then thought to be the best toastmaster in New York. He had been a pupil of Father at Williams, and no one, from my undergraduate days, ever gave me more encouragement in writing. It is the fashion of young men now to minimize the ability and influence of both Mabie and his close friend Henry van Dyke, but no two men in New York, in the nineties, showed more helpfulness to unknown writers, and it saddens me today to see such indubitable Christians thrown to the lions by young aliens who do not take the trouble to read their books.

Henry M. Alden, for so many years editor of *Harper's Magazine*, came occasionally to the Club. Like Mabie, he had been one of my father's pupils, and I suspect that Father and I were among the very few men who ever read Alden's *God in His World: an Interpretation.* The old gentleman certainly kept his passion for mystical theology out of the pages of his magazine. R. W. Gilder, editor of the *Century*, was quicker of tongue and pulse than Alden, and his mournful Madonna-like eyes and mobile face betrayed the lyric poet. I attended once or twice the 'literary evenings' in the Gilders' home on East Fifteenth Street, but some of the poets and poetesses in that collection seemed too self-conscious for my rural taste. E. C. Stedman, however, who was always self-

conscious and a trifle too assertive and 'bright,' was to
me a stimulating companion. I liked Brander Matthews,
also, after I had grown accustomed to his puns and
paradoxes. Laurence Hutton, friendliest of Scotchmen,
was soon to be a neighbor of ours in Princeton; and I enjoyed talking with Charles Dudley Warner and 'Joe'
Jefferson and George Kennan of Siberian fame and James
Whitcomb Riley and the humorous C. H. Webb who had
edited *The Californian* in the eighteen-sixties and had
served as foster-father to Mark Twain's story of *The
Celebrated Jumping Frog.*

None of these men are living now, and even before their
passing some of them were forgotten. I remember sitting
one night in the Club with Frank Stockton, a year or two
after *The Red Badge of Courage* had been published. 'Who
was that young fellow who went up and came down like
a rocket?' asked Stockton; 'Was it *William* Crane?'
'Stephen,' I replied, and in fact Crane was then a member
of the Club. There was a whimsical smile upon Stockton's
dark, gentle, tired face, and perhaps he was hinting that all
our little rockets will come down in time. I do not think
he cared for the idols of the hour. I sat with him on another evening when Richard Le Gallienne strolled in, arrayed in black knee-breeches, silk hose with silver buckles
over the instep, and a flowing black Windsor tie. Stockton seemed alarmed at this apparition. 'For God's sake,
what have we here?' he whispered; and I tried to calm him
by explaining that this was the author of *The Religion of a
Literary Man.*

But let us go back from New York to Princeton, which I
was always glad enough to do. There was nothing in New

York for me — and there is not to this hour — except a few congenial men. I was primarily a teacher, pre-occupied with a fascinating task. That was my career, and I wanted permanently satisfying conditions for it. One of these was a home of our own, and in 1895 we had built one on Mercer Heights, opposite the Marquand estate. Eco-nomically it was a risk, for we still had the Williamstown house on our hands and my income from writing was then under a thousand dollars a year. But we borrowed money, secured a New York architect, and had an at-tractive and commodious house, with a far-sweeping view over the meadows to the east and south. Once more I could have the pleasure of planting trees and weeding a lawn.

We were living in the new house in 1896, when the Sesquicentennial was celebrated; and we bore our modest share in the entertainment of the University's distinguished guests from other American colleges and from Europe. I had not seen such a blaze of gowns and hoods and flags since the Heidelberg celebration of ten years before. President Eliot brought the greetings of American univer-sities, and Professor J. J. Thompson, of Cambridge, England, the felicitations of universities abroad. On Alumni Day, October 21, Henry van Dyke, representing Clio Hall, read his Commemoration poem *The Builders*, and Woodrow Wilson, for Whig Hall, delivered that ora-tion on *Princeton in the Nation's Service* which expressed in essence the policy which he afterward championed as President of the University. The President of the United States and Mrs. Cleveland reviewed the torchlight pro-cession from the steps of Nassau Hall. On the anniversary day itself, October 22, President Patton announced the assumption of the university title: 'From this moment

what heretofore for one hundred and fifty years has been
known as the College of New Jerse↗ shall in all future time
be known as Princeton University'; and President Cleveland, then in his final year of office, delivered one of the
most notable of his addresses to the American people.

The extraordinary success of this celebration was due
largely to the efforts of Professor Andrew F. West, who
had a genius for organization. He was a teacher of Latin
and had been renowned for his clever interpretations of
Horace, but one of his colleagues prophesied that after the
'Sesqui' was over, West would never do a stroke of
scholarly work again. And he never did, finding his talents
fully employed in university politics and in planning for
the Graduate School, of which he became Dean. He had
many delightful personal qualities, and a strong following
among Princeton men; and his opponents made an error
whenever they underestimated his power. He became, as
everyone knows, the most formidable fighter — with the
possible exception of Henry Cabot Lodge — that Woodrow Wilson ever had to face.

But in 1896 there was no hint of any real dissension in
Princeton. The happy family of Princetonians was growing bigger: that was all. The new endowments announced
at the Sesquicentennial were devoted to the purposes of
scholarship, and the 'young faculty,' at last in full control
of the situation, bent every effort toward the transforma-
tion of Princeton into a real university. There were
social changes likewise. Wealthy and loyal alumni like
Taylor Pyne and Junius Morgan occupied their Princeton
estates throughout the college year. The Laurence Hut-
tons bought an old house near us on Mercer Heights, filled
it with books, pictures, and memorabilia of the stage, and

entertained lavishly. Most notable among these new-comers to Princeton were the Clevelands. Pleased by their warm reception at the 'Sesqui,' and urged by Professor West, of whom they grew very fond, they bought a house on Bayard Lane, named it 'Westland' and made it their home after March, 1897. Mrs. Cleveland charmed every-body, of course; and her husband revealed a simplicity and affability which surprised those who had looked upon him only as a stern and somewhat heavy-handed official.

On the evening of his arrival we men gave Mr. Cleve-land an informal reception in our shabby Nassau Club. He was troubled with a gouty foot, and had to remain seated with one leg extended upon a chair. The cares of state were all behind him, and we provided the old Roman with a very long and fat cigar (lifted by Junius Morgan — so the rumor ran — from the private stock of his uncle Pierpont) and watched him chuckle at the performance of two Negro minstrels whom we had imported from New York. It was not a highly academic form of entertainment, but we were not in an academic mood. He had a friendly and tactful word for each of us as we took our turns in sitting by him. He had read my father's writings on political economy, and spoke gratefully of them. Mr. Cleveland had known little about college life, but he soon settled into Princeton as if he had been born there. We found him a pleasure-giving host and guest, full of light talk which delighted those ladies who had been somewhat in awe of him at first. When he obviously did not care to discuss public affairs, I could hold high converse with him in debating the relative fighting quality of a bass as com-pared with a trout of the same weight; Mr. Cleveland al-ways defending the bass. I still possess an autographed copy of the rare issue of his *Defence of Fishermen* (Princeton, 1902, sixty copies only) privately printed by John H. Finley, with dedications to twenty-five of Finley's and Cleveland's friends. Among them are '*Andrew F. West*, who like the disciple Andrew discovers those with loaves and fishes,' and '*Woodrow Wilson*, the kindliest and best beloved of those who correct the mendacity of others.'

I hope I may be pardoned for the sin of Boswellizing if I set down a few of Mr. Cleveland's remarks to me which I remember vividly. The most interesting, historically, was his comment upon his revision of Secretary's Olney's draft of the Venezuela message in 1895: 'I got that draft from Olney and sat down at my desk that night to make some changes in it; and when I looked up, the sun was rising over the Potomac flats.'

Of the famous tariff message of 1887: 'I wrote that when Miss Smith [the dean of Wells College, which Mrs. Cleveland had attended] was visiting us at the White House. I brought it down to the breakfast table and said: "Frank, you are always telling me what a good judge of English Miss Smith is. If she says that message is all right, I'll send it in." Miss Smith read it and said it seemed all right, and so I sent it in.' It cost him the election of 1888.

His account of how his attention was first drawn to Senator White of Louisiana, whom he appointed to the Supreme Court, had the simplicity of a Sunday School story. The President, with a group of Senators, was spending Sunday in Delaware at the home of Senator Bayard. As the party broke up Saturday night, Mr. Cleveland overheard Senator White asking Mr. Bayard if there was a Catholic church in the neighborhood, as in that case he wished to attend early mass on Sunday morning. 'I made up my mind,' said Mr. Cleveland to me, 'that there was a man who was going to do what he thought was right; and when a vacancy came, I put him on the Supreme Court.'

Mr. Cleveland's old-fashioned chivalry and sense of propriety made him refrain from commenting in public upon the policies of his successor in the Presidency: an example which has not uniformly been followed since then. College reporters for the New York papers used to besiege him at Westland, and he tried usually to give them some innocuous 'copy,' because 'it may mean five or ten dollars for the boy, and that would pay his board for a week.' But one day when a persistent undergraduate asked him for his views about President McKinley's Philippine policy, Mr. Cleveland rebelled. 'That, my boy, is a rather large topic to be taken up in a brief interview which is rapidly drawing to a close.'

To professional reporters Mr. Cleveland could be extremely brusque. I was sitting one day in his bedroom while he was reading aloud to me an article which he had just written. His leg was troubling him again. He had it propped on a chair and covered with a Roman rug, and he looked more like a Roman emperor than ever. His butler knocked on the door and entered. 'Mr. President' — John always addressed him in that way — 'Mr. Blank of the *New York Times* would like to see you.' 'Tell him I'm busy.' John reappeared: 'Mr. Blank of the *New York Times* says he is extremely anxious to see you.' 'John, tell him I am discussing something with a friend, and can't be interrupted.' But John appeared once more: 'Mr. Blank of the *New York Times* says he is going to Europe.' At that Mr. Cleveland's temper broke; perhaps his leg was hurting him more than he would admit. 'John, tell

Mr. Blank of the *New York Times* to *go* to Europe and be damned!'

It was rare that his comments upon former political opponents were touched with acerbity. Of Senator George F. Hoar of Massachusetts — of the cherubic face and vitriolic tongue — Mr. Cleveland remarked philosoph-ically: 'I tell you, Perry, the recording angel is going to have a tough time of it with that old fellow. He has done so many good things and said so many spiteful things that I shouldn't know how to deal with him.'

Though he was subject to moods of depression, only once did I detect in him a real melancholy. His feeling about the Spanish-American War was well-known, though he kept it mostly to himself. But one day I was describing to him the plaster-of-Paris triumphal arch in honor of Admiral Dewey which was drawing such crowds in New York. He had not seen it. 'Perry,' he said mournfully, 'I believe that the character of the American people is chang-ing. They are not the same people that they were when I began my political life. They are more excitable, more volatile. Today they are all hurrahing for Dewey, but in three weeks they will be saying: "Dewey? Who the hell was Dewey?"' And in truth, a very little later, the Admiral, in the innocence of his heart, deeded to his wife the Washington house which had been presented to him by some of his grateful compatriots, and when the storm of criticism blew over, Dewey's name 'went off the front page' forever.

That remark about the changing character of the Amer-ican people made a deep impression upon me. I had voted for Cleveland in 1884, 1888, and 1892. In 1896, finding it impossible to support Bryan, I voted reluctantly for

McKinley; but by 1898 it was apparent that that adroit politician was following the popular sentiment in regard to a possible war with Spain. I spent a few days in Washington just prior to our declaration of hostilities. Standing in the House gallery with Congressman Sperry of Connecticut, a stanch Republican, he pointed out to me the Hearst newspapers piled upon each member's desk. 'We are going to be swept into war,' said Mr. Sperry. 'The President doesn't want it, and Speaker Reed is opposing it, but they are helpless. The Congress may break loose any minute'; and we could read even from the gallery the red headlines of the *New York Journal*. 'Get your gun!' a farmer neighbor shouted to me as I was bicycling down to my lecture on the day when the news of the sinking of the *Maine* reached Princeton; and Theodore Roosevelt and Henry Cabot Lodge, as their published correspondence now proves, were fully as eager for war as Hearst or Pulitzer.

I was only a small boy when the Civil War was fought, but I had grown up in the belief that that war was something sacred: a necessary sacrifice for the preservation of the Union and the freedom of the slave. I knew, of course, that many veterans of the G.A.R. were cashing in their military record for pensions and political office, but I believed that such aftermath of the Civil War was only a temporary blemish upon the national character, and should be forgiven in view of the sacredness of the object for which that war had been waged. But now, in 1898, learning that Spain had offered through our American Minister to yield every point at issue before President McKinley sent his war message to Congress, I became for the first time ashamed of my country. Like many college men of my generation, I had felt sincere admiration for the fine personal qualities and public service of Theodore Roosevelt, but when he began to write magazine articles setting forth his motives for fomenting the Spanish War and describing his own activities therein, my disillusion was complete; and when he wore his Rough Rider hat into a National Convention, capitalizing his military record for political advancement, I gave him up. Even today, thirty-five years later, when most of the actors in the Spanish War and in the conquest of the Philippine Islands have passed off the stage, I remain one of the irreconcilables; and still hold to the opinion of my friend William James, who wrote to Moorfield Storey in 1905, 'The whole situation has been a morally rotten one from the word go.'

Let us turn, however, to more pleasant themes. The day of the battle of Santiago, July 2, 1898, was made memorable to us by the birth of a son, a portentously big baby whom we nicknamed 'Shafter,' after the fat military hero of the hour. His next older sister, aged five, was shocked at this impertinence: 'Don't call him Shafter, call him Dove.' But the boy was not in the least dove-like, and he has long since become a better fisherman and golfer than his father. As soon as his mother was able to travel we sought refuge, as we had in 1897, in a tiny village in the Green Mountains, near the Canada line. Greensboro had been 'discovered' in the early nineties by a couple of Yale professors on a walking trip, though there were already two or three shacks on the lake, built by fishermen from Barre and Montpelier. By 1897 there were half-a-dozen summer cottages, a village hotel and a tiny boarding-house. We had marvellous air in that high altitude, restful scenery, absolute quiet; it was the unspoiled essence of primitive Vermont. The lake was perfect for bathing and boating. There were big 'square-tails' in it then, and plenty of landlocked salmon and 'lakers.'   I worked steadily in the mornings over new volumes of the *Little Masterpieces*, and fished or golfed in the afternoons.   I remember fishing seventeen trout-brooks within tramping distance of Greensboro, in our first summer there, and averaging twenty-two fish to a basket.   The food furnished at the boarding-house was not imaginative, but the trout helped; and after September first I could always borrow a dog from a native and provide rabbit-pies in great abundance.

The golf was limited at first to three holes laid out in a pasture, with tomato cans for cups; today there are dozens of cars parked in front of the clubhouse, and two or three hundred members.   Little by little our Princeton friends, hearing us whisper discreetly of this summer Paradise, followed us to Greensboro.   Winans, Hibben, Westcott, Daniels, and Collins, with their families, were among the earliest comers.   Now there are dozens of Princeton colonists living in their cottages and farms, and among them no less than three Princeton Deans, to say nothing of Deans from Harvard, Williams, and North-Western.   We all have bathtubs and electric refrigerators and garages now, with fresh fruit and vegetables from Boston and Sunday papers brought by airplane from New York.   The 'campers' think no more of driving to Montreal or Quebec for a dinner than I used to think of shooting a rabbit for supper when we were tired of eggs and fried potatoes at the boarding-house. Our children and grandchildren go to dances and movies and discuss Eugene O'Neill.   But the 'square-tails' and salmon have disappeared from Caspian Lake, and the motor-cars have ruined the brook-fishing.   There is always a magic about one's summer home, yet it cannot quite be the old magic of arriving at night at the 'Bend' after a two-days' railroad journey from Princeton, and driving in a mountain wagon up the three-mile hill through the woods, while the sleepy children try to count the fireflies or listen to the whippoorwills; nor is it the magic of wet-fly fishing along the then solitary Lamoille with friends like 'Jack' Hibben and Chester Loomis the painter. But the lake and the mountains and the sunsets are unchanged, and if the links are too crowded for comfort on August afternoons, I can sit under the pine trees which I planted thirty years ago and read a book, with half an eye open for the humming-birds hovering around the last tall blue spikes of delphinium.

As the decade of the nineties neared its close, we were settled more and more happily into the routine of Princeton from late September until June. The University was gaining yearly in solidarity of performance, in numbers and in reputation. I was in love with teaching, and though I liked to be writing a book in the spare hours, the claims of my profession came first. Our life on Mercer Heights was all that we could ask: we lived plainly among congenial friends, and we had books, music, and children. My youngest brother Lewis, after graduating at Williams in 1898, spent the following year in our home, doing graduate work for his A.M.; and after teaching at Laurenceville was called back to Williams in my old post as instructor and then professor of English. The older brothers were likewise making their way in the world, and the only real trouble at the 'Old Sod' was an unhappy tempest in a tea-pot caused by Father's publication in 1899 of his *Williamstown and Williams College*, in which he allowed himself an old man's privilege of overfrank — and in some

PRINCETON INN
ARTHUR BAVE, MANAGER.
PRINCETON, N.J.

MENU

Caviar en Canape
Little Neck Clams

POTAGE
Green Turtle Clear

HORS D'ŒUVRES
Olives   Radishes   Salted Almonds

RELEVE
Small Pattie of Oyster Crabs

POISSON
Canadian Salmon, Anchovy Sauce

Hot House Cucumbers   Pommes Parisienne

ENTREMET
Philadelphia Squab, Stuffed with Italian Chestnuts

ENTRE
Sweetbreads Larded, French Peas

ROMAN PUNCH   DIMITRINO CIGARETTES

ROTI
Philadelphia Capon, Compote of Cherries

SALAD
Lettuce

VEGETABLES
New Asparagus   French String Beans

DESSERT
Biscuit Glace   Petit Fours
Camambert Cheese   Toasted Biscuit

Café Noir

MAY 5, 1900.

A PRINCETON FAREWELL DINNER

passages regrettably unfair — criticism of some of his former academic colleagues. But this was a swiftly passing storm.

It taught me, nevertheless, the sensitiveness of any academic community, and the fierce human passions that underlie the decorous surface of professorial existence. A forest fire can be started on any smooth-clipped college campus, as Princeton was soon to learn to its cost. The bitter controversies that were to centre upon the personality of Woodrow Wilson did not begin until after the nineties, when I was no longer connected with the University and was under no necessity for taking sides. My most intimate friends in Princeton divided into hostile camps, and their differences are no part of my story. But since Wilson was destined to become a national figure and then a world figure, I should like to set down my own impression of his mind and character in the period when I saw much of him, and when, fortunately, myth and legend and calumny had not begun to distort the judgment of an observer.

When I first knew him, he was only thirty-six, but there was little that was youthful in him except high spirits, energy, and self-confidence. He had never, I suspect, been a boy of normal boyish irresponsibility. His father, who often paid long visits to Princeton and was a whimsical, forceful person, had been 'Tommy's' real comrade and had moulded his mind and behavior. The son was a true child of a manse where religion, wit, and political theorizing went hand in hand. Both father and son were idealists, phrase-lovers, and critics.

Wilson's family life was singularly happy. He was adored by his wife and daughters and by the Axson and Howe relatives who at times filled the house. He was strict with his children, particularly in regard to their habits of speech. While he had an extraordinary fund of amusing dialect stories — Scotch, Negro, and Irish — his children were enjoined rigidly from the use of slang. Sometimes they echoed his own meticulous vocabulary without really understanding it. George Armour, a book-collecting neighbor of the Wilsons, used to repeat with delight a conversation between the small Wilson girls and his own daughter. 'What is a dilettante?' asked the Wilson child. 'I don't know,' confessed the Armour child, 'do you?' 'No, but that is what my father says your father is.'

He was physically of an ascetic habit, and gave the appearance of being trained rather fine. He provided wine and cigars for his guests, but in the nineties his physician was forbidding him both alcohol and tobacco. He took little exercise except bicycling, and held himself to a stern schedule of solitary work in his study, which was guarded sedulously by his idolizing wife. Yet in those years, if not always later, he was extremely fond of company. He loved the society of cultivated women, and treated them with an elaborate Southern courtesy which was already beginning, toward the end of the century, to seem a trifle old-fashioned in the North. But in him it was genuine. For some years Mr. and Mrs. Wilson, Mr. and Mrs. Hibben, Mrs. Perry and I used to take tea with Miss Ricketts on Sunday afternoons, and unless those talks are now idealized by distance, they were exceptionally good. We rarely discussed politics. Wilson was, by the way, a great admirer of Cleveland, though he had been perturbed by the truculent tone of the Venezuela message. His review of Cleveland's second administration, printed in the *Atlantic*, was one of the ablest contemporary tributes to Cleveland's public services. I think the two men would have remained warm friends at Princeton if they had not been estranged by meddlers and by sharply diverging views of what was best for the University; but all that belongs to a later period. What we debated over the tea-cups was books and general theories of life. Our hostess was more widely read in European literatures than any of her guests, but Wilson usually outshone that little, intimate company in sheer inventiveness and pungency of phrase. I felt occasionally, not that he 'talked for victory,' but that he concentrated too much upon his own conversational game, much as some professional golfers content themselves with shooting steadily at par without regard to the shots of their opponents. This is perhaps a better rule for a golf match than for a tea-party, though it was often more delightful to listen to Wilson than to challenge the soundness of his opinions. Miss Ricketts — to say nothing of her brilliant mother — was quite capable of doing that!

We usually walked down to the college chapel service after tea was over. Wilson took his turn in conducting it, and I think no one who listened to his chapel talks could have doubted the sincerity of his religious faith. The Wilsons, on coming to Princeton, had joined the unfashionable Second Presbyterian Church, thinking that they were more needed there than in the '*First*' Church which had been recommended to us by Professor Raymond. It was left to a later decade to invent the hypothesis that Wilson was a hypocrite in everything, including religion.

No one among his intimates — though the number of his real intimates was few — had any uncertainty, in the eighteen-nineties, as to Wilson's nobility of character. Of course he had his faults. Sometimes I found it hard to excuse his impatient contempt for the dullness and slowness of some of his elderly colleagues — particularly the 'Three Snoozers' about whom West wrote a witty and privately circulated poem. His Scotch-Irish temper was quick and not always under perfect control. But his 'arrogance' and 'autocracy,' like his 'timidity' and 'vacillation,' were the invention of a later epoch. I sat on committees with him very frequently, and though he knew his own mind and never hesitated to express it, he betrayed no arrogance of opinion. In his extempore public addresses, and probably in his larger classrooms, his gift of eloquence sometimes led him into overstatements which in his quieter moods he would have been the first to criticize. I always thought, when I was his colleague, that he romanticized 'affairs,' that is to say, the practical business of the world. The word seemed to hypnotize him, as it had hypnotized two of his favorite authors, Burke and Bagehot. But I took this as a proof that he was a born college professor and was therefore inclined to exaggerate the significance of 'affairs' which lay outside his range. I used to think also that he was rather too militaristic, inclined to romanticize the Army and Navy, and expending too much eloquence in praising American achievements because they were 'American.' But all this was mere difference of opinion between two friends.

No one, I venture to say, then thought him cold or selfish. It is true that he was absorbed, day by day, in his teaching and writing, and he had the gift of intense concentration upon the business in hand. He was already composing directly upon the typewriter, and defended warmly that method of composition. We discussed it more than once, for I was sceptical. I remember his saying: 'When you find yourself at a loss for the right word, don't you light your pipe and walk across the room and perhaps look out of the window? You lose your concentration. Now I force myself to sit with my fingers on the keys and *make* the right word come.' And he was sure that the word that came was right.

It is possible, of course, that the adulation of his classes and the general recognition among his associates of his superior gifts as a speaker and writer may have spoiled him a little; but I was never conscious of it. If he had at that time any hankering after executive leadership, either in the educational world or in politics, none of us knew it. His ideals for 'the new Princeton' had been expressed in his oration at the 'Sesqui,' and when, in 1902, he was suddenly chosen to succeed President Patton, his colleagues almost without exception recognized the fitness of the choice. Yet so completely had he stood apart from all candidacy for actual office, that his election came as a surprise. I confess that I had thought of him as a man endowed by nature and training to originate theories of action and to express them with convincing skill, rather than to put them into actual operation.

The fault of the hero of tragedy, as Aristotle pointed out long ago, may be the excess of a virtue as well as the presence of a vice. If Wilson ever had any real vices, they were at least unknown to observers of his character during the 'golden nineties.' In my own opinion, his 'tragic fault' lay in the excess of that self-confidence which was one of the most fascinating of his virtues. I have heard him quote with delight the saying that while a Yankee always thinks he is right, a Scotch-Irishman *knows* that he is right. And at forty, Woodrow Wilson had already had the long habit of success. As a student of government, as teacher, essayist, and orator, he had won brilliant and unquestioned rank. He had worked tirelessly in solitude, had held himself inflexibly to his task. He had learned self-reliance. He trusted his own logic and his own instincts without much counsel from other men. It is the ancient story of heroes — and of martyrs.

For the line between superb confidence and tragic overconfidence is often hidden from the hero himself. Wilson did not cross it until he became President of his University. On the larger issues of his policy in that office, I believe him to have been right, but the sense of his own rightness and conversely of the wrongness of his opponents began to rob him temporarily of his old skill in diplomacy, his tact and judgment and patience. He was so sure that the right must prevail that he forgot the stupidity and slowness of the average man, and underestimated the power of his opponents. I venture to quote a significant remark which he made to me shortly after his election to the Presidency of Princeton. He was to address a gathering of teachers in Boston, and as I was working there, I gave him a luncheon at the University Club, inviting President Eliot, Charles Francis Adams, Richard Olney, Charles Eliot Norton, Thomas Bailey Aldrich, Dr. Crothers, Judge Robert Grant and other men who were likely to interest him. Wilson was never in better form or gayer spirits. He fascinated the Bostonians, particularly the most fastidious of them all, Charles Eliot Norton. After the luncheon I escorted him to the Trinity Place Station, to put him on the train for New York. As we were waiting for it, he spoke of his new work at Princeton, and said: 'If West begins to intrigue against me as he did against Patton, *we must see who is master!*' There was a grim smile with these words, as if he doubted as little as I did who was master. But both of us were wrong: in the subtleties of academic intrigue he was no match for West, and the game went to the more resourceful player. It was tragic overconfidence that brought disaster to Wilson's dreams for Princeton, although that disaster, indirectly, made him Governor of New Jersey and President of the United States.

VIII

THE ATLANTIC
MONTHLY

The power of writing one fine line transcends all the Able-Editor ability in the ably-edited Universe.

EDWARD FITZGERALD, *Letters*

WHEN we left for the usual summer vacation at Greensboro in June, 1899, my position in Princeton seemed permanently established. I had declined a call to Yale. Upon the death of Dean Murray, I had been assigned to his chair: the Holmes Professorship of English Literature and Belles Lettres. On personal grounds I was touched by this appointment, for I had been very fond of Dean Murray. I still have some of his eighteenth-century folios, presented by his widow and sons, together with the Leonard trout-rod which had been given to him by Professor Packard. The rod must by now have seen nearly fifty years of service, and though the second joint might be stiffer, it still does honor to its maker. The promotion to the Holmes Professorship gave me a Shakespeare course at last, and freed me, after many years, from the claims of Oratory. I was also made Director of Graduate Work in English, with some advance in salary; and the appointment of Henry van Dyke to a new chair of Literature at Princeton assured me of a congenial colleague and added to the prestige of our department. In short, the Princeton sky was cloudless; but a born New

Englander might have guessed that it was a 'weather-breeder.'

Early in July I joined Arthur L. Wheeler — then of Yale and afterward a professor of Latin at Bryn Mawr and Princeton — in a fishing trip into the 'unorganized township' of Ferdinand, in the northeastern corner of Vermont. It was a wild country then, with only a few blind 'tote-roads.' We had to pack our blankets and provisions and go in by compass, among the primeval hemlocks. We slept under a bark 'lean-to,' discovered some streams wholly new to us, and came out after ten days, ragged, unshaven, and completely happy. When we reached Greensboro, MacGregor Jenkins, Williams, '90, and already the business manager of the *Atlantic Monthly*, was smoking his pipe on the front porch of the boarding-house. Having had no answer to his telegrams, he had come up from Boston to offer me the editorship of the magazine.

It appeared that Walter Hines Page had suddenly resigned. Since 1895 Page had been assisting Horace E. Scudder — the editor of the *Atlantic* and 'literary adviser' to Houghton, Mifflin and Company — and had finally succeeded Scudder as editor on August 1, 1898. But now, he wished to return to New York to become the managing editor of a new and vast publishing enterprise — a projected consolidation of the house of Harper and Brothers and the Doubleday, McClure and Company. In this emergency, a new editor of the *Atlantic* was needed at once. I had never met any member of the firm of Houghton, Mifflin and Company, the owners of the magazine, although I knew Mr. Scudder slightly, and had seen a little of Page when he was editing the *Forum*. But Jenkins informed me that his employers had corresponded with various persons in New York and elsewhere who had recommended me for the editorship. I never learned who they were, but the gambling instinct must have been strong in all of them.

For I was wholly without journalistic experience. I had done editorial work for publishers, had contributed to various periodicals, and was the author of three or four small volumes of fiction; but the idea of editing a magazine had never occurred to me. It meant a break with the profession for which I had been trained and to which I was devoted. I do not think that my temperament was restless, and certainly my first impulse — as with the call from Williams to Princeton — was to decline. But 'Mac,' even in his early thirties a ripe diplomatist, persuaded me to smoke a few pipes over his proposal. Possibly, in my thirty-ninth year, I was susceptible to flattery, and it was pleasant to be asked to sail the boat on which I had been once or twice an inconspicuous passenger, and whose great captains of the past — Lowell, Fields, Howells, and Aldrich — I had idealized since childhood. The *Atlantic Monthly* had become one of the traditions of New England, and now, according to Jenkins, it was facing a problem which I alone could solve! To Mrs. Perry, who of course was brought into conference, 'Mac' dilated upon Boston as the home of music and pictures and literature — not forgetting to point out the excellence of its private schools for children and the fact that Greensboro could be reached by train in a few hours. In short, without saying too much about the desirability of a larger income than we were enjoying at Princeton, he blew the trumpet for Boston with a master's touch. Finally he made me promise that I would at least go back with him, out of courtesy to the partners in Houghton, Mifflin and Company, and talk the invitation over with them.

So down we went. I was presented to George H. Mifflin, the head of the firm: a vigorous and enthusiastic gentleman, a lover of horses and an expert in typography, whose passion was the making of beautiful books. Sometimes he read them a little. Mr. J. Murray Kay, the treasurer, was a portly, rubicund Scot, who had had large lumber interests in Maine, and was a mighty salmon fisherman and epicure. Longfellow's lines fitted him perfectly:

> '*A solid man of Boston.*
> *A comfortable man, with dividends,*
> *And the first salmon, and the first green peas.*'

Mr. 'Harry' Houghton, son of H. O. Houghton, the Vermonter who had built up The Riverside Press, was then in charge of that huge printing establishment in Cambridge. Like Mr. Mifflin, he considered it his job to make books faultlessly, rather than to read them. No doubt it was. I was likewise introduced to F. J. Garrison, 'the conscience of the firm,' as Mr. Mifflin proudly called him. He was a son of the famous abolitionist, and brother of the editor of the *New York Nation*; and these two sons, having only their Sundays for the task, had produced in collaboration the monumental four-volume Life of their father. 'F. J.' was a political and social reformer, as he had a natural right to be, but was also an invaluable figurer on the exact profit-and-loss account of each book of each author upon the firm's list.

All these gentlemen were most cordial in their welcome of a total stranger, and their pride in the *Atlantic* and their sense of its value as a 'feeder' of authors and books to the House was unfeigned. But all of them professed ignorance of 'literary' matters: they left such things to Mr. Scudder and Mr. Page and the 'desk-men' who had the first reading of manuscripts.

So I was shunted to the sunny rooms of the *Atlantic* to take counsel with the experts. Page was seated at his big table, looking older than when I had known him in New York. He was correcting galley proof for the September number, and he made a most irreverent remark about the 'doddering' and beloved author whose syntax he was altering. 'You won't be bothered by him very long,' he said; and I replied that I was not yet sure that I should take over the editorship. Page pushed up his spectacles and studied me with a whimsical smile. 'You have a professorship at Princeton?' he asked; and then proceeded to tell me a North Carolina story about a man who wanted to sell his sawmill for five thousand dollars. He found a purchaser, but suddenly refused to close the bargain, on the philosophic ground that he 'couldn't see what in hell any man with five thousand dollars should want of a sawmill.' The moral of this anecdote seemed to be that I had better let well enough alone. But Page wisely refused to offer any actual advice, although he did volunteer a remark which I have quoted in an earlier chapter: 'A man who won't bet on himself isn't worth a damn.' Fortified by this, I went on to Mr. Scudder.

As the interview with Horace Scudder proved ultimately to be a decisive factor in the new venture, I must say a word about that unique idealist. He was then sixty-one, a graduate of Williams, a Churchman, a prolific writer for children, and a tireless editor of textbooks and of the works of famous authors. He had contributed more pages to the *Atlantic* — most of them unsigned criticisms of books — than any other man. In 1890 he had succeeded Aldrich as editor, and in my judgment was far more laborious and resourceful than his predecessor in conducting the magazine. He was full of fertile ideas for new topics, and was uncommonly discerning in his selection of unknown and promising contributors. But these gifts were known only to his office associates, and compared with his witty predecessor he was often considered dull. He had a fastidious literary taste, and was the only magazine editor I ever knew who read Greek and Latin authors for half an hour each morning in order to keep his ear attuned to style. In his innermost mind he was never quite sure of Page's judgment, and felt that the North Carolinian was an iconoclast, although he recognized that a little iconoclasm had been a tonic for the venerable magazine. Scudder had finally retired from the editorship in order to complete his biography of James Russell Lowell. But he was continuing to serve as literary adviser to the House, and as editor of the Riverside Literature Series and other groups of books, particularly the one-volume series of the Cambridge Poets, which included both English and American writers. His own editions of Browning, Tennyson, Longfellow, Keats, and other poets, in this series, were masterly examples of competent workmanship. But rarest of the virtues of this strange compound of dreamer, 'projector,' and literary hack was his touching and unswerving loyalty to the House which had employed him for a generation. He idolized the memory of H. O. Houghton, who was thought by most persons to be an austere man, reaping where he had not sown; and I believe that Scudder would have sacrificed anything except his private honor to maintain and enhance the reputation of Messrs. Houghton, Mifflin and Company.

My long conversation with him, which was continued, after a day or two, at his summer home in Chocorua, illustrated what his intimate friend Dr. A. V. G. Allen wrote of him in the *Atlantic* after Scudder's death in 1902. Allen called him a 'philanthropist and public servant in the rôle of a man of letters.' What he strove to impress upon me was the opportunity for public service afforded by the combined offices of editor of the *Atlantic* and literary adviser to a publishing house which was then specializing in American literature and educational textbooks. He hoped that I would agree to succeed him as 'adviser' in due time. He knew that I idealized the teacher's profession, but he believed sincerely that my influence would really count for more, in the long run, if it were exerted in the field to which he had devoted his own life. Seldom have I listened to a more eloquent *apologia* for a self-sacrificing career. He had begun life with dreams of literary eminence and he was ending it as an employee of a publishing house, but his imagination envisaged every hour of hack work as a permanent contribution to the development of American culture and character. He acknowledged that this was also the aim of every true teacher of literature, but he felt that through the medium of the *Atlantic* and the House of which it was a part, the ideal aim was more sure of realization.

I cannot, after thirty-five years, recall many of Mr. Scudder's exact words, but he gave me the parting counsel to go back to Greensboro, talk everything over with my wife, and follow her judgment absolutely. I did so, and we have never regretted our decision, fantastic as it seemed to some of our Princeton friends. At a farewell dinner given by my colleagues in the following May, I tried to explain my action by an incident in that care-free fishing trip to Ferdinand, the year before. We had divided the weight of our packs as evenly as possible, and there were still an axe and a hatchet to be carried by somebody. I was the biggest fellow in the little party, and was ashamed not to shoulder the axe. In the terms of this parable, the *Atlantic* was the axe, and the pleasant life at Princeton was the hatchet. 'Now we understand Perry's choice for the first time!' exclaimed 'Billy' Magie. 'He is cursed with the New England conscience, and there-fore thought he ought to choose the more disagreeable job!'

It had not required a New England conscience, however, to perceive in July, 1899, that I had no right to leave Princeton at short notice. But the publishers of the *Atlantic* offered to divide my time with the University for one year, and I found that I could shift my lecturing hours to the last three days of each week. Accordingly I explained the situation to President Patton, sending my resignation to take effect in the following June. He happened to be in Scotland, and it was November before that indolent and delightful executive answered the letter.

On the first day of August I walked into Page's office again, and told him that I had bought the sawmill. I suspect that he thought I should live to repent the bar-gain, but he gave me his blessing and started for New York in quest of his own rainbow — for the huge publishing combination never materialized as planned, and Page contented himself by creating a new type of magazine in the *World's Work* and by a partnership with F. N. Doubleday. Fourteen years later, after notable service to many public causes, he was appointed by President Wilson as our Ambassador to Great Britain.

The *Atlantic* office must have seemed to everyone a duller place after Page had gone. But the new editor was too busy to take note of atmospheric changes. He began, on the first morning, to dictate correspondence, though he had never dictated a letter in his life. He inherited from Page an energetic and confident assistant in W. B. Parker, a Harvard man just two years out of college, but already wise in the peculiarities of authors. Later I had as assistant the brilliant Ferris Greenslet, who has since risen to such high position as a publisher, although at the sacrifice of his early career as biographer and critic. When our proof-readers at The Riverside Press posed problems too subtle for an inexperienced editor to solve, I could fall back upon the trained instinct of Miss Susan Francis, then a reader of manuscript for the House, but formerly the assistant of Fields, Howells, and Aldrich. It was she, as I have related elsewhere,[1] who, as Fields's assistant long before, had discovered in a chance copy of the *Overland Monthly* Bret Harte's 'Luck of Roaring Camp' and called her chief's attention to the new author; and it was she who, when Aldrich was studying vintages in Hungary, had to delete on her own responsibility certain passages from Hardy's *Two on a Tower* — then running serially — to avoid offending the decorums of that era. No one in the office told me that Miss Francis had edited the best modern edition of Lockhart's *Life of Scott*, but even the office-boys knew that she had rejected the manuscript of *David Harum* because it was 'vulgar' — an opinion which Mr. Page, the other reader, had unluckily shared!

Mr. Aldrich himself now resumed his former habit of

[1] *Atlantic*, November, 1932.

dropping into the office frequently. Perched upon the edge of a chair, as if about to take flight, he would often linger by the hour, entertaining me with his caustic wit and his keen shop-talk about the mysteries of editing. Himself a fastidious composer and reviser of verse and prose, he was severely critical of most contemporary writing. He pleased me once by saying of one of my own contributions to the *Atlantic*, 'That was a well-written essay'; but he added, 'You will find that you used a superfluous "of" upon the second page.' More than once I have heard him declare that he would have rejected Mr. Kipling's 'Recessional' if it had been offered to the *Atlantic* — so extreme was his dislike for the phrase 'reeking tube and iron shard.' Miss Jewett, who was present at one of these diatribes, interrupted him gently: 'Yes, T. B., but you must remember that Kipling, after all, goes down to the sea in ships and does business in great waters.' The one American poem which Aldrich would have most liked to write was, he said, Emerson's 'Bacchus' — where, amid inimitable felicities, there are surely harsh lines enough.[1]

Miss Francis once told me that Aldrich was wont to say, as he sat down at his editorial desk, 'Here goes for making twenty more enemies.' I certainly made enemies, although unwittingly. The very first was a Harvard instructor, afterward famous for the learning and bitterness of his controversial criticism. Page had commissioned a book-review from him, but he had neglected to return his galley proof. I had to correct it in the office, and when the forms were made up, there was an 'over-run' of three lines. As the magazine was just going to press, I deleted

[1] For fuller comment upon Aldrich's conversation, see my sketch of him in *Park Street Papers*.

three lines from a somewhat wordy paragraph, and forgot all about it. But immediately upon the publication of that issue, the outraged instructor strode into the office. Did I not know that an author's manuscript was something sacredly personal? What right had any editor to alter copy already accepted? And so forth and so forth. In vain I explained the mechanical necessity of avoiding an 'over-run,' and referred tactfully to his failure to return proof. Finally I remarked that there were very few critical essays ever written, even by his idol Sainte-Beuve, that would not have been improved by the omission of at least three lines. At that point the interview ended, and the critic was sulky for many a year thereafter.

A more justifiable cause for wrath was soon found in an unlucky — and, I imagine, ill-informed — sentence by President Eliot in the October number. In the course of an educational article which had been accepted by Page and proof-read by its author, Eliot referred incidentally to 'the curriculum of the Jesuit colleges, which has remained almost unchanged for four hundred years, disregarding some trifling concessions made to natural science.' Eliot was an acknowledged expert in the history of education, and was supposed to know his facts; but the editor promptly received about sixty letters from officials in Jesuit colleges, many of them to the tune of 'Why is your contemptible publication anti-Catholic?' and all of them demanding space in the *Atlantic* for a reply. Eliot, to whom I referred some of this correspondence, seemed singularly uninterested. Like Marjorie Fleming's bereaved turkey in that little girl's delightful poem, he 'was more than usual calm.' (Lovers of Marjorie can complete the couplet.) It had long been the policy of the magazine not to print controversial replies to its articles. I now think this policy was wrong, but in 1899 I felt bound to conform to it. Fortunately my stenographer was a Catholic young lady with a sense of humor and a deep loyalty to the accepted policy of the magazine, and between us we concocted sixty soft answers which may or may not have assuaged the wrath of the educators. As luck would have it, we were busy at the same time with Protestant objectors, who had violently resented what they assumed to be the pro-Catholic tone of one of Henry D. Sedgwick's articles about Italy. Later on, we faced the same situation in printing John Burroughs's incisive article on 'Real and Sham Natural History' in which he criticized W. J. Long and Thompson Seton. Both men naturally wished to reply, as did the Christian Science leaders after the publication of Philip H. Churchman's paper on the psychology of that organization. But in all these cases, and in countless others, I felt constrained to follow the inveterate policy of the *Atlantic* — short-sighted and pontifical as it seems to me today.

'But these 'thorns in the cushion' — as Thackeray, himself a somewhat unlucky editor, had called them — were not deadly, and I found the new task fascinating and exhilarating. At the outset I took bachelor quarters on Beacon Hill, with a jolly group of young painters, architects, and the invaluable MacGregor Jenkins. I fled to Greensboro for the week-ends, taking a Boston 'green bag' filled with manuscripts. As soon as Princeton opened, I went down on Wednesday afternoons, returning on Sundays by the night train. It meant travelling twenty-two thousand miles between September and June. The clear-cut division of duties forced me to work at high pressure at each end of the line, and I think I never taught better than in this final year at Princeton. Fortunately, I had the trick of sleeping and of reading manuscript rapidly.

By September, 1900, we had sold our home in Princeton and were house-hunting in two or three suburbs of Boston. Perplexed by the various alternatives, I consulted one of the most impractical men alive, the huge and genial John Fiske, then living on Berkeley Street, Cambridge. He recommended Cambridge with infectious enthusiasm: 'It's the finest place in the United States! *No one cares a damn for you*, and you can work in peace.' Accordingly we rented a house on Mercer Circle — only 'just off' Brattle Street, as the real estate agent proudly pointed out. 'But where can we pick violets?' asked our small daughters, who had been wont to roam freely in the meadows and woodlands of Princeton; and Colonel Thomas Wentworth Higginson, a new neighbor, who was touched by this plaintive question, promised to take them violet-hunting the next spring. Rents in Cambridge were high, even then, and after a few years as tenants, we bought our present home on Clement Circle, 'just off' Sparks Street, as Sparks Street in turn is just off Brattle. It is one of the physical peculiarities of Cambridge that everything, except Brattle Street, is just off something else. John Fiske was quite right in feeling that if a man really wished to work, a college town would understand that idiosyncrasy; and we found Old Cambridge, as Mr. and Mrs. Page had found it, an unpretentious and friendly community.

During that bachelor winter in Boston, when I had Monday and Tuesday evenings free, I got my first taste of the hospitality of Beacon Hill. The Aldriches, who were then living at 59 Mount Vernon Street, were very cordial: I remember particularly one supper with Ellen Terry and Henry Irving after a performance of *Becket*, and how surprised I was at the lines of old age in Miss Terry's face, and at the astonishing vigor of Irving and Bram Stoker as the men adjourned after supper to Aldrich's den on the top floor and spun yarns until three o'clock in the morning. I recall also a big dinner there in honor of Mark Twain, and how he and Aldrich, at opposite ends of the long table, chaffed each other with such rapid-fire wit that the rest of us kept silent to enjoy it. I never saw either man in such high spirits again. Mrs. Henry Whitman — so vividly sketched by 'Jack' Chapman in *Memories and Milestones* — was hospitable also. I was duly presented to Mrs. Bell and Mrs. Pratt, the brilliant daughters of Rufus Choate, and to Julia Ward Howe, who still liked to be asked to recite her 'Battle Hymn of the Republic.' Sarah Orne Jewett was spending the winter with Mrs. James T. Fields, at the once famous Fields home at 148 Charles Street. Both Mrs. Fields and Miss Jewett, in their zeal for the super-refinement of the *Atlantic*, urged me to make an arrangement with the *Revue des Deux Mondes* by which I could reprint, each month, twenty-five or thirty pages of French! 'Mac's' reaction to this delicious suggestion may be imagined. Oddly enough, though we received plenty of comment upon each number of the *Atlantic*, the most helpful and constructive criticism came, not from veteran editors like Alden, Gilder, Burlingame, and Mabie, all of whom were most encouraging, but from my younger friend Edward W. Bok, who was then creating the *Ladies' Home*

Journal, but who had no desire to see the *Atlantic* made in that image.

As a matter of fact, it had been Howells, rather than Scudder and Page, who had transformed a 'Bostonian' magazine into an American magazine. We had, if I remember rightly, more subscribers in Wisconsin and Michigan than in Massachusetts, and when we made up a California number — using only our regular contributors from that State — we might easily have chosen a dozen other states for the experiment. Beacon Hill opinion of the *Atlantic* was negligible. We were able to print only about three per cent of the unsolicited manuscripts. About half of the papers in each number were by writers who contributed more or less regularly and with whose plans the editor tried to keep in touch; one quarter were on subjects directly proposed by the editor, and the remaining quarter were unsolicited gifts of the gods. Any package of manuscripts deposited on my desk by the indefatigable W. B. Parker — after he had weeded out the obviously unfit offerings — might conceivably contain another 'Battle Hymn of the Republic' or another *To Have and to Hold*. My green bag was a Pandora's box, and any one of the strange company of men and women who drifted into the inner office in order to present their manuscripts in person might be a second Keats or a Charlotte Brontë for all the office-boy could tell. But they never were!

The circulation of the *Atlantic*, even under Page's vigorous editorship, was only about eleven or twelve thousand copies; and if I remember rightly, the largest printing in my decade of service was twenty-three thousand copies, to supply the news-stands with Grover Cleve-

land's articles on 'The Independence of the Executive.'
The great increase in circulation did not come until the
World War. Nevertheless, at the turn of the century, in
spite of the rivalry of low-priced magazines and the begin-
nings of highly sensational and 'muck-raking' journalism,
the old *Atlantic*, devoted, as its cover proclaimed, 'to
Literature, Science, Art, and Politics,' was making substantial progress. Page had bequeathed to me, as a serial,
Mary Johnston's *To Have and to Hold*, and though I
have always been sceptical as to the real value of serial
fiction to a monthly magazine, that story was precisely
in the romantic vein of the hour. Page and Jenkins
knew it would prove to be a success as soon as they
found the stenographers borrowing the galley proofs to
read during the luncheon hour. None of the later serials
which I sponsored — Miss Jewett's *The Tory Lover*, Miss
Johnston's *Audrey*, Arthur S. Hardy's *His Daughter First*,
Robert Herrick's *The Common Lot*, Mary Austin's *Isidro*,
Margaret Sherwood's *The Coming of the Tide*, May Sinclair's *The Helpmate*, and Alice Brown's *Rose Macleod* —
though they showed sound and sometimes beautiful workmanship, quite equalled *To Have and to Hold* by the test
of the stenographers' luncheon hour.

Of the non-fiction serial articles, General Schaff's *Spirit
of Old West Point* and James O. Fagan's *Confessions of
a Railroad Signalman* were the outstanding successes.
The Reconstruction series which we featured in 1901 and
to which I devoted a great deal of energy and enthusiasm,
never commanded the public attention which I thought
it deserved. In autobiography, J. T. Trowbridge's *My
Own Story* and T. W. Higginson's *Part of a Man's Life*
had eager readers. I expected much from Walter Page's

pseudonymous *The Autobiography of a Southerner Since the Civil War*, by 'Nicholas Worth.' The narrative — which Page later acknowledged, calling it a novel — was brilliantly written, but for some reason it did not attract the public except in a few sections of the South.

The *Atlantic* has always been fortunate in its 'out-of-doors' articles. Papers like John Burroughs's *Camping with President Roosevelt* — which had some amusing manuscript emendations direct from the White House [1] — and anything from Bradford Torrey or John Muir, were sure of an appreciative response. On Muir's rare visits to the office, his talk about California trees and flowers was even more wonderful than his writing, and the stenographers and desk-men used to invent errands to my room in order to listen to fragments of it. MacGregor Jenkins, with an eye to the news-stands, urged the publication of articles on outdoor sports, and we secured excellent papers on golf, tennis, tramping, and swimming. My own contribution to this series, a defence of 'Fishing with a Worm,' is still, after thirty years, a subject of ironic comment by my fellow anglers, and I shall never live it down.

The technique of *Atlantic* short stories, in those days, conformed mainly to the patterns of the eighteen-nineties. That they were expertly written is evidenced by such names as Alice Brown, Sarah Orne Jewett, and Edith Wharton. We printed some of the last short stories by Howells and Aldrich; and a new note was struck now and then by Jack London, John Buchan, and Mary Austin. After some years of alienation, Lafcadio Hearn began again to send us his marvellous sketches of Japan. It was on the whole a dull decade for American poetry; but I

---

[1] Printed in the paper on Burroughs in my *Praise of Folly*.

recall with especial pleasure William Vaughn Moody's noble 'Ode in Time of Hesitation' written on the Philippine theme in 1900, Edwin Arlington Robinson's haunting 'Calverly's,' and the faultless tiny lyrics of my friend Father Tabb. Only the other day, when I was praising Robinson's 'Aunt Imogen' to his face as one of his finest poems, E. A. R. gently reminded me that I had once rejected it for the *Atlantic*, on the ground that it was too difficult for a magazine reader to grasp at one reading. Perhaps I was too timid about 'Aunt Imogen,' but at least I atoned for that blunder by persuading the sceptical House to publish Robinson's *Captain Craig*.

Our list of *Atlantic* essayists was a brilliant one. John Fiske, Brooks Adams, Woodrow Wilson, Goldwin Smith, William Garrott Brown, Paul Elmer More, William James, and William Roscoe Thayer knew how to write! And so did Edmund Gosse and Havelock Ellis and Norman Douglas and Alice Meynell. The crackling humor of Dr. Crothers and the suave irony of Agnes Repplier found congenial readers. I think I was the first editor to encourage Gamaliel Bradford's biographical studies; and though he had not then invented his formula for 'psychography,' this earlier work seems to me not inferior on that account. What hours of talk, and how many letters, did that gallant invalid and I devote to the discussion of 'psychography,' and how stubbornly unconvinced did I remain until the end!

I differed sharply with Page as to the value of those critical essays for which the *Atlantic* and the New York *Nation* had been famous. Such essays seemed to me essential for the maintenance of literary standards. But Page, in spite of — or possibly because of — his early philological training at Johns Hopkins, had become contemptuous of all literary criticism. To him it was mere 'Talkee-talkee': he declared that 'the hope of American literature now is not in men who produce or who feed on literary criticism.' This point of view seemed to me boyish, though it has plenty of advocates today; and I was immensely proud to print such critical essays as Mrs. Meynell's on 'Charles Dickens as a Man of Letters,' W. C. Brownell's 'Henry James,' and Henry James's own papers on Zola and Balzac. I allowed and even encouraged C. C. Everett to dilate on James Martineau, and Edmund Gosse on Mandell Creighton and Louise Guiney on Lionel Johnson — to say nothing of my rashness in letting Andrew D. White, a sound historical scholar, contribute excessively long and learned articles on Fra Paolo Sarpi, Hugo Grotius, Thomasius, and Stein! In Page's judgment — and he was a far better journalist than I — such critical and historical essays were 'sinkers,' and I suspect that secretly the loyal 'Mac' Jenkins agreed with him. 'Mac' may remember, if he ever sees this page, how he once besought me, with actual tears in his eyes, not to print another short story by Henry James, since he was trying desperately to persuade the American News Company that the *Atlantic* was not really a 'high-brow' periodical!

But being tolerably stubborn by nature and a college professor by training, the editor held to the notion that the *Atlantic's* first duty was to Literature. Mr. Burlingame of *Scribner's* told me that the worst error an editor could make was to underestimate the intelligence of the public; yet I think now that I overestimated the public interest in purely literary questions. We printed too many papers, I imagine, about European writers. My device of securing regular letters from England, France, Germany, Italy, and occasionally even from Mexico and Japan, could not overcome the indifference of our subscribers to international affairs. The United States, even then, was far more 'isolationist' than I supposed. Page used to say that our people had no real interest in politics, except in those crises where politics seemed likely to affect business; and certainly our articles on economic and social questions provoked more immediate comment than anything we printed on politics, art, science, or literature. Vigorous papers on economics by such experts as Taussig, Carver, Bullock, W. M. Daniels, C. A. Conant, and A. D. Noyes secured instant attention. Yet I endeavored to publish competent group reviews of the important books in each of the various fields, not yet sensing the fact that daily and weekly journalism was already undermining the type of 'authoritarian' criticism long represented by the *Atlantic*.

After all, I am not trying to write a chapter in the history of that magazine, but rather to comment upon the fresh interests which were thus suddenly brought into my own life. I made thousands of new acquaintances, and among them, I trust, were more friends than enemies. Emerson noted in his *Journal* that 'Life consists in what a man is thinking of all day'; and for ten years a considerable portion of my days was devoted to public questions, to contemporary authors and to the problems of a publishing house. Although I had never had any business training — except what was involved in earning my own living after I was twenty — I could grasp the fact that the *Atlantic* must pay its monthly bills and purchase only such manuscripts as it could afford to buy. I had an amusing and sometimes trying half-hour each month with Mr. Kay, when I submitted the proposed scale of payment for each contributor to that month's issue. I learned that the *Atlantic's* original rate of payment had been modelled upon *Blackwood's* and was five dollars a page of seven hundred words. Gradually it went up to seven dollars, and I understood now why my first contribution, in Aldrich's reign, had brought me precisely thirty-five dollars. It was five pages long; nothing could be simpler! By Page's time the 'space' rate was supposed to be ten dollars a page, although verse and specially commissioned articles were sometimes paid at a higher figure.

Of course those authors who desired more money or circulation than we could offer went elsewhere. In my collection of autographs is a postcard written to me in 1905 by William James: 'You are a true gentleman — not an editor! Thanks!' This tribute was due to my releasing to him a paper which I had already accepted for the *Atlantic*, but which he now wished — 'a horrible temptation,' as he wrote me — to send to *McClure's*, a monthly which then boasted a circulation of seven hundred thousand copies. The 'horrible temptation' was not, I take it, a large honorarium, but the chance to reach seven hundred thousand readers. And I remember one 'blue Monday,' when a United States Senator from Massachusetts had set a price of seven hundred dollars upon an essay which I had asked him to prepare, but which luckily was not ready. I had to write him that we could not possibly afford the luxury of printing the essay. And just then Booker Washington came in, with the proof of one of his articles. 'Will our usual "space" rate, say one hundred dollars for the article, be satisfactory?' I asked, still thinking about the Senator. 'Perfectly,' said the Negro; '*I don't write for money.*'

I have left Mr. Kay waiting for me in his office for the monthly checking up of accounts. I had exactly one hundred and forty-four pages to pay for, and if the total did not much exceed fourteen hundred and forty dollars, Mr. Kay was complaisant enough. But sonnets bothered him: they contained precisely fourteen lines, and why should not all sonnetteers be paid the same wages for their toil, say ten dollars a sonnet? And two sonnets could be printed on a page; which meant that that page cost twice our usual space rate. And why should one short story cost more than another? Wasn't a story only a story, after all? And Mr. Kay, who was personally one of the kindest of men, would intimate that it was the firm's money, and not mine, which I was thus proposing to lavish among distressed authors, and that it was his disagreeable duty, as treasurer, to curb any extravagance. When the monthly discussions reached this point, there was only one card that I could play: I shifted the subject to sea-trout and salmon. In five minutes Mr. Kay would pull from his desk his fishing logbook of the last season, and after showing me how often he had been 'high rod' on his stretch of river, he would 'O.K.' all of my estimates with a smile.

The weekly 'Powwow' of the firm, attended by all the heads of departments and presided over by Mr. Mifflin, likewise served for me as a Graduate School of Business Administration. We listened to reports from the readers of manuscripts, discussed copyrights and royalties, the projects of rival publishing houses, and the further plans of authors already upon our list, together with their exact rating according to Mr. Garrison's figures of profit and loss. Certainly the firm was carrying some distinguished names without any adequate financial return, yet it felt that something must be sacrificed for the dignity and glory of the 'list.' In most cases, however, I perceived that the scale of values discussed in the Powwow was not at all the scale of values to which a professor of literature was accustomed. Professors of literature might rate *The Country of the Pointed Firs* much higher than *Rebecca of Sunnybrook Farm*, but if one of these works sold ten times as many copies as the other, that settled the question of the relative importance of the two authors. There was nothing more to be said. Messrs. Houghton, Mifflin and Company were among the most upright and successful publishers in the United States, but I confess that I thought sometimes of the sermon which my old friend Dean Murray vowed he would preach some day upon the text 'Nothing damns like Success.'

In the field of politics, I endeavored to keep the magazine non-partisan. Page, although a Democrat by inheritance, had accepted McKinley's expansionist policy and was a warm admirer of Roosevelt. It was he who had put the American flag on the cover of the *Atlantic* in June, 1898; and as late as June, 1904, he wrote to W. R. Thayer: 'The impulse that moved the people when we went into the war with Spain was the best possible evidence of the sound moral instincts of our democracy. It was the sanest, humanest, most generous act of our time.' [1] I must by contrast have seemed to my employers a very lukewarm patriot, for though I accepted fair-minded articles on both sides of the questions then in controversy, I wrote

[1] *The Training of an American*, p. 271.

signed editorials against the annexation of the Philippines, and made no secret of my own anti-militaristic views. I had been profoundly stirred in 1898 by the Czar's proposal for an international conference; and the resulting Hague Convention of 1899, disappointing as it was in many ways, seemed to me then the herald of a new era. After coming to Boston I joined the American Peace Society, and attended Lake Mohonk Conferences in the interest of arbitration and disarmament. Later, I supported the League to Enforce Peace, and then the League of Nations, and served for some years as a trustee of the World Peace Foundation. But though I spoke and worked to the best of my ability in this noblest of causes, I felt, during my editorship, that I had no right to turn the *Atlantic* into an organ of the peace movement, and I made no attempt to do so.

There was then no law compelling American periodicals to publish the names of their owners and editors. Except when they wrote signed contributions like any other authors, the names of the *Atlantic's* editors had never appeared in the magazine. It was supposed to be an impersonal organism, and its conductors were beings far removed from what Mr. Scudder called 'the glare of publicity,' of which he had a horror. When I began to initial my editorials and book-reviews and to write some personal 'Toastmaster' addresses to subscribers in January of each year, commenting upon the course which the *Atlantic* was taking, and explaining its policy, I was breaking with tradition; and was thought by some persons to be lessening the dignity and anonymity of the editorial function.

Never but once, however, did the owners express any

disapproval of the editorial policy, and that was after half-a-dozen years of service. Rollo Ogden, then of the *New York Evening Post* and now of the *New York Times*, whom I had once succeeded — though never rivalled! — as third baseman of the Williams nine, proposed early in 1905 a series of brief 'Letters to Literary Statesmen.' His scheme was to compare the political opinions of writers like Balfour, Roosevelt, Cabot Lodge, and John Morley, as expressed before they ever held office, with their words and actions after they assumed real political responsibility. The 'Letters' were to be signed 'Alciphron,' and knowing Ogden's gift for brilliant satire, I accepted his proposal with joy. It was the kind of writing I coveted for the magazine. The 'Letter to Theodore Roosevelt' appeared in the March number; only two pages, but each sentence sparkled, and I was sure that the President would be as delighted by it as he had been with the sallies of 'Mr. Dooley.'

Then Washington dropped a bombshell! Senator Lodge wrote to 'Harry' Houghton that the 'Letter' had given serious and painful offence and that the pages containing it had been torn out of the White House copy of the *Atlantic*. To Mr. Houghton and Mr. Mifflin the Senator's word was final. They asked that an apology be sent and the 'Letters' abandoned. I wrote as courteously as I could to Senator Lodge, explaining that the 'Letter' was, in my judgment, harmless and amusing political satire, written and published without any intention of giving pain. Then I informed Mr. Mifflin that the 'Letter to Arthur J. Balfour' was already on the press for the April number, and could not be recalled; but since the owners did not seem to approve of my editorial judgment, my resignation was now in his hands. I went home to Cambridge, and remember going out to dinner that night in high spirits. I had a wife and three children to support, and had been able to save only a little money; but I felt somehow that the fishing was going to be good. The next morning Mr. Mifflin asked me to withdraw my resignation. He and Mr. Houghton did not wish in any way to influence my editorial decisions, and if I thought the 'Letters' should be continued, the firm would back me. Accordingly I made an equally beautiful gesture: inasmuch as the spirit of the 'Letters' had evidently been misunderstood, I would arrange with their author to terminate the series in April. This was done; and no 'Letter to Henry Cabot Lodge' — who was, I believe, the next Literary Statesman in line for treatment — ever appeared in the *Atlantic*, although I still consider it an attractive theme.

I have no illusions as to the value of my services as 'literary adviser,' which began after Mr. Scudder's death. I took over the general editorship of the *Cambridge Poets*, and in that capacity read all the page-proofs of More's *Byron*, Dodge's *Spenser*, Noyes's *Dryden*, Boynton's *Pope*, George's *Wordsworth*, and Sargent and Kittredge's *English and Scottish Ballads*, besides engaging Neilson to edit the *Shakespeare* and F. N. Robinson the *Chaucer*. Scudder had enjoyed such 'knitting work,' as he called it, and had performed it with more devotion and competence than I could bring to the task. I wrote prefaces to many special editions printed by the House. In the weekly Powwow I argued for or against thousands of books; sometimes cajoling the House against its better judgment to risk something upon a new poet or to try once more a book by some veteran whose prose was savory and yet hitherto unsalable. Of two achievements as 'adviser,' however, I am inordinately proud. I did persuade the House to publish the full text of Thoreau's *Journals* in fourteen volumes, edited by Bradford Torrey and F. H. Allen, as well as the ten volumes of Emerson's *Journals*, edited by Edward W. Emerson and Waldo Forbes. That, at least, was something worth doing!

Those ten years of employment by a publishing house were a great enrichment of my experience. The duties involved, although demanding time, energy, and constant preoccupation, did not, after all, absorb my other interests completely. I still wished to write something more permanent than editorials, book-reviews, and anonymous essays for the Contributors' Club. I lost somehow the desire to write fiction myself, but each day at Park Street gave me some new impressions about that art, and when Houghton, Mifflin and Company asked me to prepare a book on the subject, I looked over my Princeton lecture notes, and published in 1902 *A Study of Prose Fiction.* There are scores of books upon that topic now, but mine was then almost a pioneer volume. It suggested new methods of approach to the field of fiction, was promptly adopted by many colleges and schools, and has apparently been one of the most influential of my books. Perhaps I thought less of its vogue among academic persons than I did of the praise it won from men like Edward Sothern the actor, James Huneker the art critic — who wrote me that he had read it three times — and professional fiction writers like O. Henry. Two years later I printed a volume of essays and addresses with the title *The Amateur Spirit.*

Mr. Mifflin was most generous in urging me to take all

the time I wished for writing and lecturing, and for a good many years I was called upon to address colleges, clubs, and other organizations. I shall comment later upon the danger of these excursions into the field of popular lecturing: that mixture of prophecy and play-acting, as Carlyle dubbed it so long ago. But the danger is less in closely written addresses prepared for formal occasions. During the years of my editorship occurred the centenaries of the birth of Emerson, Hawthorne, Longfellow, Whittier, and Holmes, and a little later came the anniversaries of Lowell, Whitman, and Parkman. It happened that I was called upon to make commemorative addresses upon the work of these writers, and I did my best to present their achievements to twentieth-century audiences who could not be expected to share fully in my own respect and enthusiasm for these figures of the past. The tide was already running against most of them; how strongly, I did not then perceive.

In 1904, when Professor Barrett Wendell of Harvard was lecturing in France, I was asked by President Eliot to take over Wendell's lectures in 'English 28,' dealing with English authors of the eighteenth century. It was one of my favorite literary periods, and twice a week I forgot all about contemporary problems in the pure pleasure of talking to a roomful of agreeable boys about Defoe and Fielding, Pope and Swift, Gray and Goldsmith, Horace Walpole and John Wesley and the 'Great Bear' himself. It was the first college teaching I had done since June, 1900, when we had attended the last of the farewell dinners, bidden good-bye to our friends and driven away from our home in Princeton. The romance of teaching — for I always held it to be a romance and always shall —

then seemed to be ended for me; but I discovered that President Eliot, in 1904, was by no means sure about it.

My father's full and happy life came to a close in 1905. He was seventy-five, and his last years had been clouded by invalidism. My sister had sacrificed her own teaching career in Albany in order to help her mother at the homestead, and Mother's serene days crept on until her quiet passing in 1916. What my father's life and death meant to his oldest son is too sacredly intimate to be set down here. Many eulogies of him have been written, but I like best the final words of my brother Carroll's book, *A Professor of Life*: 'He loved truth and honor and fairness; but mostly he loved friendship and little children. He cared nothing for riches, and only a little for fame. Some measure of the last he gained, and he knew what to do with it. He forgot it. If we hold with Bronson Alcott that Heaven is a place in which we shall be able to get a little conversation, it is certain where you will find my father. You will find him, directly he has gotten "the lay of the land," where the wit is the keenest, the humor most humane, the laughter the heartiest, and the hope for mankind the most sure.'

I went back to work, and there was work in plenty, for I had already begun one of the most fascinating of those 'outside' tasks which I seemed destined to be carrying in addition to the editorship. It was a Life of Walt Whitman. John Burroughs, an intimate associate of Whitman in the old Washington days, had been promising for years to write this book. When he finally abandoned the enterprise, Houghton, Mifflin and Company asked me to undertake it, and Burroughs, with whom my relations had become most friendly, offered every assistance. Whitman had died in 1892. I had never seen him, though I had read him ever since I was an undergraduate, and was fairly familiar with what had been written about him in America and Europe. But even a dozen years after his death, though legend and myth had been busy, there was no thorough-going biography except the book by an Englishman, H. B. Binns, which appeared while my own work was in progress. Fortunately I was able to draw upon a mass of untouched manuscript material. Not only John Burroughs, but Edward Dowden in England, E. C. Stedman and Gilder in New York, Weir Mitchell, Talcott Williams and Horace Traubel in Philadelphia, and dozens of other friends of the poet, loaned me their Whitman letters and gave their personal impressions of the man. Most helpful of all was the widow of William D. O'Connor — Mrs. Ellen M. Calder, of Providence — who entrusted me with the priceless collection of Whitman letters preserved by O'Connor and herself. Ultimately she bequeathed to me all of this correspondence, together with her entire collection of Whitman first editions, many of them inscribed by the poet.

Some epochs and phases of Whitman's life remained obscure, as they do even today, after another generation of investigators have done their utmost. John Burroughs, for all his apparent frankness in long conversations with me, never gave a hint as to Walt's considerable share in the composition of Burroughs's *Walt Whitman as Poet and Person*, published in 1866. I am indebted to these interviews with Burroughs, by the way, for an excellent Roosevelt story. We were tramping from his farm on the Hudson over a steep hill to his favorite retreat, 'Slabsides,' where he had promised to cook for me over an open fire the same luncheon of steak and baked potatoes which he had recently offered there to President and Mrs. Roosevelt. Halfway up the hill 'Uncle John' paused to ask solicitously: 'Are you sure this hill isn't too steep for you?' At forty-five I had retained a boyish pride in my hill-climbing ability, and in fact I had been holding back for fear of tiring my host. So I replied, perhaps a little dryly, that I thought I could make it. 'You should have seen Theodore climb this hill!' exclaimed Burroughs. 'He clenched his fists and gritted his teeth and came up like a race-horse!' 'I thought you said that Mrs. Roosevelt was with you,' I remarked. A puzzled look came over 'Uncle John's' face: 'She was, and there was something queer about it. She didn't seem to make the slightest effort, and yet she got to the top just as soon as he did!'

In the very middle of this long struggle to produce from all available sources a really veracious Life of the 'Good Gray Poet' came a letter from President Eliot asking me whether I would accept a call to Harvard. A famous professorship, held in succession by Ticknor, Longfellow, and Lowell, and vacant since 1886, might be offered to me, with full freedom as to the courses which I might desire to give: 'it will be for you to select the work you would prefer to do within this great field of literature — English, French, Italian, and Spanish.... I hope it will look attractive to you.' This was early in August, 1905, and it appeared that the Corporation hoped to make the appointment in 1906. President Eliot's proposal was certainly 'attractive,' but there were some practical difficulties about accepting it at once and under the conditions that were first suggested. I was under contract to complete the *Whitman* by June, 1906, and I felt that I ought not to desert the *Atlantic* immediately, at least not until after we had celebrated its fiftieth anniversary in November, 1907. Then Mr. Eliot, after some correspondence, and conversations at the Saturday Club, proposed an appointment on a half-time basis, to continue until I should feel that I could fairly leave the *Atlantic* in other hands; and when I told him that I had been counting on a holiday in Europe as soon as my book was done, he offered to defer the beginning of my Harvard courses until February, 1907. Mr. Mifflin, who was a zealous Harvard man and who agreed with Mr. Eliot on most matters except politics, very graciously fell in with the half-time arrangement. It was precisely what we had carried out during my first year of service for the firm. And so, to pass over for the moment one of the most important personal decisions which I have ever been called upon to make, I became in March, 1906, a professor at Harvard. As will be noted in another chapter, the chair to which I was elected was, fortunately, not precisely that originally proposed by the President. There were no teaching duties for a year to come. I shall comment later upon my first impressions of the University where I was to spend the remainder of my life.

By June the *Whitman* was in the printer's hands. For the first time in the seven years since coming to Boston, I felt a bit fagged. I can see clearly enough now that I had been trying to do too much, and that my wife was right in pointing out that no one could do his best work if he were functioning as editor, lecturer, teacher, and author, all at the same time. I had endeavored, it is true, to keep in careful physical training. Such portions of the summers as I had been able to spend in Greensboro were always tonic; in the spring and fall at Cambridge I had tried to get a couple of afternoons each week for golf; and occasionally I had snatched a brief holiday for a fishing trip in northern New England or Canada. What those trips meant, and still mean to me, I have told in my book of fishing essays, *Pools and Ripples*, and it need not be repeated here.

I felt an immense relief in leaving the *Atlantic* for six months in the capable hands of Ferris Greenslet. Mrs. Perry, the three children, and my brother Lewis — who had now won his professorship at Williams and was planning to spend a year in Paris and Oxford — sailed with me on the *New Amsterdam*, bound for the Hook of Holland. It was exactly twenty years since Starr Cutting and I had sailed for Germany on the *Pennland* with our heads full of dreams; and some of those dreams had come true.

Unluckily, the Perrys had given hostages to fortune in the form of some oysters eaten at Hoboken the night before sailing, and as soon as we reached Brussels, on our way to Switzerland, our daughter Margaret came down with typhoid fever. We took the top floor of a *pension* kept by some kindly Swiss people, recommended to us by the Hibbens; and a skilful Belgian doctor, with a tall, blue-eyed nurse sent over from the London Hospital, pulled the invalid through. But we had an anxious eight weeks. Lewis stayed by us loyally, and toward the end of that hot summer he and I took some short walking trips in the Forest of Ardennes and the valley of the Meuse, visiting Liège, Namur, Rochefort, and other places which were to witness heavy fighting during the German invasion of Belgium in 1914. By the middle of September we all escaped to Switzerland. The children, with the English nurse, were placed in a French school at Wilderswyl, near Interlaken, kept by the daughter of that painter in whose family Mrs. Perry had lived in 1887. Snow was already falling on the mountains, but Lewis and I climbed a few passes, and were on the Gorner Grat while a Williams friend of ours was making the last ascent of the Matterhorn for that season. Then Lewis left for Paris, to join 'Bill' James, who was beginning to paint; and Mrs. Perry and I, relieved at last from anxiety, betook ourselves to Florence and then to Rome.

Never before or since did Italy seem more entrancing to us than in that autumn. We were too tired to attempt much sight-seeing. In Florence we took Italian lessons for two hours each morning, but for the most of the day it was enough to revel in some of our favorite pictures and to read dozens of Italian novels. I remember the sunshine in the Piazza Indipendenza as I sat writing a Toastmaster essay for the January *Atlantic*, and I meditated a good deal upon Longfellow, whose centenary was coming in February, 1907. I had promised to write about him in the magazine. But otherwise I followed Tolstoi's advice to 'stop thinking.' We saw few Americans, though we were entertained charmingly by Mrs. John Alexander, who was then ninety-three, and her daughter Francesca, who had written *The Story of Ida* and had been made famous by Ruskin's praise of her drawings. Francesca was already growing blind.

We passed November and December in Rome. Many of our warm friends were there, especially Mr. and Mrs.

James Ford Rhodes of Boston, the William Roscoe Thayers of Cambridge, and the Jesse Carters of Princeton. Carter was then the Director of the American School of Classical Studies. He was lecturing that winter, in what he called his 'hypodermic style,' on the Roman occupation of Britain, and among his auditors might be seen Rudyard Kipling, assiduously taking notes. Mr. Kipling was writing his *Puck of Pook's Hill* stories, and remarked to Carter that he did not wish to let the critics catch him in any errors of fact! We dined out a good deal with these agreeable companions, and the days were filled with the inexhaustible interests of Rome. Signor Boni took us to the Forum to show his latest excavations; we drove out to Frascati and Hadrian's Villa and Horace's Sabine Farm; we had an audience with Pope Pius X and were, I hope, a little the better for his blessing. In short, we did in Rome as good Americans do. The first copy of the *Whitman* reached me here, with the first press notices, and the book was obviously scoring. We had a happy Christmas with Lewis and the children, for he had brought them down from Switzerland. The day after Christmas I left my wife and children to finish their winter in Rome, and sailed home alone from Naples. The *Canopic* was a slow boat, and I had finished the Longfellow article — writing in the smoking-room — long before we crawled into Boston Harbor, the decks covered with ice and a pitiless north wind blowing.

I found the dovecot at 4 Park Street fluttering with excitement. May Sinclair, an English novelist whose *Divine Fire* had been among the outstanding successes of that era, had written for us a serial entitled *The Helpmate*, beginning in the January number. It opened with a 'bedroom scene' which would be thought innocuous today, but which instantly cost us many subscribers. The manuscript had been belated, and I had not seen the proofs, but my first task on reaching the office was to dictate letters defending the lady against the charge of corrupting American morals. As I had not yet read a word of the story, I fear that these letters to angered subscribers were too detached to be convincing.

There was another pile of letters awaiting me, and these were more angry still. They were from Traubel, Harned, Platt, and other admirers of Whitman — idolaters all — who resented as slander some statements in my biography of the poet. Documentary proof was demanded, and I was in a delicate position. I had had my facts from responsible men like Stedman, J. T. Trowbridge, Gilder, Talcott Williams and others who had known Whitman well, but I could not expose these friends of mine to the picturesque abuse which Traubel was pouring upon me in the *Conservator* — the organ of the 'Whitmaniacs.' So I made no public reply, contenting myself with dictating some of those 'soft answers' which actually increase a correspondent's wrath instead of allaying it. I had, however, the vulgar comfort of discovering that the more bitterly the *Conservator* attacked the book, the better it sold. John Burroughs praised it to me, but apparently changed his mind later. The whole episode taught me what I should have known long before, namely, the suspicion and jealousy felt toward the college-bred which has lurked in our democracy from the beginning. Both Whitman and Burroughs were marked examples of this distrust of 'the professors.'

Aside from that initial flurry over *The Helpmate*, 1907

was a fortunate year for the *Atlantic*. We had two subscribers for each one that was lost. It was, alas, the year
of Aldrich's death, and his touching poem on Longfellow,
printed in March, was the last he ever wrote. He made a
beautiful manuscript copy of it for me to keep — and died
before that month was over. In November came our
fiftieth anniversary. We celebrated it with all piety. There
were two survivors of the contributors to the first volume:
J. T. Trowbridge — the story-writer and poet — and
Charles Eliot Norton. I persuaded both of them to give
us their reminiscences of the early days, and even tried to
seduce Trowbridge into composing a poem in praise of
the flying-machine of the Wright brothers, to match his
once famous 'Darius Green and his Flying-Machine,'
written half a century before. But as to further verse-
writing, that jolly old gentleman balked. He had the same
complaint and excuse as 'Uncle John' Burroughs, when I
once suggested a topic for an essay, 'I'd do it, Mr. Perry,'
said Burroughs, dropping into dialect, '*if I could only
git het up enough so's I could flow!*'

Mr. Norton offered us, however, an unpublished poem
by Lowell, the first editor, and we gave it the post of
honor; but I fear it was better for window-dressing than
as a poem. Mr. Howells told the story of his own editorship, and never wrote with more wistful charm; and Page
produced a vigorous paper on 'The Writer and the
University' — a plea for post-graduate training of professional writers. A survey of American progress during the
preceding half-century seemed advisable, and 'Literature'
was entrusted to T. W. Higginson, 'Science' to Henry S.
Pritchett, 'Art' to H. W. Mabie, and 'Politics' to Woodrow Wilson. All of these papers were workmanlike, but

Wilson's remains the most significant, particularly in its forecast of coming political and governmental changes. My own contribution to the anniversary number was entitled 'The Editor who was never the Editor' — a sketch, drawn from his unpublished correspondence, of F. H. Underwood, the real projector of the magazine. He was almost forgotten by 1907, and is quite forgotten today. It happened that when the *Atlantic* was celebrating its Diamond Jubilee in 1932, Mr. Sedgwick asked me, as a former editor, to contribute a paper; and I could not help pointing out in it that the cleavage which had stretched between 1857 and 1907, vast as it was, seemed much narrower than the gulf which separated 1907 — the climax of the Theodore Roosevelt era — from the America of 1932.

This mention of Ellery Sedgwick calls to mind that day in 1908 when the new 'Atlantic Monthly Company' came into existence. Mr. Sedgwick, a young journalist of tested capacity, persuaded Mr. Mifflin to transfer the ownership of the *Atlantic* to a new organization in which Sedgwick held the controlling interest. I had long felt that a magazine which was financially independent of a publishing house had some great advantages. While I had never chafed as much as Page did over being a publisher's 'hired man,' [1] I knew well enough that a salaried employee must lack something of the independence, the initiative, and the driving power that come with ownership. The new company announced, indeed, that it contemplated no changes in the policy and editorship of the magazine. But it was known, of course, that I had expected before long to resign from the editorship

[1] See *Life and Letters of Walter H. Page,* pp. 67–70.

in order to devote myself wholly to college work. Finally I agreed to stay until August 1, 1909, thus completing precisely ten years of service.

Ten years. That was as long as the siege of Troy! But, alas, those 'forts of folly' against which I had been fighting seemed as strongly entrenched as ever. I was willing enough to let a younger and far better journalist take his turn in conducting the campaign. And as for the publishing business, that mystical *aura* which my idealistic friend Horace Scudder had plainly seen floating over it was after ten years of close observation no longer visible to me. Nevertheless, I wished to leave some pleasant memorial of my service with the magazine and the House, and I dedicated to Mr. Mifflin a volume entitled *Park Street Papers*, including some of my Toastmaster addresses and the commemorative essays which I had published on Hawthorne, Longfellow, Aldrich, Whittier, and Underwood. All of these men had been a part of the *Atlantic* tradition.

And then, just as I was arranging my courses for full-time teaching at Harvard, came another fork in the road. President Eliot, then in his last year of office, invited me to serve, for the year beginning in September, 1909, as the Harvard lecturer at the University of Paris and the other universities of France.

IX

FRANCE

Fair stood the wind for France
When we our sails advance;
Nor now to prove our chance
Longer will tarry.

MICHAEL DRAYTON, *Agincourt*

THE exchange of lecturers between Harvard and the Sorbonne (i.e., 'The University of Paris') was due originally to the energy and generosity of a young Harvard man, James Hazen Hyde. Beginning in 1898, the year of his graduation, he had arranged for the annual visits to Cambridge of distinguished French scholars, who lectured under the auspices of the *Cercle Français*. René Doumic was the first lecturer, followed by Edouard Rod and other well-known men of letters. André Tardieu had come in 1908, and in 1909 Abel Lefranc. In 1904, however, Mr. Hyde had succeeded in persuading the authorities of Harvard and of the Sorbonne to establish also an annual course of lectures in English upon the United States; the lecturers to be appointed by Harvard, but to be recognized as serving temporarily upon the staff of the University of Paris and of such provincial universities as might desire their services. The real aim of this interchange of professors was felt at that time to be not so much the stimulus of technical scholarship as the promotion of friendly relations between the two countries.

Professor Barrett Wendell was the first of these American lecturers. He took his responsibilities and social privileges with the greatest seriousness, and later described them in one of the best of his books, *The France of Today*. He was followed, in due order, by Professors Santayana, Coolidge, and Baker of Harvard and Professor Henry van Dyke of Princeton — who was my immediate predecessor in the lectureship. It should be noted that the present exchange of professors between Harvard and the Sorbonne is on a different basis from that originally planned by Mr. Hyde. Nowadays the scholars representing the two universities give regular courses, as they would at home, to students who are candidates for degrees. There is no longer any attempt to interpret one country to the other; and the Harvard professors in France are not expected to give public lectures upon the United States, although some of them continue to visit the provincial universities. But in 1909-'10 the original plan, as described in Wendell's *France of Today*, was in full force. The lecturer was supposed to hold the attention of a miscellaneous audience in the Amphithéâtre Richelieu and to interpret to France — in an unofficial 'Ambassadorial' capacity which had pleased vastly the imagination of Barrett Wendell — the institutions, the ideas, and the ideals of the United States.

Accordingly I agreed to deliver twenty-five lectures between the end of November and the first of March, and thereafter to spend a few weeks in visiting a dozen provincial universities, giving one or two lectures in each city. My theme was to be 'American Types' as exhibited in representative men, in sectional and national characteristics, and in literature; a theme broad enough, surely, to cover anything that I might wish to say. There was no time, before sailing, for the preparation of my lectures, but I shipped to Paris a big box of books together with some old lecture-notes, cleared my *Atlantic* desk for the last time, late in July, and sailed from Quebec with my wife and daughters on the ill-starred but very fine boat, *The Empress of Ireland.*

In those days the *Empress* boats went into Liverpool, instead of calling, as now, at Southampton and Cherbourg. The voyage was singularly restful. For the first time in ten years — save for one holiday of six months in Europe — I could dismiss all home problems from my mind. The tumultuous 'Roosevelt era' was over, and President Taft's administration had opened peacefully enough. President Lowell seemed quite competent to manage the affairs of Harvard; but if either Taft or Lowell were to blunder, it was now Ellery Sedgwick who could be responsible for admonitory articles in the *Atlantic Monthly.* I had hung that shield upon the wall. I could not even take very seriously the current talk about strained relations between the great European Powers. We had as one of our fellow voyagers an English ecclesiastical dignitary who is now a famous Bishop. As I walked the deck of the *Empress of Ireland* with him he maintained stoutly that it was in England's interest to declare war on Germany at once, before the Kiel Canal could be made any wider. I was shocked at this bellicose attitude of the man of God, and asked him if he could really see, in imagination, a triumphant Prussian lieutenant standing guard in front of the Bank of England. 'Yes,' declared the future Bishop, 'I can, if we don't strike first!' Five years later I often recalled this shipboard conversation, but the Prussian lieutenants have not yet been posted in front of the Old Lady of Threadneedle Street.

We showed our daughters London and Salisbury and Stonehenge, and then crossed on a rough night from New Haven to St. Malo. There we were joined by Mlle. Chesneau, a school-teacher in Paris, whom we had engaged to travel with us for a few weeks in order to polish our sadly rusted conversational French. She would allow no word of English. In the evenings she read aloud to us, and I can still feel the shiver in her voice as she rendered — ostensibly for the benefit of the children, but to her own authentic terror and delight — Conan Doyle's *Le Chien des Baskervilles*. On the coast of Brittany — for we stayed some weeks at St. Briac and Dinan — she chose, appropriately, Victor Hugo's *Travailleurs de la Mer*. But nothing, even in Victor Hugo, and even after we had helped some English boys to capture a real octopus at low tide among the rocks of St. Briac, gave us such a vivid horror as Conan Doyle's huge phosphorescent dog, dressed up in French! We made our pilgrimage to Mont St. Michel, and thence to Guingamp and through the Black Country to Quimper. We visited Douarnenez and Audierne, Concarneau and Carnac, and the spell of Breton enchantment which they cast upon us is not yet broken. Then we journeyed leisurely into the Touraine country, which is never more lovely than in September.

We reached Paris on October first, and went into winter quarters in a friendly little hotel on the left bank — the Hôtel du Quai Voltaire. It was noisy and not overclean, but the chef was an artist. We had a tiny salon on the first floor, and a few books and prints and flowers soon made it homelike. The Seine ran under our bedroom windows, and the bookstalls stretched temptingly along the Quai. The very first title that caught my eye was

Lawrence Lowell's *Government of England*! We entrusted
our daughters to a boarding-school at Groslay, eight miles
north of Paris, but Mlle. Chesneau continued her strict
supervision of our French exercises and conversation.   I
had babbled fluently enough in French ever since the days
in Strassburg, but I had never been trained to write it
accurately, and it was a salutary although humiliating
experience, in one's fiftieth year, to wrestle with 'my
aunt's gloves are reposing under the bureau of my grandmother.'

I devoted the forenoons to the task of blocking out the
twenty-five lectures, for I intended to speak, as at home,
from carefully arranged notes rather than from manuscript.   The afternoons began to be filled at once by social
duties.   Coached by the efficient French secretary of Mr.
Hyde, I proceeded, in silk hat and frock coat, to make
solemn official calls upon the Minister of Public Instruction, the Rector of the University of Paris, and the Dean
of the Faculty of Letters.   The latter was Alfred Croiset,
and when he discovered that I had read one of his books
on Greek poetry he relaxed his official formality and welcomed me like a man and a brother.   I had almost no
personal acquaintance with men of letters in Paris, but
one of the most delightful of them, Abbé Ernest Dimnet,
was among our first callers.   He was then teaching in the
fashionable Collège Stanislas, and I had printed one of
his short stories — written in impeccable English — in the
Atlantic.   He introduced me to two of his closest friends.
Emile Legouis, Professor of English at the Sorbonne, whose
work on the youthful Wordsworth had been so distinguished, and Auguste Angellier, the poet, who taught
English at the University of Lille for two days a week

during the spring and fall, and had made his reputation among scholars through his book on Robert Burns. To hear these three Frenchmen talk together — using English out of courtesy to me — was a revelation of the high spirits, the accuracy, and the cleverness with which English may be spoken by men to whom it was not the mother tongue. Bergson's English was to me equally remarkable, and André Chevrillon's.

We knew of course a few persons in the American Colony, which was estimated that winter at thirty thousand. The proportion of saints to derelicts in this floating society defied computation, though it did not strike me that the percentage of derelicts was any higher than it had been in Berlin or Rome. The saints do not always betray themselves at dinner parties, nor do the derelicts. The Robert Bacons did the honors of the American Embassy at that time, and were most hospitable and thoughtful, entertaining the just and the unjust with equal courtesy. But the purely French dinners were naturally more interesting to us than any functions in the Colony. Our friends the George P. Bakers of Cambridge had given us letters to many of their Paris acquaintances, and after the preliminary cards had been exchanged in the French fashion, we began to climb long flights of stairs in the Latin Quarter to attend dinners given in our honor by professors at the Sorbonne or the Collège de France. We soon grew accustomed to seeing the host and hostess seat themselves at the middle of the table in order to facilitate that general conversation which is the ideal of French dinner parties. But long after we had acquired a tolerable courage in exchanging views with the guests on either side of us, we found it terrifying to be coaxed into addressing the whole table.

Of course we made constant social blunders, however mercifully they were overlooked. Neither of us discovered when we first met Madame Dieulafoy — an archaeologist who had worn male attire during her explorations in Persia and was allowed to continue to dress as a man in Paris — that her faultless masculine evening clothes, exactly matching her husband's, were a disguise. She looked and talked like a Parisian lawyer with a high-pitched voice, and both my wife and I addressed her all through a dinner as 'Monsieur.' At another dinner, when we had returned to the drawing-room for coffee, I found myself cornered with a plump, light-haired gentleman arrayed in one of those unstarched pleated silk shirts which were just coming into evening wear in Paris. I did not know his name. He was extremely affable and replied '*Mais, parfaitement!*' to everything that I said. I was tired from lecturing that afternoon, and as often happens when one is speaking a foreign language, I mounted one subject and rode round and round on it without being able to dismount. And my unlucky theme was this: that no one was really happy unless he had to work for a living. Upon this excellent morality I played all the variations of which my French was capable, and whenever I paused in the weary round my new acquaintance would give his en-thusiastic assent with another '*Parfaitement!*' At last someone kindly interrupted this performance, and then asked me, 'What *did* you find to talk about with Count Boni de Castellane?' Castellane, who knew English as well as I did, had just squandered the Gould millions and had never done a stroke of work in his life!

It is only fair to match such misadventures with one piece of good fortune. I had taken a lady in to dinner without catching her name. Across the table some guest mentioned Pasteur, and to make conversation I asked the lady whom I had taken in: 'Who wrote that charming life of Pasteur which we were all reading a few years ago?' Her beautiful face flushed with pleasure. 'I am so glad,' she exclaimed, 'that you like my husband's book about my father!' She was Madame Valléry-Radot, and her husband, who was just opposite us, was promptly and publicly informed by his wife of my delight in his book. I told him how often President Eliot of Harvard had praised and quoted that biography.

At one dinner given to us by a well-known *savant* who was popularly supposed to be the original of Anatole France's *Monsieur Bergeret*, we had the pleasure of meeting Captain and Madame Dreyfus. Though the once-famous 'affair' was an old story then, it is needless to say that there were no representatives of the clergy or the army at that dinner. Dreyfus came into the men's dressing-room in company with a professor of Sanscrit, and I supposed at first that he was another one. We had a long talk after dinner about United States Steel and Standard Oil, for his son was about to visit America to study the methods of these corporations. I liked Captain Dreyfus very much, though when he told me that he was coming to hear me lecture upon Poe, I could not help wondering how a man who had lived through his Devil's Island experiences could find anything really thrilling in the imaginary horrors invented by Edgar Allan Poe. Also, I missed a luncheon with another defender of Dreyfus, Anatole France, for the reason that that gifted personage went suddenly into mourning for a lady.

Mr. Hyde, with his customary hospitality toward the

American exchange professors, gave me half-a-dozen elaborate Sunday-evening dinners, where he gathered the leading scholars, authors, artists, and government officials of Paris. I was presented with a list of the name and address of each guest — there were over twenty at each dinner — and within a day or two I was expected to leave my card. All sorts of invitations followed: to receptions of new members of the Academy, where we listened to Pierre Loti and other notables, and to dinners of various literary organizations, where I was allowed, fortunately, to respond in English to the toasts. Only once, during the whole winter, did I have to make an after-dinner speech in French. The Marmite Club was about to honor an aviator who had just performed the then unparalleled feat of circling the Eiffel Tower and returning safely to the landing field. Baron D'Estournelles de Constant, whom I had met in Boston at a World Peace Conference, insisted that I should represent the country of the Wright brothers, and that I should speak in French. I did not dare to write out an address, for fear of forgetting it, but I learned all the aviation terms which I could cull from the newspapers, and inflicted the nauseous compound upon those four hundred polite Frenchmen. They preserved perfect decorum, and indeed applauded vigorously. Then came the turn of the hero of the evening. He looked precisely like an embarrassed captain of an American football team when summoned to speak in public. He rose slowly, bowed profoundly to each corner of the room, opened his grave lips, closed them in sheer terror, and sat down. He could fly, but he had not the courage to attempt a speech! I took a fancy to that fellow, and told him so.

The world of the theatre was excited in that season over

the first performance of Rostand's *Chantecler*. It was a relief to us to discover that many of our learned French
friends were as much puzzled as we by the obsolete words
employed by the poet to decorate his glittering dialogue.
We attended occasionally the opera and plays at the
Français and the Odéon, but the evenings were too crowded
for regular theatre-going. We could not return in kind the
hospitalities which were showered upon us, but my wife
served tea every Saturday in our little salon at the Quai
Voltaire, and the room was filled with academic and literary persons, with now and then some gorgeous apparition
from the American Colony. What curious flashes of memory still light up individual figures seen in those winter
afternoons and evenings: Pierre Loti in his wig; Mounet-
Sully's gratitude as I lighted a cigarette for him — for he
was already almost as blind in a drawing-room as he was as
King Edipus upon the stage; George Moore with his silky
French and the feline watchfulness of his greenish eyes;
and that polished leader of the Young Turk party, re-
splendent in Paris clothes and moving his cigarette lightly
as he replied to my impertinent question, 'Were you not
obliged to execute a good many of your opponents?' with
a deprecatory '*Mais non, Monsieur, seulement vingt-six.*'
What a language for conspirators is French! 'Twenty-six
men shot' seems crude and cruel in English; but '*seulement vingt-six,*' on the lips of that Young Turk, seemed a
negligible though doubtless regrettable detail, a concession
to the onward march of Progress. And why should a
French deadbeat, addressing me on Christmas Eve as
'*Cher Maître,*' succeed in borrowing twenty francs, when
he could never, with that fishy face of his, have borrowed
it in English?

But after all, I was in Paris to lecture professionally, rather than to receive fugitive or memorable impressions. On Tuesdays and Fridays at five I appeared in frock coat and silk hat at the Sorbonne, was ushered by the *appariteur* into the waiting room, and was thence escorted by him, at the precise minute, into the Amphithéâtre Richelieu. It held nearly a thousand auditors, and except for one day when the flood-waters of the Seine made access to the Sorbonne difficult, there were always some persons standing. The 'publicity' had been competently handled, it is true, but the fact remained that many residents of Paris were sincerely interested in the United States. About half the audience was French, although only one or two hundred were students enrolled at the Sorbonne. There were soldiers, priests, journalists, and even a group of actresses from the Théâtre Français who came to study 'diction'; and there were plenty of Russians, Germans, and Orientals, besides some of the motor-car wing of the American Colony. Contrary to the French professorial custom, I spoke standing, and to make it easier for foreigners to understand what was said, spoke so deliberately that I could present only about three-quarters as much material in one hour as I could in a classroom at home. But I never had better listeners. Once, when the Seine flood was at its height and the lighting system of the Sorbonne was put out of commission, the *appariteur* appeared just as the great hall grew dim, and placed a single wax candle by my desk. I finished the last ten minutes of a Whitman lecture by the light of that one candle. It was a singular lesson in optics to observe how much illumination of the amphitheatre one candle could supply, and a still more singular lesson in courtesy as the audience listened without a whisper and quietly dispersed. How white their faces looked by candle-light!

What I tried to emphasize in those Paris lectures was, first of all, the European and particularly the English inheritance of our original colonists, and the gradual modification of their intellectual and political outlook under new physical conditions; then the relation of eighteenth-century figures like Franklin and Jefferson to the European movement of ideas and to the later American democracy; and what was really new in such literary pioneers as Irving and Cooper. I stressed the European affiliations of Emerson's Transcendentalism, the influence of Longfellow as an interpreter of the European scene, and the relationships of men like Whittier and Garrison to English liberalism and radicalism. But I discussed also, in connection with Lincoln and Mark Twain, some of the indigenous qualities of American humor and satire, and the contributions of our various sectional types of character to the gradual moulding of public opinion in the United States. In fact I was dreaming then, and for many years thereafter, of writing some day a History of American Literature upon a somewhat different plan from anything attempted up to that time; and for that reason I declined the offer of a Paris publisher to issue a French translation of the Sorbonne lectures, feeling that such a publication would be sketchy and premature.

I suspect, however, that my array of facts and theories about the interrelationship of European and American points of view proved less effective upon the platform than the biographical interpretations of such figures as Emerson, Poe, Whitman, and Lincoln. Yet it is easy for a lecturer to delude himself as to the actual impression made

upon the mind of his composite audience. They may
listen courteously enough, but there is no available yard-
stick or cardiogram for the measurement of their thoughts.
When philosophers like Bergson and Boutroux came up
after my lecture on Emerson to express their pleasure, it
was natural that a weary speaker should imagine that his
performance had really been excellent. Perhaps it was! It
may be noted that the provincial universities, making
their own selection from the list of Paris lectures, chose
Walt Whitman in preference to any other subject, with
Poe as the second choice, followed by Franklin and
Fenimore Cooper. But the living American about whom I
was most often questioned in university circles throughout
France was William James.

I had many opportunities, while in Paris, of listening to
lectures delivered by professors at the Sorbonne and the
Collège de France. The subject-matter of these lectures
seemed to me neither more nor less substantial in scholarship than the lectures given by first-class men in Germany.
But there were striking differences in the mode of presentation. The Frenchmen, sitting immobile behind a desk and
reading quietly from manuscript, seemed a different order
of beings from such orators as Kuno Fischer and Von
Treitschke. Apparently they made no physical effort to
hold the attention of their audience. There was nothing
remotely resembling the emotional fire and fury which
may be observed in any political gathering in France or
Italy. Nor was there anything of the yearning sub-
conscious ethical intention which often imparts a wistful
eloquence to English lecturers who seem to suffer bodily
torment from being exposed to view upon a public platform. The French scholars appeared to have passed be-

yond all that. Their facts and their emotions were transmuted somehow into the ordered beauty of a symmetrically designed discourse, flowing from paragraph to paragraph in consummate perfection of phrase.

When Alfred Croiset lectured on Plato, and Gustave Lanson on Montesquieu, they did not seem to lift their voices above conversational pitch or raise their eyes from the manuscript, and yet they riveted the attention of hundreds of listeners. Of course the listeners were trained also, and did not need to be prodded awake by such sharp devices as Jesse Carter's witty 'hypodermic' thrusts. One need not enlarge upon the technical methods of French academic lecturers, since many of them — like Bergson, Bedier, Legouis, Feuillerat, Cestre, Baldensperger — have spoken frequently in American universities. It is true that from boyhood they have undergone a far more exacting intellectual discipline than most of their American colleagues; that they carry a somewhat lighter teaching load — often only two or three lectures a week; and that they are less burdened with committee work and other administrative details. But taking all such matters into account, the fact remains that the best French lecturers reveal a combination of mastery of their subject with artistic skill in its presentation which I have never seen matched — except here and there in some gifted individual — in any other country.

Our chief experience in Paris was over by the first of March, and we set forth as itinerant messengers of goodwill to visit eleven provincial universities. First came Lille, Nancy, Dijon, and Lyons; then an indolent month of Easter holiday in the South; and then Grenoble, Montpellier, Toulouse, Bordeaux, Poitiers, Rennes, and Caen.

The efficient secretary of Mr. Hyde had arranged everything, even to the hotels and time-tables. In three of the
universities there were two lectures, and in the others but
one, all chosen by the local authorities. Usually the young
persons studying English in the various Lycées were
marched in to my lectures in order to test their ability to
understand spoken English, and they were obliged to sub-
mit written reports to the Ministry of Public Instruction in
Paris. At Toulouse, for example, I was reported to have
used a very provincial American accent; but an amused
official of the Ministry explained to me afterward that the
Toulouse standard of spoken English had been set by a
young Scotch *lecteur* from Glasgow!

Everywhere in these provincial centres of learning we
were received with official courtesies and with warm personal friendliness. The only awkward moment was at the
opening of the lecture at Lille, where the Dean of the
Faculty of Science was called upon to preside. He was not
in good temper, and introduced me by saying that a professor from Harvard — with its immense wealth and
magnificent buildings — must of course look down upon a
poorly equipped provincial university like Lille. I could
not let that pass. Remembering that Pasteur had once
been Dean of the Faculty of Science at Lille, I described
the shabby and ill-furnished laboratories in which he had
first made those experiments which resulted in such incal-
culable benefit to France and to the world, and turning
to the Dean I assured him that Harvard would be only too
happy to exchange the most expensive of its buildings in
return for one Pasteur. That remark won the audience,
though it may not have mollified the grumpy Dean.

But usually the officials were delightful persons — none

more so than that eccentric Rector of Dijon, who had drawn me solemnly aside after a Paris dinner in December in order to inquire what brand of Burgundy I would prefer to have served at his dinner for me in March. And what a dinner that proved to be, with its 'Soles James Hyde, Filet de boeuf Roosevelt, Riz de veau Harvard, Glacé Edgar Poë' and wines that only a scholar and a Burgundian could have selected! A formal reception commonly preceded or followed each lecture. My wife was never quite certain what she ought to wear at these gatherings, but high-necked gowns for the ladies and frock coats for the men predominated even at official dinners in the provinces. The main function of the receptions seemed to be the toasts to Harvard and then to the local university; to the United States and then to France. I hope I rose to such patriotic exchange of compliments without disgrace, although privately I consider champagne a treacherous beverage. My friend Baldensperger may remember that at Grenoble these four toasts, drunk in mid-afternoon, were followed by black coffee plentifully laced with cognac, to the secret alarm of the abstemious Yankee visitor, who was obliged straightway to mount the platform and expound Walt Whitman with precision.

At Bordeaux my wife was barely saved from a grave social error by the tact of our host. He was a Scotch Jacobite by descent and a famous wine merchant by profession, and he had escorted us through what seemed miles and miles of his *caves*, discoursing mainly about the mysteries of claret. He declared that he had himself tasted (of course without swallowing) eighty-four different vintages that morning, and that such exercise was highly beneficial to one's health. Wearied out at last, Mrs.

Menu

Potage mousseline.

Soles James Hyde.
Filet de bœuf Roosevelt.
Riz-de-veau Harvard.

Sorbets au Kirsch.

Petits pois à la française.
Dinde truffée.
Salade d'endives.
Foie gras Usona.

Glace Edgard Poë.
Petits fours.
Desserts.

La Tour Blanche.
Saint-Émilion.
Vosne-Romanée.
Champagne.

(On the scroll:)
The Broughton
House
Jim Kilteridge
Powers at play
plated City
Etta masterpiece
Park Street Papers

A DIJON DINNER CARD (1910)

Perry asked if she might have a glass of water. Our host, well over eighty but a superb figure still, looked at her with amazement. 'Madame, you are the second guest of the Johnstons since 1745 to ask for water when under our roof. The other was President MacMahon, when I was showing him these very *caves*. *"Water?"* I said. *"We have no water!* But inasmuch as you are the President of the Republic, I will send a boy out to see if he can find some." And, Madame Bliss Perry' — with a deep bow to his guest — 'I shall consider it an honor to do the same for you!'

I must not, however, give the impression that the kindly professors who entertained us in these provincial cities were really convivial in their tastes. As a rule they were anything but that. Even at elaborate dinners in Paris I had noticed that the academic guests usually took but a single glass of wine and smoked not more than one or two cigarettes. The majority of these Paris pundits had come up from the provinces and had retained their frugal manner of living. In the smaller universities we met many a distinguished scholar who spoke frankly of his own peasant origin and who lived on a salary of twelve hundred dollars a year. In their intellectual ardor and their ascetic simplicity of life, they made us think of the old unsophisticated days at Williams and Princeton. They were more likely to ask us to luncheon than to dinner, as involving less formality, and at these luncheons the children were often present. We had already discovered one infallible method of making conversation: all French fathers and mothers were delighted to talk about their children and about ours. One does not often risk this topic with Bostonians, but it is a sound opening for the conversational game in France.

The lectures in Lyons were over by the middle of March, and the holiday month began. We spent long hours in the sunshine of Avignon, Orange, Arles, Nîmes, Les Baux, and Carcassonne; plucked some laurel leaves from Petrarch's garden at Vaucluse; and settled for a fortnight at Bormes, between Hyères and Saint Raphaël. Here the Mediterranean lay six hundred feet below us. The cherry and peach trees were already in brilliant white and pink against the green-grey background of cork and olive groves, and stone-pines which reminded us that we were almost in Italy. Three or four companionable professors from the Sorbonne were staying at our hotel, and best of all, our friend Angellier the poet had a villa near-by. He was in delicate health and could not walk far, but we strolled slowly under the cork and olive trees, and talked about books and men and poetry. Lanson, the historian of French literature, was one of the group of professors at the hotel, and Angellier loved to chaff him. I have quoted in my *Study of Poetry* one of these comments on Lanson, for it contained an original metaphor about reading verse:

'There goes Lanson! His big book is carrying all the treasures of French literature down to posterity like a cold-storage transport ship. But he published a criticism of one of my poems which proved that he did not understand the poem at all. He had studied it too hard! The words of a poem are stepping-stones across a brook. If you linger on one of them too long, you will get your feet wet. You must cross, *vite, vite!*' The delightful Angellier died not long afterward, just when his friends Legouis and Dimnet were confident that he was to be elected to the Academy. He crossed the stepping-stones to the other world, *vite, vite*.

After this enchanted oasis on the French Riviera, we

took the road again to visit seven more university towns. Everywhere there was the same kindness; the same expert guidance by professors of the fine arts and of local history in visiting ancient churches and monuments of art; the same professional talk about books with ambitious young teachers who had Paris as their ultimate goal and many of whom have since arrived at the Sorbonne, the Ecole Normale, or the Collège de France. Doubtless, under the polished surface, there were the jealousies, the heart-burnings, and the disappointments incident to academic life everywhere, but we saw nothing of it. These professors knew that I had been trained in Germany, and I was struck by their scrupulous fairness in discussing their professional rivals in that country. One evening at Rennes I was the guest of half-a-dozen scientists who compared the work then being done in their special fields at the various French universities with that which was going forward in Germany; giving the palm, now to Germany and now to France, with a dispassionate detachment at which I marvelled. Nowhere, during that year in France, did I meet with the opinion that war with Germany was in any way imminent, though the French mind was too realistic to deny such an ultimate possibility. For ten years my thoughts had been directed to international peace more constantly than to anything except my professional work and my family, and on the whole I felt encouraged at what I imagined to be the steady although slow advance of international good-will.

Both my wife and I wished to revisit Germany before going home, and we thought that our daughters, who had had excellent instruction at Groslay and spoke French readily, could profitably add to their knowledge of German before entering Radcliffe. As my duties in France came to an end on May 5, we decided to spend a couple of months in Weimar, with brief visits to our old friends in Strassburg and Berlin. My final task in Paris was to help Ambassador Robert Bacon in selecting an auditorium at the Sorbonne for Theodore Roosevelt, who was on his way home from Africa and was billed for speeches in Berlin, Paris, and London. I should have been proud to serve as one of Roosevelt's gun-bearers in Africa, but I had no desire to listen to him again on the platform. When we reached the Gare de l'Est on the morning of May 7, the newsboys were crying extras with the news of the death of King Edward VII. He had been extremely popular in Paris, and the French press commented with kindly understanding upon some aspects of his character which were left untouched by English journalists. That scene in the Gare de l'Est, with the black-bordered extras fluttering everywhere, was destined to be my last glimpse of Paris until long after the War.

I cannot say that our attempt to recapture the charm of Germany, after more than a score of years of absence, was a brilliant success. Germany had changed, and not, we thought, for the better. The new Industrialism was triumphant. I could not find a trace of my old quarters in Strassburg, that section of the city having been 'improved'; new professors had posted their spring courses at the University, and there were more uniforms on the streets than ever. Weimar, it is true, had altered very little, but it must be admitted that Weimar in the twentieth century is a trifle dull. We were in a pleasant *pension*, took the usual walks and drives, played tennis for a small fee on the Grand Duke's court, and went piously to the famous theatre. But our daughters took an inexplicable distaste for the German language: they simply would not drink from that Pierian spring. We left them for a visit to Berlin; but that, too, was a disillusion. Berlin had grown monstrously, but the bigger it was, the uglier it looked. Some of the old professors who had treated me so hospitably in 1886–'87 were now immortalized in bronze and marble in front of the University, but that did not increase my cheerfulness of mood. The daughters of the Von Holst family seemed glad to see us, and the big-hearted W. C. Dreher, now the Berlin correspondent of London and New York papers, gave us a supper in the Zoological Garden and assured us that all talk of war was nonsense: Germany was too busy making money to run any risks. And Dreher was one of the best-informed journalists in Berlin. Back we went to Weimar, still searching for something which we could no longer find. One day I stopped at a bookshop — the window was full of the works of Oscar Wilde and Upton Sinclair — to leave some kodak films to be developed. When I gave my name to the proprietor, he grew excited: 'Are you the discoverer of the North Pole?' For Peary had just accomplished his greatest feat and had reached Europe on his way to the United States. But I had to confess that I was not the explorer: I could not even rediscover the Romantic Germany of my youth. Again we drove and walked and played tennis and went to the theatre; and in the mornings I sat in a shady garden and wrote a little on the *History of American Literature* which I hoped to finish some day — and never have finished, or shall. By and by we did the sensible thing: Rip Van Winkle ought to have thought of it when he was low in his mind: we bought tickets for London.

Just before leaving Weimar I received notification of my election on June 1, 1910, to the American Academy of Arts and Letters. There was no very tangible glory attached to this honor, but it was pleasant to be thus remembered by one's fellow writers at home. The Academy had been founded in 1904, its fifty members having been chosen from the membership of the National Institute of Arts and Letters. Mr. Howells was still President, but among the older members Saint Gaudens, Stedman, Clemens, John Hay, MacDowell, McKim, Norton, J. Q. A. Ward, Aldrich, Jefferson, and Gilder were already gone, and of the forty-seven living members at the date of my election, there are now only four survivors. For many years we were a homeless company, but since 1923 the Academy has been housed in its own beautiful Administration building at 633 West 155th Street, New York, to which an Auditorium has now been added. So far, so good; but whether an Academy has really helped American writing, painting, music, and architecture, who knows?

Back in London, then, with rising spirits; another glimpse of Oxford and Cambridge and the cathedral towns on the East Coast as we journeyed North; a tramp over the battlefield of Marston Moor and around Ecclefechan and Dumfries; finally the Lake Country again, and the *Empress of Ireland*, homeward bound. Two of my brothers were waiting on the dock at Quebec, together with our son, aged twelve, whom we had left in boarding-school during our absence. His sisters, with ears sharpened by their sojourn in Europe, declared that their brother had a highly objectionable American accent! We reached Greensboro too late for any fishing, but the delphinium was still in bloom, the lake seemed more lovely than ever, and Harvard University, then in its second year under the leadership of Lawrence Lowell, would not open for another month. So we rested and were thankful, and soon found that our pleasure in the American accent was unimpaired by residence in France.

X

HARVARD: THE COCKPIT
OF LEARNING

I have been a looker on in the Cockpit of Learning these many years.
ROGER ASCHAM, *The Schoolmaster*

The best and most fruitful conception of a university or college is the ancient one of a society or guild of scholars associated together for preserving, imparting, increasing, and enjoying knowledge.
PRESIDENT A. LAWRENCE LOWELL,
At War with Academic Traditions in America

I: LOOKING IN AT THE WINDOW

MY GRANDFATHER, Baxter Perry, had been graduated from Harvard in President Kirkland's time, but I cannot recall that my father had any special veneration for that seat of learning. In my own undergraduate days, few students in the smaller New England colleges knew anything whatever about Harvard. The 'inferior institutions' imagined that Harvard looked down upon them, but the more cruel truth was that she was not thinking of them at all. The first Harvard undergraduates I ever saw were on the porch of a hotel at Bar Harbor in the summer of 1879. Half-a-dozen of us Williams boys, cruising along the Maine coast and held at Mount Desert by a southeaster, fell into conversation with these Harvard youths. They were extremely courteous, but when they asked politely, 'Where *is* Williamstown College?' we were young enough to be annoyed.

I suppose I knew at that time the names of a few Harvard professors. The one most familiar to me was that of Louis Agassiz, who had died in 1873. I had studied Goodwin's Greek Grammar, and was aware that Child was an authority on English Ballads. I had read Professor Lowell's poems and essays, and knew that Longfellow and Holmes had once been professors likewise. Asa Gray, the botanist, was a distant kinsman of ours, and I had seen Charles Eliot Norton at Ashfield. Oddly enough, considering the ineffaceable personal impression which President Eliot usually made, I cannot recall when and where I first saw him.

By 1886, when Harvard was celebrating its two hundred and fiftieth anniversary, I was studying in Germany, and during the nineties, whether at Williams or Princeton, I had very few opportunities of meeting Harvard teachers. When we came to live in Cambridge in 1900, I knew possibly a dozen professors. In the Department of English, for example, I had happened to meet Barrett Wendell and George P. Baker. I knew that Child was dead, and that A. S. Hill, Wendell, and Briggs had devoted much of their energy to teaching undergraduates to write, but the courses offered by the English Department in Linguistics and Literature were then much less known to the general public than the courses in composition.

By the tests of productivity and of interesting personalities the leading department at Harvard, in 1900, was that of Philosophy. In this unrivalled 'philosophical menagerie,' as Professor Palmer termed it, he was himself the senior exhibit, with William James, Royce, Münsterberg, and Santayana as his associates. All of them except

Santayana wrote for the *Atlantic* and were constantly in evidence in Boston and Cambridge circles. Although Norton had retired from active teaching in 1898, he and Shaler—the geologist and professor of things-in-general — were among the best known of the Harvard group. Both men had welcomed me warmly when I first came to Cambridge. I printed Shaler's *Reminiscences* in the *Atlantic*, and Ruskin's letters to Norton, although I objected strongly and without avail to Norton's deletion of many of Ruskin's affectionate personal greetings to his correspondent. I was always a little in awe of Mr. Norton. I saw him occasionally at the Tavern Club and always at the Saturday Club. In his own library at Shady Hill he was a charming host, and like my friend Robert Grant I found Norton's 'bent for disillusion' singularly fascinating. 'Not only,' writes Judge Grant,[1] 'did I relish hearing false claims or premises stripped of their glamour, but his judgments, even when most gloomy with respect to immediate values, were compact with infinite riches in a little room — riches of finished speech, however withering.'

On two occasions, in his library, after seating me by the fireplace and waiting until the cigars were drawing well, Mr. Norton proceeded to give an elaborate analysis of Theodore Roosevelt. In both instances, his mild opening phrase was this: 'Of course the man is a Barbarian.' But he said it so gently and with such a disarming smile that I was sure — perhaps mistakenly — that 'T. R.' would have enjoyed it as much as I did. To his old friends he was finely loyal. I remember dining at Shady Hill one evening with Mr. Howells and Arthur Sedgwick, just after the publication of Henry James's *The American Scene*.

[1] *Fourscore; an Autobiography,* 1934.

After dinner Howells read aloud some passages from it for our delectation. I hope I was not in a controversial mood, but I did not really like this much-discussed 'third manner' of Henry James. (Neither, for that matter, did Henry's older brother William. 'There *isn't* any third manner,' William once remarked to me. 'Poor Harry has simply changed his stenographer, and the new one records all of his hesitancies and ellipses.') Whenever Howells paused in his reading of striking passages, Mr. Norton, perhaps mischievously, insisted on asking my opinion of the style. I maintained that with all its marvels, it was artificial and affected, and I could not help contrasting it, in my own mind, with the perfection of Mr. Howells's reminiscent writing in such books as *Literary Friends and Acquaintance*. I did not utter this conviction aloud, however. Arthur Sedgwick, I thought, was on my side, but neither our host nor Mr. Howells would allow that those glittering pages had any flaw. Two or three days later I happened to meet Mr. Norton. 'I think I may tell you,' he said, with his wonderful and slightly malicious smile, 'that Mr. Howells agreed with you entirely about *The American Scene*, but he would not admit it.'

Professor Norton's cousin, President Eliot, was likewise a fastidious master of speech, with a mind as inquisitive as Norton's, although less subtle and far more vigorous. As I have said of him elsewhere, [1] 'he was an *amplificator imperii*, an enlarger of the empire of man's estate. His mind was Roman rather than Greek; he cared little for speculative subtleties, he distrusted introspection, and was deaf to some of the rich voices of the past. He read John Locke

[1] At the unveiling of the bust of President Eliot at Eliot House, on the one-hundredth anniversary of his birth, March 20, 1934.

rather than Plato, was more interested in Pasteur than in Virgil, and in commenting on the Bible story of Mary and Martha, he made it clear that he preferred Martha. He was primarily an organizer and administrator, with an imperial grasp of fact.... It is true, of course, that sculpture cannot suggest all of the fascination which was felt in Mr. Eliot's living, speaking presence: in his flawless courtesy of bearing, his habit of deferential listening, his swift, benignant smile, and above all, the tones of his incomparable voice. It was usually low and grave; sometimes hauntingly wistful; but when he was moved by moral indignation it rang — as someone said of Dryden's couplets — like a bronze coin thrown down on marble.'

Mr. Eliot belonged to my father's generation, and from the first year of our settling in Cambridge, his kindness to me could scarcely have been greater if I had been his son. I do not think that he was particularly interested in the purely literary features of the *Atlantic*, but he read all its articles on education, economics, politics, and social reconstruction, and was a frequent contributor. I happened to meet him on the platform of various public meetings in Boston and Cambridge, and sometimes had the ill-luck to precede or follow him as a speaker. I say 'ill-luck,' because all the rest of us must have felt, 'What can the man do that cometh after the King?' And yet, as many other men of my generation have testified, we could not have had a more considerate and encouraging listener. How flattered I felt in 1902, when he suddenly found himself unable to give a promised address at the University of California and asked me to take his place! I did my best with a speech on 'Poetry and Politics,' about which I remember nothing now except the remark of D. O. Mills, the veteran banker and Regent of the University. As soon as the formal exercises were concluded, Mr. Mills poured out for me a very tall glass of whiskey-and-water in President Wheeler's library, and pronounced with finality: 'Mr. Perry, Poetry is a fine thing, but Business is *the* thing.' That was the voice of a whole era.

Yet if there was one spot in the United States which seemed as yet deaf to such a voice, in the opening years of the twentieth century, it was Old Cambridge; steeped as it was in the traditions of Harvard College and typified by the leisurely charm of Brattle Street. The Graduate School of Business Administration, designed to 'establish business as a profession,' was not invented until 1908, and did not attain its present prominence until after the World War. In 1900 the gracious outward aspect of Old Cambridge was in harmony with its inner spirit. Brattle Street, and even the streets 'just off' Brattle, looked as secure as an English cathedral close, and there was among its old American families the sense of continuity, of assured social position, which was a part of that English tradition which lingered in Boston and Cambridge until well into the twentieth century. Brattle Street was like an island in the stream of new and alien races swarming into Greater Boston; an island also in the stream of suburban Americans attracted to Cambridge by rapid transit, by the development of manufacturing interests, and by the growth of Harvard University. Possibly Old Cambridge could count fewer men of world-wide reputation than in 1850, and yet within half a mile of the Craigie House there were probably as many men of personal distinction as could be found anywhere in a similar radius, outside of the great European capitals. Family still counted for something, but money for very little. A typical figure was President Eliot, riding his bicycle every morning on his way to market or for tranquil exercise. I recall that he once appeared on his bicycle at our house at Mercer Circle at 7.15 A.M. to invite me to lunch with an Englishman who had just arrived. Luckily I was shaved and nearly dressed, and came down to find Mr. Eliot examining curiously some vellum-bound seventeenth-century quartos in my study — about the last things in which I should have supposed him to be interested. There were very few telephones in Cambridge then. Today, if a President of Harvard were arranging an extemporized luncheon party, his secretary would be telephoning the professor's secretary — but it would be much later than 7.15 A.M. There were no motor cars as yet, and but few private carriages, though Mr. Howells could no longer have said, as he did once, that there was but one carriage in Old Cambridge and that was owned by a publisher. Social life was simple. Calling had not yet gone out of fashion, and for such occasions, especially on Saturday and Sunday afternoons, gentlemen were accustomed to don their silk hats. Richard H. Dana the Third, a lover of the old ways, was one of the last dwellers on Brattle Street to wear a silk hat really well.[1]

As newcomers to this Old Cambridge, my wife and I were naturally looking at Harvard from the outside. Yet it was obvious that for generations the college had set its stamp upon the community. There were many Harvard professors, for example, in Saint John's Church — really the Chapel of the Episcopal Theological School — where we sat on Sundays under the preaching of Dean George

[1] In this paragraph I have quoted freely from my *R. H. Dana (1851-1931)*, Boston, 1933.

Hodges. He was a singularly able, liberal, and spiritually minded man, like ourselves an immigrant to Cambridge, and, I suspect, never really at home or happy there. Mrs. Perry, who was born in New Haven, educated at Smith, and had been a professor's wife at Williams and Princeton, was tolerably familiar with the innocent provincialism of typical college communities. In our first year or two in Cambridge, we used to collect Harvard stories. One of hers was the remark of a Cambridge lady upon whom my wife happened to be calling, on the day of a Harvard-Yale football game. Casting about for fruitful topics of conversation, they hit upon the fact that two brothers, one representing Harvard and the other Yale, were that day playing against each other. 'Perhaps it isn't so strange as it seems,' hazarded the Cambridge lady; 'you know that it often happens that one of two brothers is brighter than the other.' Her guest, brought up in Yale loyalties, assented politely. I was able to match this with a remark made to me by the Cambridge lady's husband, after a dinner in their house. The men, while taking their coffee, mentioned a then newly published book, *Who's Who in America*. I remarked that I was finding it useful in the *Atlantic* office, inasmuch as it gave biographical information about most of the men who had achieved national prominence. Whereupon our host asked, with entire seriousness, 'Wouldn't the *Harvard Quinquennial Catalogue* answer every purpose?'

There was a strong Harvard flavor, naturally, in those 'paper, discussion, and supper' clubs in which Cambridge abounded. We joined the Query Club and the Junior Shop Club, and are indebted to them for many enduring friendships. The Query Club still held to the old convention of frock coats and high-necked dresses; the Junior Shop Club, made up almost entirely of young Harvard professors and their wives, ventured boldly upon dinner coats and evening gowns. The 'papers,' supposed to be the shop-talk of a specialist, were not too technical, and the suppers were excellent. Occasionally we attended dinners in the Back Bay, which was then none too easy of access from Cambridge. I joined a good many — perhaps, in view of the amount of night work which I was carrying, too many — of those agreeable men's dining-clubs which are a peculiar institution of Boston. Aldrich introduced me to the Jury Club, whose twelve members dined monthly at some Boston hotel. We had a bibulous retired Admiral, I remember, and a couple of flaming Irish journalists from the Papyrus group. I had supposed that all the Fenians were dead!

A personification of ancient Boston and Harvard respectability was the Examiner Club, founded in 1863 by some of the contributors to the famous Unitarian organ, *The Christian Examiner*. Its original aim was 'the discussion of some topic of general interest,' and it met monthly at Young's Hotel. Among the older members were a few survivors of the 'Conscience Whigs' and the 'Cotton Whigs' of the eighteen-fifties; men who still hated or loved Daniel Webster and liked to talk about him. There were old-school reformers like Edward Atkinson and Gamaliel Bradford, Senior, who shared my father's views on the tariff. Our most picturesque figure was Edward Everett Hale, who had written 'The Man Without a Country' for the *Atlantic* in the very year of the founding of the Club. The phrase 'grand old sloven' — once applied to Montaigne by Emerson — might with equal affec-

tion be applied to Dr. Hale, and the carelessness of his
dress was matched by the reckless inaccuracy and vigor of
his talk. Our treasurer, who was responsible for the selection of the food and wine, was a venerable librarian and
epicure named Denny, who might have stepped straight
out of the pages of Charles Lamb. He startled me once by
asking the chemical composition of the ink used in the
Harvard Library, and when I pleaded ignorance, he remarked with deep satisfaction: 'I asked that question
once of Justin Winsor, and *he* could not answer. I always
said he was destitute of the very first qualification for a
librarian.'

A more gentle figure of the past was Mr. Josiah Phillips
Quincy, who as a boy of six had been the marvellous
'little Josiah' of Bronson Alcott's Temple School in 1835.
His questions and answers to his teacher are faithfully recorded in Miss Elizabeth Peabody's *Record of a School* and
Mr. Alcott's *Conversations with Children on the Gospels*.
Emerson, who often visited the Temple School, wrote in
his *Journal* for 1836: 'Little Josiah Quincy, now six years,
six months old, is a child having something wonderful and
divine in him. He is a youthful prophet.' But 'little
Josiah,' when I knew him, had long ceased to talk theology.
He had even written dramatic poems and worldly fiction
for the *Atlantic*. He disliked the cigars selected for us by
Mr. Denny, and always brought a supply of his own,
which he used to offer me with an Old-World hesitancy and
elegance. It was from him that I learned that he happened to be calling upon Emerson on the day when the
1856 edition of *Leaves of Grass* arrived, with its famous 'I
Greet You at the Beginning of a Great Career. R. W.
Emerson' emblazoned in gilt letters upon the cover.[1]

[1] Reproduced in my *Walt Whitman*, edition of 1906, p. 114.

Emerson had written those words to Whitman in a private letter in 1855, and Walt saw no reason why he should not make them public. 'At no other time,' Mr. Quincy wrote me, 'had I seen a cloud of dissatisfaction darken that serene countenance.'

Although I was a member of the Examiner Club until 1910, and met there many vigorous men of my own generation, I find that my memories of their talk are vague. That private dining-room in Young's Hotel seems now a dusky, shadowy place, with but a dim light upon the faces of a few old men, who represented something that has long since disappeared from Boston. But perhaps the dimness is only the haze from those cigars presented to me by Bronson Alcott's favorite pupil, 'little Josiah' Quincy.

The Harvard coloring in some other Boston clubs was even more marked than in the Examiner. The Saturday Club, which I joined in 1903, had at that time thirty-five members, although some of these, like Mr. Howells and Judge Holmes, were no longer residents of Boston. Yet every member of the Harvard Corporation, save one, was enrolled in the Club, besides ten or a dozen Harvard professors. Mr. Norton was then President. It is obvious that it was a temptation to some members to utilize Club dinners for informal discussion of the various business of Harvard College. In fact, James Russell Lowell had been a sinner in this respect as far back as 1866, when he wrote to Norton concerning a recent dinner of the Club: 'With me it was a business meeting. I sat between Hoar and Brimmer [two members of the Corporation] that I might talk over college matters.' I confess that as a newcomer to Boston and Cambridge I was amazed at the annihilating frankness with which Harvard men discussed the personalities and policies of their Alma Mater. The phrase 'Harvard indifferentism' had already been coined, but though it was accurate enough as describing a small and sophisticated group of undergraduates, indifference was surely not a characteristic of the alumni. If they disliked some fact or tendency pertaining to Harvard, they never hesitated in public or private to express their views. Astonished as I was at first by this broad latitude of criticism, I came gradually to see that it was one of the priceless traditions of a freedom-loving university.

Those leisurely monthly dinners of the Saturday Club opened many doors of friendship. Although I met many of the Saturday Club group at other clubs also, there were some men like Edward W. Emerson, Alexander Agassiz, William Lawrence and George A. Gordon whom I rarely saw elsewhere and whose conversation was always rewarding. 'General conversation,' the ideal aim of dining-clubs, is difficult to secure when there are more than ten at the table, but even on crowded days at the Saturday Club and in spite of the 'business of Harvard College' which was bound to intrude at times, there was always the chance of sitting next to some real person like Major Higginson or Dr. Henry P. Walcott or President Eliot, members of the Corporation though they were! I recall the touchingly simple question asked by Mr. Howells on the occasion of his very last visit to the Club. He was then an old man, and disinclined to meet strangers. But discovering that he and President Lowell had never met, I asked Mr. Howells if I might not bring Mr. Lowell over to sit next him. *Is he a friendly person?* ' asked the novelist with some anxiety. I could assure him on this point. The two men, thus shaking hands for the first time, had long been members of both the Saturday Club and the Tavern Club, where 'friendly persons' do not wait to be introduced; but more than thirty years had gone by since Howells had deserted Boston for New York.

The history of the Saturday Club has been written in two stout volumes,[1] and that of the Tavern Club in one,[2] and I should not naturally allude to these clubs in this chapter, were it not that I am attempting to describe the various indirect paths which I happened to follow in gaining an acquaintance with Harvard men and Harvard ways. The ever delightful Tavern Club, which has long had its home in Boylston Place, Boston, with the Bear for its totem, is as unacademic a retreat from sorrow as can be discovered anywhere. Yet Harvard men are in the majority of its varied membership. Its first President, Mr. Howells, was indeed a perpetual example of the saving truth that a college education is not essential to a real education; but his seven successors in the Presidency of the Tavern all had some association with Harvard. When I joined the Club in 1905, the splendid figure of Major Henry Lee Higginson sat in the Tall Chair. In the immortal line of Mark Howe — official historian and unofficial poet of the Tavern — Higginson was

'The Bear's — the Ursa's — Major.'

I was still, in the midsummer of 1905, looking in at the windows of Harvard College from the outside. I knew next to nothing about its graduate schools and the larger problems of Harvard University. But having been

---

[1] *Early Years of the Saturday Club (1855–1870)*. By Edward W. Emerson, 1918. *Later Years of the Saturday Club (1870–1920)*. Edited by M. A. DeW. Howe, 1927.

[2] *Semi-Centennial History of the Tavern Club*. By M. A. DeW. Howe, 1934.

for half-a-dozen years in daily contact with Harvard graduates as human beings, and having found that most of them were 'friendly persons,' I was in a mood to look favorably upon that letter of President Eliot which offered me a professorship. Whatever else might be true of Harvard, I could not believe that an institution headed by Charles W. Eliot was dominated by any considerations of Circulation and Advertising. At No. 4 Park Street one was trained to speak respectfully of Circulation and Advertising, for without the protection of those Twin Deities what would become of the magazine? 'When my master goeth into the house of Rimmon to worship there, *and he leaneth on my hand*, and I bow myself in the house of Rimmon; when I bow down myself in the house of Rimmon, the Lord pardon thy servant in this thing.'

It is a very human prayer, but I did not wish to be repeating it for the rest of my life.

II: LIFTED IN

'I hope it will turn out,' President Eliot wrote me on March 21, 1906, 'that your pecuniary situation will be fully as good as it is now, and that the nature of your work will be more congenial, comfortable, and influential.' With these kindly words he lifted me into the cockpit, on the half-time arrangement.

There were some amusing aspects of this appointment. In the first place, I did not know exactly what I was accepting. The Smith Professorship 'of the French and Spanish Languages and Literatures and Professor of Belles Lettres' was the title of the chair which I had been offered in 1905, with the explanation which I have already quoted: 'It will be for you to select the work you would prefer to do within this great field of literature — English, French, Italian, and Spanish.' I wrote Mr. Eliot at once that though I had a reading knowledge of French and Italian, and a very little Spanish, I did not possess accurate scholarship in any of the Romance languages. In his opinion, however, the previous holders of the Chair had 'made it almost entirely a professorship of belles lettres and English literature, with an excursion by Ticknor into Spanish literature, and by Longfellow and Lowell into Italian literature.... The Smith Professor could not appropriately be a philologist in the technical sense, literature rather than linguistics being the appropriate field of this professorship.' This was an assuredly clear statement, though it may be open to question in its interpretation of the actual courses given long ago. Mr. Eliot was equally clear in his dislike of the term 'Belles Lettres' and in his unwillingness to have it perpetuated at Harvard. I think he associated it somehow with the Scottish Presbyterian Universities of the eighteenth century! What label he would invent for me, and whether the Corporation and Overseers would approve, of course I did not know; but as I had already borne (and survived) such awesome titles as Professor of 'English and Elocution,' of 'Oratory and Aesthetic Criticism,' and of 'English Language and Literature and Belles Lettres,' the question of my future academic label did not worry me. Many months went by without any further word from President Eliot.

Finally the University *Gazette* of March 16, 1906, gave the official notice of my appointment as 'Professor of English Literature,' with an explanatory note which, as I afterward learned, was written by Mr. Eliot himself in the office of the *Gazette*:

'This Professorship of English Literature replaces, and is in succession to, the Professorship of Belles Lettres hitherto attached to the Smith Professorship of the French and Spanish Languages. The incumbents of the combined Professorships have been George Ticknor, from 1817 to 1835, Henry Wadsworth Longfellow, from 1836 to 1854, and James Russell Lowell, from 1855 to 1886.'

Up to this time there had never been a chair of 'English Literature' at Harvard, the term 'English' being considered elastic enough to cover both linguistic and literary courses; and to my embarrassment the newspapers made a good deal of my election as 'the successor of Ticknor, Longfellow, and Lowell.' I did not belong in that galley, of course, and though I did not mind the chaffing of a few friends, I had an uncomfortable feeling that the public was getting the impression that Harvard was landing a bigger fish than it had actually caught. Fortunately the situation was soon clarified by the promotion of a brilliant young scholar, J. D. M. Ford, to the Smith Professorship of the French and Spanish Languages; and W. H. Schofield's appointment to a chair of Comparative Literature indicated a growing recognition of the interrelation of various European literatures.

Although President Eliot wrote me, a week after the *Gazette* appeared, that 'the appointment meets with cordial and universal approval,' I knew well enough that such a miracle was impossible. Without raising the question of my qualifications for a professorship, it was felt by some of my future colleagues that the President had carried through the appointment without due consultation with the Department of English — although as a matter of fact some members of that Department had been

taken into his confidence. Barrett Wendell evidently
had not, and he talked a good deal about the abuse of
Presidential power. A comic situation arose on the very
day when the newspapers announced my election. I was
lunching at the Tavern Club, as usual in those days, and
as I went up to the dining-room several men called out
their congratulations. By some ironic fate the only
vacant chair at the round table was the one next to
Wendell. I did not expect him to welcome me to Harvard, and he was too honest to pretend to do so. He
opened the conversation with some reference to Byron,
and before long was attacking violently his *Vision of
Judgment*, the famous satire written as a parody of
Southey's eulogy of King George Third. Wendell maintained (perhaps with his tongue in his cheek; I was not
sure) that Southey's poem was better than Byron's, on
the ground that Southey was on the side of the established order of society, while Byron's satire was subversive
of it. I do not usually care for a literary debate while
eating lunch, but I could not let anybody exalt Southey's
poetry over Byron's, and I contradicted every assertion
that Wendell made. For half an hour this battle was
waged, and Wendell told someone as he left the Club
that he had not had such an enjoyable conversation for
months. But Harvard was not mentioned.

I have described in earlier chapters my first faculty
meeting at Williams, before I was twenty-one, and the
first faculty meeting at Princeton, a dozen years later.
Compared with those experiences, I must confess that
my first faculty meeting at Harvard, in the spring of 1907,
was disillusionizing. We met at four in the afternoon in
that beautiful Bulfinch room in University Hall which

in my grandfather's time had served as the college chapel. Tea was served in an anteroom, and after President Eliot had called the Faculty of Arts and Sciences to order and the secretary had begun to drone out the minutes of the previous meeting, professors kept strolling in for the next quarter of an hour, tea-cup in hand and still talking. The older men took seats at the long table; the others sprawled in big chairs or upon the side benches. Trained as I had once been in the punctilious decorum and strict parliamentary procedure of the Princeton faculty, the Harvard customs seemed to me shockingly indecorous. Nothing could spoil Eliot's impeccable dignity as a presiding officer, and I marvelled at the patient courtesy with which he listened to motions and remarks made by men who did not even take the trouble to rise in addressing the chair. And I observed that when a man did rise, it was ominous, for the chances were that he was one of the recognized bores who wanted to make a speech!

Of course, being a stranger to University Hall, I missed the historical key of the situation. The truth was that the faculty meeting had sought to preserve the informality of a committee meeting long after it had outgrown the conditions for effective working. When a community has grown into a city, it can no longer be governed by the admirable methods of the primitive town-meeting. I reflected with amusement upon Mr. Eliot's own behavior at faculty meetings when he was a young assistant professor, for he had told me that in that early period he had no interest whatever in faculty discussions and desired to spend the hour upon his own work. Unluckily the table in the faculty room seated at that time only seventeen men, even with some crowding, so that young

Eliot could not find elbow room for writing. With characteristic daring, he asked President Walker if the faculty might not have a larger table. 'Why, Mr. Eliot,' exclaimed the President, 'a new table would cost *money*, and Harvard College *has* no money!'

And now, after more than forty years, there was indeed a little more money and a longer table, but precisely the same indifference to what some members of the faculty might be saying! As Eliot sat there at the head of the table, he looked old and indifferent. No one doubted his ability, even then, to master any assembly if he chose, but he reminded me somehow of Lancelot as umpire of the lists in *The Last Tournament*, when he saw the rules of knighthood broken, but made no sign. By 1907, the real work of the faculty was done off-stage, by small committees, and the talk in the faculty meetings was largely supererogatory. During President Lowell's administration the meetings declined in frequency and significance, and now under President Conant a smaller representative body, the 'Council of the Faculty of Arts and Sciences,' is functioning in their place — the faculty assembling as a whole only four times a year.

My colleague F. N. Robinson and I have had many a laugh over the deplorable scene which made memorable my first attendance upon a meeting of the English Department. The gentle Dean Briggs was presiding, and the business of the afternoon was the approval of the courses proposed for the next half-year. If accepted by the Department, they were then submitted to the Committee on Instruction, who in turn presented them to the Faculty for final adoption. Professor X indicated his desire to offer again a course on 'The English Bible,' which he had already given with marked success. But Professor Y, whose nerves were often out of tune, made sudden and violent objection: declaring that Professor X was ignorant of Hebrew, and that it was a disgrace to the Department and to Harvard that a course in the Bible should be taught by a man who could not read the Old Testament in the original. Professor X naturally resented this attack upon his scholarship, particularly as Y was himself ignorant of the Hebrew tongue. I happened to be sitting between X and Y, and as their voices rose higher and higher, while their gesticulating fingers shot across my face and the sweet-natured Briggs writhed in humiliation for his Department, I saw the Cockpit of Learning at its worst. If 'rare Ben Jonson' had been presiding instead of Briggs, he might have enjoyed the quarrel for a season, but surely he would have ended by taking X and Y, one in either hand, and knocking their hot heads together.

Both X and Y are dead long ago, but that scene taught me something about the jealousies and animosities that may underlie the decorous surface of a department; and I am tempted to set down another instance of the emotional instability of justly famous teachers. Within a few months after I had begun work at Harvard, the French Ambassador, M. Jusserand, was to receive an honorary degree. It is customary in such ceremonials to appoint some professor to escort the candidate — walking with him in the Commencement procession, and taking him to his assigned seat upon the platform. President Eliot asked me if I would escort the Ambassador. I could not decently decline, although I have little love for the pomps of college Commencements, having seen too much of them all my life. Besides, to wait in Cambridge for Commencement Day meant a loss of three days of fishing! Nevertheless I walked with the friendly M. Jusserand, just as I walked in later years with Henry James and with my brother Lewis, when they in turn were candidates for honorary degrees. Not until autumn did I learn that my endeavor to be courteous had had dire consequences. Another professor, it appeared, had considered that the honor of escorting the Ambassador should have been his, and that President Eliot had passed him over with the deliberate intention of insulting him. For two years he refused to speak to Eliot. He wrote me a letter, however, explaining that he knew that I was innocent of having done him an intentional injury, and that the fault lay wholly with the President. I kept that letter as a curiosity, and should not mention it now except to illustrate the pitiful misunderstandings and rivalries which sometimes fester in the professorial heart. Yet when faced by the real troubles of life — as distinct from imaginary maladies — such men often act with silent and magnificent heroism. Ours is a queer profession.

Hitherto I had known little of departmental psychology. At Williams I had had but one colleague in the field of English, and at Princeton only two or three; and in those colleges, after we had once settled upon a fair division of our labors, each man went his own way. But now I began to perceive that the English problem at Harvard was not so simple. One had to reckon with the 'filiopietistic' loyalty to the methods of dead masters: if Child had taught Milton or Bacon in a particular way, that was the way to teach those courses still. One had to reckon also with the prescriptive right to certain authors or fields, claimed by men already giving instruction in them. I remember my surprise when an exceptionally competent young professor wished to offer a new course in one corner of a great field, large enough for half-a-dozen specialists at once. But the cautious Department felt compelled to refuse the request: Professor Z was already lecturing upon that general period, and his feelings would be hurt if any portion of it were assigned to another man.

Obviously, a new member of this Department had to walk delicately. Here was a brilliant array of prima-donnas, each supreme in a chosen rôle: men like Briggs, Wendell, Copeland, Robinson, Baker, and the famous Kittredge, with younger scholars like Neilson and Greenough coming on. But it was difficult for a stranger to discover any common denominator of their activities. What was the underlying philosophy of the Department, its ideal aim, its relation with liberal studies as a whole? I had no intimate friends in the Department, and there was no one to explain its state of mind, if indeed it had one. Fundamental questions were avoided in our meetings; the precious time was consumed in the discussion of wearisome administrative details. The separate parts of the English machine seemed to be in competent hands, but how were the parts related? One was tempted to think, with the old lady who listened to one of Emerson's discourses, that 'it had no connection save in God.' Years afterward, when I had grown accustomed to our irresponsible individualism, I remember that a colleague in English said to me gloomily: 'We *have* no real Department, and never have had.' But we were then six hundred miles from Cambridge, salmon fishing, and he had had no luck that day.

The steel core of the English work at Harvard, then as now, was in the solid linguistic and historical courses covering the period from the earliest Anglo-Saxon writers to the decline of the Elizabethan drama. These courses were essential for candidates for honors in English and for the higher degrees. My own graduate work in Germany had been largely in this field, but I had ceased to teach Anglo-Saxon and Chaucer after going to Princeton, and during the dozen years before coming to Harvard I had fallen quite out of step with the philologists. I had, and still have, deep respect for the science of linguistics, but the very best I could say for myself in 1907 was the remark of the futile Mr. Brooke in *Middlemarch*: 'I went into that a good deal at one time.' An out-of-date philologist is worse than none.

But I could be trusted, Dean Briggs thought, with 'English 7^b,' a large lecture course covering the period between the death of Swift and the publication of the *Lyrical Ballads*, for in the eighteenth century I had long felt at home. Then Schofield, desirous of new courses for his Department of Comparative Literature, proposed that I should offer something on 'Types of Fiction' in the eighteenth and nineteenth centuries, the material to be drawn partly from Continental and partly from English novelists. The idea was to follow the currents of Realism, Sentimentalism, Romanticism, etc., as they swept from one European country to another. We had to study Russian fiction in translations, but a portion of the assigned reading might be done in French, Italian, or German, at the preference of the student.

It was in these two courses, 'English 7^b' and 'Comparative Literature 12,' that I began my half-time work in

February, 1907, after returning from the holiday in Italy. In the next year, 1907–'08, I find that I gave a course in Tennyson, to be given alternately with one on Carlyle; and, for graduate students only, a Comparative Literature course on 'Political Satire since the Renaissance.' In 1908–'09 I was offering a new course on 'Lyric Poetry,' and wondering whether my colleagues in the Department would sanction a course on Emerson. Finally they did, with the remark that in their judgment Emerson was the only American author worthy of having a course devoted exclusively to him. Perhaps they were afraid that I might offer a course on Walt Whitman! As far as I am aware, this was the first Emerson course to be given in any American college; and when my friend Dr. George A. Gordon heard of it, he remarked grimly that he had himself been graduated from Emerson's own college, and had heard the seer mentioned at Harvard precisely three times.

But when the year 1909–'10 opened, and Lawrence Lowell was succeeding Eliot as President of Harvard, I found myself, as has been told already, expounding Emerson, not in Sever 11, but in the pleasant land of France.

III: STAYING IN

Thus it happened that my full-time service at Harvard did not begin until the autumn of 1910. I was turning fifty, and I stayed in that fascinating Cockpit for another twenty years, when I became 'emeritus.' Both of my old friends, Wilson and Hibben, during their terms in the Presidency of Princeton University, tried to persuade me to return thither, and there were various other calls to teaching and administrative positions which did not tempt me in the least. I had changed direction too many times already. I now wanted, above all, to teach; and I thought then, as I do still, that after one has learned his way around, Harvard was a teacher's Paradise.

This is not saying that there were no corners of that paradisiacal garden susceptible of improvement, nor that Presidents gifted with imagination, like Lowell and Conant, may not from time to time announce, like Signor Pococurante in Voltaire's *Candide*: 'I shall have another garden laid out tomorrow upon a nobler plan.' It should be remembered that by 1910 the old 'free elective' system once championed by President Eliot had passed into a kind of twilight of the gods. We were struggling with the new theories of 'concentration and distribution' of studies, with a faculty adviser for each student — although the student was not really obliged to follow the advice. He could still 'shop around' a good deal, as in a huge department store. The achievements of President Lowell in establishing the 'general examination,' the tutorial system and the 'reading period' — to say nothing of the Houses with their libraries and resident Masters and Tutors — were still in the future. For all but a small minority of ambitious undergraduates, incoherence in the choice of courses and the mechanical accumulation of course-credits were still the order of the day.

A full-time professor was then supposed to give two and a half courses of three hours each, although in the large lecture courses the third hour was usually delegated to the assistants for conferences, quizzes, or written tests. Many professors increased this schedule by repeating certain of their courses at Radcliffe, either through pure altruism or with the aim of eking out the still slender professorial salary. President Eliot had explained to me that

THE TEACHER AT HARVARD

a Harvard teacher was under no obligation to offer
courses at Radcliffe, and I never did so. There were
always more Harvard applicants for work in English than
we could handle effectively. We had three general groups
of courses: those restricted to undergraduates; a 'middle
group' where supposedly qualified undergraduates sat
side by side with graduates; and an 'upper group' for
graduates only. Also, we offered 'research courses' —
'English 20' — to individual candidates for the Ph.D.,
intended to guide the student in the investigation of material for his thesis.

My own work fell in all of these groups. 'English 28,'
for instance, was a survey course in literature, for freshmen, given by several different professors, each taking a
certain period. 'English 41,' which I was asked to take
over after Wendell gave it up, was another survey course
open to any undergraduates who had never elected
'English 28.' To tell the truth, I preferred at that time
to be assigned to another course, but was too proud to
ask for it. Yet '41' proved to be the most widely elected
of any of my courses. I hope that it was never considered
a 'snap,' but the numbers rose to six hundred until
finally I admitted only three hundred — which happened
to be the capacity of Sever 11 — and kept a waiting list
of applicants. The success of these large lecture courses
for undergraduates — a reasonable skill on the part of
the lecturer being taken for granted — lies almost wholly
in the selection of proper assignments for reading and in
the devotion of the assistants in conducting the 'third
hour' conferences. I took my turn in these conferences,
naturally, for a lecture system without them, however
successful in France or Germany, does not work for
American boys.

The middle group courses faced a peculiar difficulty. The teacher had to present his material in such a way as to meet the needs of two different types of men: properly qualified undergraduates who were candidates for the A.B., and graduates who were bent upon securing an A.M. or Ph.D. degree. The professor had to be the judge of the qualifications of undergraduates, and a boy's rank in other subjects was not always an indication of his ability to grasp Emerson or Carlyle or Lyric Poetry. Unless one happened to know the graduate student personally, it was equally difficult to assess his qualifications in advance. Usually about one quarter of a middle group course, comprising altogether perhaps one hundred or one hundred and fifty men, would be graduates of other institutions; for there were relatively few graduate students from Harvard. Those institutions represented every variety of training and of no training. My own courses open to graduates were what were then known in the Department as 'luxury' courses — which meant, not that they were special delicacies, but that they did not belong in the list of those solid linguistic courses essential for the Ph.D. The theory was that if a graduate student spent most of his time, let us say, on Gothic, Anglo-Saxon, and Middle English, a course in Carlyle or Tennyson or Emerson would give him some measure of variety for his programme and do him no harm, though it was not likely to help him directly in his oral examination for the Ph.D., which rarely touched, in those days, upon nineteenth-century literature.

We were still in bondage to the mechanical 'course-system' of credits, which is disappearing today. But during my term of service, an A.M. could be secured by four 'B's' in any approved list of courses; and a 'B' under Robinson or Kittredge needed more steady daily work than the average graduate student would give to a course on Lyric Poetry or Types of Fiction where the majority of the class were undergraduates. I always read the graduate blue-books and other papers myself, instead of leaving them to the assistants, and devised various methods of putting extra work on the advanced men, but in the lectures I had to keep in mind the capacities of the undergraduate majority.

My purely graduate courses, such as Political Satire and the English Critical Essay, were easier to manage. Sometimes I limited them to a Seminar of a dozen men, for the discussion of texts, with but little lecturing; in other years there might be forty or fifty students, with lectures for their general guidance, but with the stress laid upon the thesis prepared by each man. In the 'English 20' courses to direct the research of Ph.D. candidates, I met each man by himself in my study in the Widener Library, usually once in two or three weeks. These conferences often took many hours, but it was, I trust, real teaching, whereas in lecturing one cannot always know whether he is teaching or not. I happen to be one of the men who enjoy the excitement of lecturing in big courses. Although I worry about the lecture beforehand and afterward, I find that the mental and physical stimulus of holding the close attention of a large audience is a thrilling experience. If one puts the very best he has into it, he is limp when the lecture is over, and needs an hour's rest — though he cannot always get it — before proceeding to another classroom. But I think I have often worked as hard with the mind of a single graduate student in my study as I ever did with the six hundred men in 'English 41.'

The case of these graduate students was often pitiable. Most of them were poor in purse — though perhaps a true scholar ought to be poor. Cambridge is an expensive city, and the University has thus far been unable to provide adequate quarters for graduate students in the Arts, or anything like the opportunities for social intercourse now offered to undergraduates who can afford to live in the Houses. Many of the graduates of the smaller Southern and Western colleges had married early, and had been saving a few hundred dollars in the hope of securing an A.M. or Ph.D. from Harvard, and thereby bettering their chances of professional promotion. They appeared in Cambridge without knowing the precise requirements for securing these degrees, since the printed statements were somewhat ambiguous to a stranger. Their programmes for study were perforce hastily approved by the authorities, for hundreds of cases had to be passed upon within a couple of days. Misfits evident at once could be corrected, and the authorities were kindly, but often months went by before the new graduate student recognized his predicament. Sometimes it appeared that his college training had been grossly deficient, though his marks had been high enough. He was supposed, for instance, to be able to use French and German as tools in his graduate work, but no one had really examined him in those subjects, and often he could not use them at all. The pace set in his linguistic courses was a stiff one, and soon he felt a stitch in his side. Then he jumped to the conclusion that his real obstacle in this race was 'philology,' and he began to worry and then to curse and then to seek out some professor who would listen to his troubles.

Perhaps I did not have more than my fair share of these interviews, but I had a great many. I was not identified with any of the philological courses, and the graduate students who had what they thought was a literary turn of mind sought me out for advice. They had no idea that I had ever gone through a rigid philological discipline myself, and I think that G. L. K. would have been amused to hear me defend the emphasis which the Department and Division were laying upon that side of the necessary training of a teacher. To the sentimentalists who believed, in Stuart Sherman's phrase, that attention to linguistics was 'killing the poet in them,' I pointed out that if a poet could be killed by a year or two of hard work on the early stages of Germanic or Romance languages, the quicker he died the better. To the modernists who wished to confine their work to the eighteenth and nineteenth centuries I replied that the main thing was to learn to paddle one's own scholarly canoe, and that if some of the most skilful canoe-men at Harvard chose to exercise and teach their craft upon the rough upper reaches of the river instead of upon the broader and smoother currents lower down, it was the duty and privilege of a pupil to learn from the master on those waters where the master loved to teach. After the pupil had once learned what the linguistic specialists had to impart, he would be free to paddle his own canoe on any waters he preferred!

Thus did a very rusty and at best inept philologist, who was himself giving 'modern' courses, preach patience and docility and loyalty to the Powers that Were. But at heart I felt that the requirements for the Ph.D. in our

Division were — not too severe, for they should be severe — but too inelastic and unchangeable, recognizing too little the value of equally important disciplines in parallel fields. I remember that we once refused to give a candidate any credit for a year spent in the graduate study of Catullus at the University of Munich. He wished to substitute this for the Harvard course in Gothic, and I thought that for a teacher of literature there was more virtue in Catullus than in the language of the excellent Bishop Ulfilas. Very recently, it is true, the programme for the Ph.D. in our Division has been modified. With no loss in severity, it allows for more flexibility of choice in the fields to be covered.

One characteristic of this 'lost gregarious horde' of graduate students never ceased to surprise me. I was aware that ours is not yet a book-loving country, and that only a very small proportion of the college-bred are real readers. But I could not understand why the men who were proposing to devote their lives to the teaching of literature brought with them to Harvard such ignorance of European books and of the general history of thought. We have long ceased to expect any familiarity with Greek, save from a very few, and it was seldom that the graduates knew more Latin than their half-forgotten Cicero and Virgil. Fortunately some of them were obliged to pick up some mediaeval Latin in the progress of their work. But the great majority of them knew nothing, at first hand, of such European figures as Petrarch, Erasmus, Rabelais, Diderot. They did not even know their Goethe and Voltaire, their Franklin and Jefferson. If they had ever sat up half the night reading Rousseau and Wordsworth for the sheer pleasure of it, they would have had some counterweight for Irving Babbitt's diatribes against the dangerous Romanticism of these authors; but they came to his brilliant lectures without any preparatory personal experience with the authors whom he attacked. As for the history of thought in Europe, their minds were usually blank. It is curious that in taking over from Germany the conception and methods of the doctorate of philosophy, American universities paid so little attention to Philosophy itself. The 'fact' men triumphed. Exact information, in a limited field, was demanded of Ph.D. candidates, and no one will quarrel with a demand for exact information. But in more than a score of years of attendance upon examinations for the degree of Doctor of Philosophy, I recall scarcely a question dealing with the contributions to thought which were made by Plato or Aristotle, Descartes or Spinoza, John Locke or Kant.

Another thing that puzzled me at Harvard was the persistent faith, among undergraduates and many teachers, in the value of courses in Composition. This tradition went back to the days when John Quincy Adams held the Boylston Professorship of Rhetoric and Oratory, a chair subsequently filled by 'Ned' Channing, Child, and A. S. Hill. Surely these men, followed by such expert teachers of composition as Briggs, Wendell, Copeland, and the rest, could not have labored in vain! Although it was known that Child and Wendell, toward the end, had grown sceptical of the value of 'themes,' there was a comfortable creed that the graduates of Harvard wrote better than the graduates of other colleges. I kept to myself the dreadful secret that in ten years of reading manuscript for the *Atlantic* I had never observed that

Harvard men wrote any better than Yale men or Bowdoin men or men like Howells and Aldrich and John Burroughs who had never gone to college at all! It seemed to me that writing was a highly personal craft, to be perfected only after long practice, and that it made little difference where or how the practitioner learned the rudiments of his trade. Many years afterward, I admired Professor Grandgent's courage in declaring his fear that Harvard students 'write rather poorly, and speak worse.' [1] Having been myself in youth an enthusiastic teacher of English composition, and in middle age infected somewhat with Wendell's scepticism as to its unique worth as a college study, I may be allowed to unburden myself of some truisms:

(1) The mechanics of English composition can be taught. They are taught well in hundreds of schools, and may if necessary be imparted to such college students as have failed to receive proper instruction. Beyond this field of mechanical correctness lies the domain of literary art, and art in writing is mainly a matter of self-discipline, although the practitioner may be helped by expert criticism. (2) We expect too much, however, from the teachers of English in American colleges. They have had to shoulder a great part of that burden of accurate training in the mother tongue which was formerly carried by means of daily drill in translating Greek and Latin. Year after year in the Harvard Graduate School, I used to notice that the best writers were the Canadians who had kept up their classics. No boy well trained in Latin or Greek composition ever found difficulty in expressing himself clearly in English. It was hoped that drill in

[1] S. E. Morison, *Development of Harvard University, 1869–1929*, p. 104.

the modern languages would ultimately supply the discipline once given by the classics, but thus far the results are disappointing. (3) Undergraduates with literary ambitions should have the opportunity for writing verse, prose, drama, fiction — any literary form they prefer — under competent instruction. This individual instruction is, however, very costly, both in time and money, and it should be limited to students of special promise. Even from these youths one should not expect immediate triumphs. One cannot make bricks without straw or a work of art without materials, and very few undergraduates have read enough, experienced enough, pondered enough, to have even the raw material for a literary masterpiece.

Let us come back to what one of my brothers called 'the overarching Harvard': a true Cockpit and Paradise of Learning, where petty flaws and neglected corners may be pardoned and forgotten. Its fascination for me, as a teacher, lay in its freedom. I do not mean merely that 'academic freedom' of thought and utterance which was defended so courageously by Presidents Eliot and Lowell. I had no subversive economic or social views to express, either in the classroom or in public. Whenever my good father made a vigorous speech against protective tariffs there were certain newspapers and public men who demanded that he should be deprived of his professorship; but times had changed, and no one cared much what a professor of English literature might be saying to relieve his mind. I disliked publicity, and avoided topics that might furnish 'copy' for the newspapers. My classroom was 'dukedom large enough,' and I think few men were ever happier there. That very lack of co-operative team-work which my gloomy colleague criticized when he declared 'We *have* no Department' left us free, as individuals, to teach in our own fashion and to try, within reason, any experiments we pleased.

I was supposed, for instance, to be lecturing to graduates on Political Satire since the Renaissance, but inasmuch as it was necessary to show them first what political satire was, I could take material, if I liked, from the Old Testament and from Aristophanes. Since the classic English school of satire was founded upon Roman models, I joined forces with Morris Morgan of the Latin Department and took my students in to hear him lecture upon Juvenal and Horace, and he brought his men into my room to hear about Dryden and Pope. I wish now that we had carried this collaboration in Comparative Literature courses much further than we did, particularly in studying international influences upon the development of types of fiction. But the point is that professors were free to seek out many inventions. I experimented for a while with 'pass' and 'honors' grades, determined by examinations of different degrees of difficulty, although based upon the same required reading; and as long as the grades were handed in promptly at University Hall, there was no one to say how they were determined. Instead of a regular lecture in the Emerson course I escorted the class, year after year, to Concord, to visit the Old Manse and the Emerson House and Sleepy Hollow, and I know that many boys learned more in those sunny afternoons than I could ever have taught them in Sever 11.

I was too preoccupied with my own classes to know much about what was going on in the University. Fortunately I had little committee work, and was quite out of touch with the complicated machinery of administration which was housed in University Hall. I fear I was jealous of University Hall, for it had developed the habit of robbing the English Department of some of our best men — Briggs, Hurlbut, Greenough, Murdock, and, for one year, Lowes — in order to utilize them as Deans. It is, I am told, an honor to become a Dean, but it is one dearly purchased if it means the temporary or permanent end of a scholar's productivity. The whole tendency of American institutions is to breed ten administrators to one real teacher. I used to pass University Hall with something of the small boy's dread of passing a cemetery: for teachers lay buried there under their roll-topped desks. Only once did I get a cheerful picture of it, and that was during a holiday in Florence in 1928. George W. Cram, the Recorder of the University, was likewise in Florence, and one day we tramped out to a hill-town beyond the Certosa to see the frescoes in the ancient church and incidentally to try a cup of the mulled wine for which the local restaurant was famous. In that one excursion I heard more amusing gossip about the machinery of University Hall than I had picked up in twenty years at Cambridge.

Likewise I was too ignorant of the personal history of the men whom I was trying to teach. One could place the graduate students roughly, for one knew the colleges from which they came and something about their records and their plans. But I never knew even the names of the majority of students in the big undergraduate courses, nor their preparatory schools nor their Harvard groupings and social affiliations. I had to leave all that to my assistants who read the blue-books and conferred personally with the men. I trust that my natural sympathies, like my father's, were with the poor, the aliens in race, the 'untouchables'; but I did my best to treat each student precisely as I treated every other. I admit that when a boy came up to the desk one April, just as I was about to begin what I thought was an important lecture, and asked me confidentially what sort of trout-reel I considered the most reliable, I caught the lad's spring-fever, and had no difficulty in remembering his name.

The response of these undergraduates to a teacher's efforts seemed to me wonderful. Many of them, naturally, had no particular interest in literary questions, and had elected one of my courses because the rules for 'distribution' obliged them to choose one course in Literature. But once inside the classroom, they met me halfway. The real work of the course had to be done by the student himself, in mastering the handbooks containing the facts essential to a knowledge of a given period, and in interpreting and reflecting upon the assigned masterpieces. The lectures were designed to assist in an intelligent approach to the writers chosen for study, and not as a substitute for what each boy was expected to discover for himself. It was the business of the assistants to find out through conferences and written tests exactly what each student was accomplishing; and it was the professor's business to superintend all that, and to make each lecture hour interesting and profitable to the whole class — an impossible but fascinating enterprise.

I imagine that very few of the students realized — if

they happened to see the professor strolling down to the
Yard for a 'nine-o'clock,' carrying a green bag full of
books and lecture-notes, and smoking an after-breakfast
pipe — how many hours he had given to the preparation
of his lecture and how inordinately anxious he was that
it might go well.

First, as to preparation. I will illustrate from 'English
41,' one of those survey courses which are supposed to
be easy enough for an experienced teacher. We began
with some reading from *Beowulf*, in translation, some
English and Scottish ballads, and a little Chaucer; then
some pre-Shakespearean drama, half-a-dozen of Shakespeare's plays, Spenser, a little Jacobean drama, then
Bacon and Milton and so on down the centuries until
we reached authors that were still living, like Kipling.
It is obvious that upon each topic selected as the subject
for a lecture in such a course, new biographical and critical material is constantly appearing. This new material
may be too technical to mention in the classroom, but
the teacher is bound by the honor of his profession to
keep informed of it if he can. He distinguishes sharply,
however, between 'keeping abreast' of the new knowledge,
and 'research,' which means adding to it oneself. Here,
for instance, are some letters, just discovered, by Swift
or Gray or Horace Walpole: a conscientious teacher feels
that he should examine these letters before lecturing
again upon the writers. That is merely 'keeping abreast,'
although the mass of new material has now become so
great that no one scholar can possibly be in touch with
all of it. John Lowes's *Road to Xanadu*, on the other
hand, is based upon true 'research' into Coleridge's
reading and into the workings of a poet's mind. Even keep-

ing abreast, a much more humble effort, is no holiday affair.

I choose for illustration four English authors on whom I happened to be lecturing at Williams in the eighteen-eighties, at Princeton in the eighteen-nineties, and at Harvard in the nineteen-twenties: Fielding, Byron, Thackeray, and Browning. It is clear that the lecturer, at the outset, should have read the entire work of each author. Then comes the task of thinking, for, as W. C. Brownell used to say: 'To produce vital and useful criticism it is necessary to think, think, think and then, when tired of thinking, to think more.' The third stage is the selection and arrangement of such significant facts, conclusions, queries, as can be presented to a class in fifty minutes. All this is preparatory to the actual delivery of the lecture. But we will suppose, as in the case of the four authors just named, that the teacher continues to lecture upon these men, at intervals, for forty years. If he has had any vigorous intellectual life of his own, his opinion of the four authors is bound to change somewhat with each yearly reading. This or that aspect of their personality or their art gains or loses in significance; no one can read Byron at sixty-five with the eyes of twenty-five. The teacher has changed, and the mood of his classes changes with the years or with the shift in literary fashions. In the eighteen-eighties one could allude to a passage in George Eliot or in Tennyson and be fairly certain that the allusion would be understood; in the nineteen-twenties one was equally certain that the allusion would not be understood. It was safer to quote Hemingway or D. H. Lawrence. It is true that the teacher may find his old notes on Byron useful in certain respects, but chiefly as a record of the development of the teacher's

critical sense or of his classroom methods. I am by no
means sure that I taught Byron any more effectively at
sixty-five than at twenty-five, but I could not help teaching him differently.

Once, when I was going up to my library in the evening
for two or three hours of final preparation for the next
morning's lecture, one of my daughters protested. 'What
are you going to talk about tomorrow?' she asked. 'Sir
Walter Scott,' I answered. 'I suppose,' she remarked with
fine sarcasm, 'that you never heard of Scott before?' But
my familiarity with the subject of the lecture was the
very reason why I had to sharpen my senses afresh by re-
reading his pages and by re-thinking my old conclusions
before I could venture to re-shape another talk on the old
and glorious theme.

Very likely I re-shaped too anxiously, in the dread of
repeating myself. Dr. George Gordon told me that he
never 'preached a sermon but once' and that was during
the actual half-hour of delivery. When he had prepared
what he had to say, he dismissed it from his mind until
he reached the pulpit, and as soon as he had finished his
discourse he could dismiss it from his mind again. I
wish I could say that! I worry over a lecture for days and
weeks beforehand, enjoy the actual hour of teaching
enormously, and then suffer acute misery in reflecting
how I might have bettered the instruction. Old John
Sullivan, a guide on Lake Nicotaus, once paid me a great
although undeserved compliment. The trout were coming
in fast that morning, and John, regarding the process
with shining eyes, exclaimed: 'I do like to watch a fellow
fish who doesn't get *excited!*' But in reality I was deeply
excited — too deeply to let John suspect it; and I have
sometimes wondered whether my pupils realized the

intensity of feeling which underlay a decorous classroom manner of dealing with certain books and men. Perhaps I gave myself away when I read poetry aloud.

How many of us conductors of courses there were, under the great hospitable roof of 'the overarching' Harvard, each one of us convinced, naturally, of the transcendent importance of his own theme! We could never have gone on without that faith, and when a man loses it, it is time for him to stop teaching. Even though he does not and cannot lose his zest for his subject, the years take their toll of his physical energy, and he comes to realize that he should give place to younger men. 'I retire,' said Mark Hopkins when he gave up the Presidency of Williams at seventy, 'that it may not be asked why I do not retire.' One need not have been a pupil and colleague of Mark Hopkins to recognize the old gentleman's wisdom. He knew his world.

When Samuel Johnson wrote his final *Idler* paper in 1760, he remarked: 'There are few things not purely evil, of which we can say, without some emotion of uneasiness, *this is the last.*' I cannot affirm that I faced my final lecture at Harvard in May, 1930, 'without some emotion of uneasiness,' but the kindness of my pupils carried me through the ordeal. They gave me some rare editions of books that I was known to like, and arranged to have a portrait painted for the University. I thanked them as well as I could. But I did not really need any fresh evidence of their regard, for I was sure of it already, and I cannot remember whether I told them in words that I was fond of them. They knew it, anyway.

Then I drove out to Milton with my son, and celebrated the new freedom with a round of golf. It was forty-nine years since I met my first class at Williams.

XI

EMERITUS

Indeed we are a crazy company, yet we live in His sight, and shall work the time appointed to us, and shall rest after that in peace.
OLIVER CROMWELL, *Letters and Speeches*

A man's life is his whole life, not the last glimmering snuff of the candle.
HAZLITT, *On the Past and Future*

They might look upon transience all day long, yet be in company of the gods.
A.E., *The House of the Titans*

JUST below the Burnt Hill Rapids on the Southwest Miramichi, the river quiets and broadens into a great pool which we call 'the Pond.' If one has taken his canoe at the Bridge, twenty miles upstream, he has found plenty of rough water before he reaches the head of the Burnt Hill Rapids, and these, the most dangerous on the river, call for a coolness and skill beyond the reach of the amateur. As the guide takes the last plunging slope at the foot of the rapids, he swings sharply to the left; and all at once there is silence and smooth water and an easy landing-place, for this is the Pond. It is growing late, too. Perhaps we lingered too long at Slate Island, where we thought the salmon might be rising. But there will be plenty of time before dark for all there is to do. We have only to drag the canoe up the beach, cut a little wood for the fire, carry the blankets into the old camp, eat supper, light another pipe, and look across the river to see if that doe is still coming down in the twilight to browse and drink. We watch the nighthawks while the dusk comes on, we grow drowsy and silent and a bit weary, perhaps, after the long day on the river, and then we turn in, to dream of the shining and sullen and treacherous Miramichi. Sometime, of course, we must go on down the river, but not yet, not yet.

'Which things,' as Saint Paul remarks, 'are an Allegory.' An emeritus professor has reached the Pond. A long stage of his journey is over. He can rest and dream and think — and no one cares what he thinks, either. He has become a 'Superannuated Man.' Did not Charles Lamb testify, 'It was like passing out of Time into Eternity — for it is a sort of Eternity for a man to have his Time all to himself'? I have no doubt that the nine o'clock bell still rings every morning in the Harvard Yard, but I never hear it, even when the wind is in the east. It is not deafness, but the Higher Indifference. I can even listen with tolerable complacency to the medical specialist who points out that there are 'circulatory changes' after one passes seventy: one should not run upstairs, like Lawrence Lowell; one ought not to shovel snow; one should remember that tobacco is not a Fountain of Perpetual Youth, although G. L. K. has apparently proved it. I really like these specialists, particularly when I compare their solemn admonitions with their own habits of eating and drinking and smoking and overworking as much as they please. Of course their advice is sound; most of it, except the cardiographs, is to be found in Cicero's *De Senectute*. No doubt I shall discover some day that the steep eighth hole on the Greensboro links speaks of Old Age more eloquently than Cicero, and even now, when my tall son gives me a hand instinctively as I climb in hip-boots up a slippery bank from

the Lamoille, I know what it means. At seventy-five it is
time to take in sail — just a little.

And perhaps it is time, now that one has reached the
Pond and is not hurried any more, to think over the
nearly completed voyage, to take account of its chances
and mischances, to wonder whether this course or that
might have been better. Yet this depends upon one's
temperament. Some retired professors hate to look back;
like President Eliot, they are not interested in the past
but in the future. I have known one who spent his new
leisure in designing a boat, though he knew he could not
hope to sail her long. Some content themselves with
pitching horseshoes in Florida, or driving to California
to see just how much mileage is left in the old car. Dean
Briggs and I have been known to sneak over to Braves
Field together, to watch a new third-baseman. Some
raise chickens, though the wiser prefer tulips. But more
often they continue to potter about in their accustomed
libraries and laboratories, like old sea-captains hanging
around the wharves; they endeavor, usually in vain, to
bring that unfinished *magnum opus* to completion. Some
of them like to write letters to the newspapers about
politics and philanthropies. Some, like Emerson's old
Greek professor, Popkin, resolve that they will now 'read
the authors'; and many of these veteran readers, like my
father, report that they never knew the true enjoyment
to be had from books until they began to read with no
specific purpose. Others maintain their curiosity about
the world: my Grandfather Deacon Smedley averred
that he disliked to die, because he could then no longer
read the *Missionary Herald* every month and find out
precisely what each missionary station was doing. 'The

full Eternal mundane spectacle' continues to unroll before such men and to fascinate them as spectators long after they have ceased to act. And among my emeritus friends who do nothing whatever, there is one who maintains that when all other bodily and mental resources fail — except eyesight — there is one pleasure which is heightened and enriched from year to year: the pleasure of watching a landscape.

Yet for the men who yield to the temptation to review the past, this impulse to assess and analyse, to take account of stock — like Robinson Crusoe with his wrecked ship — is very strong. As I study the log of my own journey, here in this latest camping-place above the Pond, it is clear that I might have kept a straighter course if it were not for the perpetual struggle between Vocation and Avocation. The course was laid, after some preliminary fancies for other callings, for Teaching, but it is only too evident that I have spent much time — in one instance, the greater part of ten years — in doing something else. I like to believe that a teacher's best work is a summary and application of all of his experience to the immediate teaching task, and that few professions afford such opportunity for utilizing apparently unrelated material. An ancient proverb asserts, 'There is that scattereth and yet increaseth' (like Dean Briggs), but I dare not apply that comfortable doctrine to myself. The Avocations, I fear, have interfered with the Vocation.

One cause is not far to seek. I have had to pay my own way since I was twenty, and a teacher's salary at that time was very small. If one wished to study in Europe, to marry and build a house, to educate the children, to

meet doctors' bills and life insurance, with something over
for church and charities, to say nothing of books, music,
travel, and other needful recreations and a reserve laid
aside for the inevitable rainy day, a teacher without
private means was obliged to earn something in addition
to his salary. The easiest and indeed the only way for me
to earn anything was by writing and lecturing. Neither
of these avocations, it is true, was wholly unrelated to my
professional work, and, indeed, considered with a charitable
eye, they might be called an outgrowth of it.

There, for instance, was the shy but secretly ambitious
young fellow in Williamstown, earning his living by
trying to teach college boys to speak and write. He had a
passion for Browning. When groups of Browning lovers
in neighboring cities and colleges invited him to talk to
them about the poet and to read some lyrics and dramatic
monologues, it was a twofold discovery: he found that he
could hold a miscellaneous audience and also earn a fee.
The fees were diminutive, but as with the first cases of a
doctor or lawyer, the professional recognition counted
for more than the money, and yet the money meant
additional independence at a time when every penny was
important. It was exciting, when at Princeton, to join
my friends Wilson, Mabie, Arthur Hadley, and Brander
Matthews in giving University Extension lectures in
Philadelphia. We all had faith in that attempt to bring
academic subjects before a general audience. My topics,
for a while, were likely to be taken from the field of fiction:
it might be those newly discovered British authors,
Kipling and Stevenson, who are now, as I am told by
undergraduates, quite out of fashion.

I was really uplifted, as was William James, by the

experience of lecturing in that strange summer university for the people, the original Chautauqua, in the wilds of Western New York. Those audiences had an intellectual hunger for the very best that one could give them. The same may be said for the summer sessions of the University of Chicago, where President Harper once urged me to spend a week. Even after coming to Harvard my outside lecturing continued, for President Eliot's friendly hope in 1906 that 'your pecuniary situation will be fully as good as it is now' proved to be an iridescent fancy. The plain fact was that though we lived as economically as possible, we could not send our children to good schools and to college and meet the other necessary expenses of life in Cambridge without some addition to the college salary. That modest source of income was at least secure, and there would be a pension at the end if one lived long enough; but in the meantime I kept on giving public lectures when the dates did not interfere with college engagements. At the peak of this activity, during the four years preceding the World War, I find that I delivered nearly fifty lectures a year. More than sixty were given, first and last, in the Brooklyn Institute alone. After the War, when our children were no longer in college and the Harvard salaries were materially increased, I was able to abandon 'the platform,' though I do not know how many Phi Beta Kappa orations and Commencement addresses I was still persuaded to deliver.

Looking back at it, I find that this experience, based though it was upon financial necessity, had something to be said for it. I spoke increasingly, as the years went on, upon American writers and public men like Jefferson, Hamilton, Webster, Emerson, Whitman, and Lincoln.

The response of the audiences, whether in Virginia, Carolina, Texas, California, the Middle West, or in New England, confirmed my faith in the underlying idealism of the American people. There have been times during the sleek materialism of the post-war epoch when many persons have doubted the existence of this idealism. I do not: I have watched the faces of too many thousands of my fellow citizens. It was a good education for the speaker, if for no one else. Physically, it was a continual excitement and an unceasing strain. There is a sense of power in facing a strange audience and in knowing that you can 'make 'em laugh, make 'em cry, make 'em wait,' as Wilkie Collins once said that a novelist must do. But to do it well one must keep in perfect bodily condition, must be able to sleep well on trains, and 'To confront night, storms, hunger, ridicule, accidents, rebuffs, as the trees and animals do.'

I was glad enough, at sixty, to give it up. To tell the truth, I was always a little afraid that that horse might run away with me. For there are more subtle temptations in this calling than the mere temptation to go beyond one's physical strength. Carlyle's phrase about the mixture of prophecy and play-acting, in the public lecture, is fiercely true. In speaking without manuscript before large audiences, there is always the danger of forcing the note, of exaggerating, of extemporizing convictions upon the spur of the moment, and sometimes, alas, of 'speaking in yesterday's faith, hoping it will come back tomorrow.' A teacher can maintain his intellectual integrity in the classroom more easily than in Faneuil Hall. Even his colleagues begin to suspect him as soon as he turns into a 'spell-binder.' They are sure that if he talks well to a

Woman's Club about the latest novel or the latest play there is something wrong with him: he will be giving 'radio hours' next, or writing for the Hearst newspapers. In short, he has become, in their judgment, a 'popularizer' instead of spending his time on 'research'; and it is true that there are few teachers nowadays like Louis Agassiz, whose gift for research was doubted by no one, but who was never happier than when he was standing in front of a blackboard in a crossroads schoolhouse before an audience of farmers, armed with a clam-shell and a piece of chalk.

If lecturing to popular or academic audiences, up and down the country, absorbed many of the days that might have been given to pure scholarship, the same must be said of that other avocation of writing books. It is true that a college professor is supposed to be 'producing' something, and that in my own case, both at Princeton and Harvard, the university authorities generously proposed that my schedule of hours should be somewhat lightened in order that I might have more time for writing. But in the tolerably long row of books which bear my name upon their fading covers there is only here and there any evidence of original research into recondite sources. I hope I have added a little to the world's knowledge of Whitman and of Emerson and of some other lesser men; at any rate, I have examined many thousands of manuscript pages which few other eyes have seen. If my contributions to scholarship are fewer than might be wished, it is too late now to regret it. My first ambitions as a writer were in the field of fiction, and when I turned later to biography and criticism and literary history, I was choosing subjects

that were more interesting to me than to the general
public.

The question of money, fortunately, has affected me
very little, as regards the number or the character of my
books. When stories or essays ran in my youthful head,
I wrote them, and when I discovered that they would pay
for coal bills and life insurance I was delighted; but I
should have written them in any case. Some editing of
textbooks for schools and colleges might not have been
undertaken as a purely missionary enterprise, but I
never approached one of these tasks without feeling that
it was worth doing, irrespective of the possible royalties.
'No one but a blockhead ever wrote except for money,'
declared Samuel Johnson, but that was not one of his
best shots. Each of my books has brought me a little
money, but my best satisfaction, as I review fifty years
of miscellaneous authorship, is found in those bits of
writing where money played no part. The centenary
addresses at Bowdoin on Hawthorne, on Longfellow and
Lowell and Dana at Cambridge, on Parkman in Montreal,
and on Goethe in Cambridge, were written simply to obey
the injunction 'Let us now praise famous men.' When
Bruce Rogers devoted his consummate art to the designing of limited editions of Emerson's *Compensation*
and Hawthorne's *The Old Manse*, I was proud to be asked
to write the prefaces, as I did later for Conrad's *Victory*,
Galsworthy's *Patrician*, Carlyle's *Sartor Resartus*, Wal-
ton's *Compleat Angler*, and Edwin Arlington Robinson's
Selected Poems.

I have taken great pains with many brief memoirs
intended for a very limited circle of readers. One
may spend weeks in composing a memoir of some fel-

low member of the Massachusetts Historical Society,
knowing that it will never be read by more than a few
dozen men; but knowing also that for the next hundred
years some scholar will be bound to turn to that memoir
for authentic information. I have written for the Academy
of Arts and Letters tributes to old friends like T. W.
Higginson, John Burroughs, Woodrow Wilson, and W.
C. Brownell, and to other writers like Henry James,
Marion Crawford, and William Vaughn Moody. When
the aged Dr. Edward W. Emerson grew weary and confused
with his task of writing personal sketches for the *Early
Years of the Saturday Club*, I wrote for him the character-
izations of eight of the early members of the Club: Dwight,
Lowell, Motley, Whipple, Prescott, Whittier, Hedge, and
Estes Howe. It meant months of labor and only a hand-
ful of readers; but someone must be drafted for this Old
Mortality rôle if any memory of the past and respect for
sound literary achievement is to survive.

I have already mentioned the books which I wrote
before coming to Harvard, and must comment briefly
upon some of the later ones. *The American Mind* (1912)
was utilized first as the Earl Lectures in Berkeley, California, and repeated in the Lowell Institute in Boston as
well as in the Brooklyn Institute. It was a preliminary
study for the projected *magnum opus*. In 1915 I published
Carlyle in the 'How to Know the Authors' series, an
enterprise which some of us expected to be a real contribution to popular education for adults. But the World
War was now providing other types of education. I
spent the first five months of 1917 in the Library of
Congress, writing *The American Spirit in Literature* for
the 'Chronicles of America' series issued by Yale Univer-

sity. This book would clarify my mind, I hoped, upon some of the topics to be treated in the *magnum opus* — that *History of American Literature* in two stout volumes which I was now under formal contract to finish by 1920. I still think that *The American Spirit in Literature* was a good little book, but for many years the only two men in Cambridge who were known to read it were H. J. Laski — the English writer then teaching at Harvard — and a Russian Jew who kept a delicatessen shop and borrowed the book from my wife. Laski liked it. The Russian Jew confessed that he had to look up a good many words in the dictionary.

When 1920 came, only a few chapters of the *History* were drafted. I still had a good deal of spade work to do in the seventeenth century and in the first half of the eighteenth. The nineteenth was easier, for I had already written upon many of its leading authors. I did not propose to touch the twentieth century at all, as being still too near us for any true historical perspective. But as I worked away, I grew more and more baffled, partly by the lack of first-hand investigation of some periods that are still obscure, and partly because I was not sure that the generalizations which I had been forming so slowly were sound. A mere encyclopaedic record of books and men was not what I wished to produce. Finally, under the stress of college teaching and of other literary tasks that had to be done at once or not at all, I began to postpone the *History* from year to year, until at last I awoke to the fact that I could leave it cheerfully to some younger and stouter scholar. Many of them are coming on. My notes, useless to anyone else, will some day make a big bonfire.

Thus it happened that in 1920 I published a very different book, *A Study of Poetry*, which I needed as a textbook for one of my classes and which was also, like *A Study of Prose Fiction*, aimed at the general reader. It represented more learning and labor than the *Prose Fiction*, but it was not such an immediate success. If anyone in Cambridge, except my own students, read it, I was unaware of the fact. Perhaps it was already out of date in Cambridge, although the letters which came from Oxford, Paris, Munich, and Calcutta were pleasant to receive. I took a year's leave of absence, then, to write *The Life and Letters of Henry L. Higginson*. Major Higginson, a dear friend for twenty years, had died in 1919. He was a noble, whimsical, generous soul, and when his family asked me to prepare a biography, it was a congenial task. Many persons go to Symphony Hall nowadays without even thinking of the founder of the Orchestra, but to those who loved him he remains an unforgettable figure.

The Praise of Folly (1923) borrowed its title from Erasmus, and contained some of my Phi Beta Kappa and Commencement addresses, together with a few biographical and critical studies which I wished to preserve in book form. By 1926 I was able to persuade Emerson's heirs and publishers that a selection of striking passages from the ten volumes of his *Journals* would reach a new public and increase Emerson's fame. Twenty years earlier I had been of some slight assistance to Dr. Edward W. Emerson in his task of editing the original manuscript of the *Journals*, but now, though he lived to see *The Heart of Emerson's Journals* published, his mind had become too clouded to let him understand and enjoy the popular success of this volume. His long and patient labor of love in editing his father's writings was reward enough for that modest and brave gentleman.

This roll-call of books is too long already, but I must add two or three more items. *Pools and Ripples* (1927), a volume of fishing essays, owes its title to my son, who has been my companion upon many lucky and unlucky days, ever since he brought in his first basket of trout at the age of seven. A friend once showed me a letter about *Pools and Ripples* from Lord Grey of Fallodon, in which that statesman and fisherman expressed his special liking for a sentence describing a river in midsummer drought. To be praised by the author of *Fly-Fishing* was reward enough for writing the book. But it amuses me to think of the number of copies of *Pools and Ripples* and *Fishing with a Worm* which I have autographed for fellow anglers who could not be bribed, I fear, to read one of my 'scholarly' volumes. However, as Thackeray once exclaimed, 'One ought to be glad if they like anything!'

The first book I wrote after retiring in 1930 was *Emerson Today*, a little volume of Vanuxem lectures at Princeton, designed to show the present scope and character of Emerson's influence. Then came a solid year of work upon the biography of Richard H. Dana 'the Third' (1851–1931). Like the *Higginson*, this book was commissioned by the family of my friend, much as a family in the Renaissance might commission a portrait for an altar-piece. But I tried to paint the portrait honestly. 'Dick' Dana was not a man of outstanding intellectual endowment, and he lacked the humor and subtlety of Major Higginson. Yet he presented an interesting problem of personal traits inherited from famous ancestors, and he had rendered notable service to many fine causes, especially that of Civil Service Reform. He deserved more recognition than he ever won from his contemporaries, and I wrote his Life knowing it would be read only by a dwindling circle of his surviving friends. And that was my very last book — until this one.

The writing of books! '*Thou carriest them away as with a flood*'; they are like the green and dry leaves on the foaming surface of the Miramichi in high water, rushing down the Burnt Hill Rapids to float for a few hours in the Pond. Everything goes downstream in time, except the work of a few men who 'lie like a rock in the bed of the river' — as someone has said of Mr. Justice Holmes as he went to his grave. But if a man chooses to write books, the least he can do, and all he can do, is to write them as well as he is able. Of all the literary men whom I have known, Gamaliel Bradford had the most passionate concern for recognition, which he called 'glory.' At nineteen, it is true, he wrote in his *Journal*: [1] 'I wish that I could reveal the intense longing which I have to write something great: not for fame, not that the world may praise; but to know — not to dream, or fancy, or hope — but to know that the Spirit of Beauty has laid her finger upon me and consecrated me to her service.' But forty years later, in 1927, he is writing to Miss Alice Brown: [2]

'Pray do search your heart, and search it again, and see if you really mean that you do not care for glory. It is hard for me to believe it, because ever since I first drew the breath of conscious intellectual life to write

[1] *Journal of Gamaliel Bradford* (1933), p. 5.
[2] *Letters of Gamaliel Bradford* (1934), p. 287.

beautiful things and *to be praised for doing so* has been
the supreme thing in the world for me. You say it is
enough to write the beautiful things. But the only possible way that we — or I — can know that they are
beautiful is to have them praised. The greatness of
Shakespeare is the glory of Shakespeare, and for me
nothing less than the glory of Shakespeare would be
enough.

'After which, of course I agree with you that the
millions of individuals who make up glory are perfectly
contemptible, like you and me. This is one of the many
reasons that make life a damnable thing. But it has its
good points.'

Bradford never wrote a more revealing letter. I do not
agree with him that life is 'a damnable thing,' for I have
found it precisely the opposite, though I have never had
to bear the pain, disappointment, and sorrow which he
faced so bravely. And surely, in the letter just quoted,
the woman's argument runs deeper than the man's. 'It
is enough to write the beautiful things.' Then watch
them go downstream with all the others, if one must;
but I suspect that it is wiser just to watch the Miramichi
itself on its sure way to the Atlantic, and to forget about
your own books.

For it is the privilege of the Superannuated to forget,
as well as to remember; to forget old anxieties and errors,
old wrath and suspicion, all the unlucky guesses and
bad investments of money or of time. One may also
forget all Doctoral Dissertations and stupid meetings of
committees on this or that; forget twenty-five years of
climbing Beacon Hill to attend sessions of various Peace

Societies, and twenty-eight years of service as a Trustee of one's Alma Mater: thankless jobs, these last, but like most thankless jobs, well worth doing. But it all passes, like a summer cloud, and any evening, as one rests here by the river, brings its lesson of patience. Perhaps it is raining far up in the mountains, and there will be flood water tomorrow, with salmon beginning to work their way upstream; perhaps the drought will continue for another day or week or month. No one knows, and fortunately no one can do anything about it. Our strength is to sit still. Possibly it is a sign of lessening vitality when you refuse to grow excited over political, social, economic, and educational changes that would once have prompted you to anger and alarm. Yet it may be a sign of a new dispassionate wisdom, of an awareness that things are what they are, and that Nature and human nature will not be hurried. What a passionate political speech I made for Grover Cleveland in that campaign of 1884! How excited I was over Gladstone's fight for Home Rule in Ireland! How sure I was in 1896 that a victory for Bryan would mean financial dishonor! When Wilson succeeded in getting the Panama tolls exemption bill passed, I thought a new day of international good-will was dawning! And now, with vast political changes evident all around the globe, with Washington at the testing-point of our economic stability and perhaps even of the world's peace, with my native State of Massachusetts overrun by aliens and preferring, at the moment, to be governed by venal and unscrupulous politicians, I can nevertheless lay me down to sleep and not even write a protesting letter to the *Boston Evening Transcript*!

My wife, whose instinct in such matters is so often

truer than mine, holds that the World War 'took it out of' our generation, exhausting our capacity for emotional and moral reaction to events. For four years it was a daily succession of knock-down blows, hopes deferred or hopes defeated, and after that long tragedy, how was it possible that faith in the visible progress of humanity could burn as brightly as it did in the days of our youth?

How constantly were we deceived! In that first week of August, 1914, I was camping on Big Greenough Pond, above Errol, New Hampshire. Anxious to get the latest news from Europe, I tramped at dusk three miles through the woods to Errol, and could pick up only one tattered page of a *Boston American*, which announced that Great Britain had entered the War. I climbed back through the darkening woods, thrilled by the conviction that since England had taken its stand for the right, the fighting would be over in a couple of months! I thought then, as even Theodore Roosevelt and my friend William Roscoe Thayer did in those early weeks, that Wilson's policy of strict neutrality was the proper one officially, however impossible neutrality of thought might be. Like most Americans who gave heed to the subject at all, I felt that Germany's invasion of Belgium was a crime against international honor and against humanity, but I could not see, even after the sinking of the *Lusitania* and for all my sympathy with the Allies, that it was the present duty of the United States to take up arms. The 'intellectuals' along the Atlantic seaboard had grown, by 1916, more and more outspoken in their feeling that we ought to 'go in,' but my farmer neighbors in Vermont kept saying: 'It's natural for you people who have lived in Europe to be interested in this War, but we don't know anything about the right and wrong of it.'

The Middle West was equally apathetic. In June, 1916, I had to make Commencement addresses at the Universities of Iowa and Nebraska, and stopped over in Chicago to witness the Republican and Progressive National Conventions. Nowhere west of the Hudson, except from one red-headed Canadian Pullman conductor between Detroit and Chicago, did I hear a single person assert that the United States should enter the War. In Boston most of my friends were highly belligerent, and impatient — to say the very least — with President Wilson. Just before the November election, President Eliot asked the Saturday Club to take a straw vote as between Wilson and Hughes. Of the seventeen members present at that luncheon, only three, including Mr. Eliot, voted for Wilson. (Oddly enough, when a similar straw vote was taken in the campaign of 1928, a strong majority of these same Brahmins voted for 'Al' Smith!)

We were in Washington, as I have said, from February 1917, to June. An obstinate group in the Senate was still blocking the President's proposal to arm our merchant ships, but by March it was apparent, at last, that he could count upon the support of the country. The turning-point came when the 'Zimmermann note' was transmitted to the Senate. My wife and daughters happened to hear it read, but I was over in the Library of Congress that day, trying to keep my attention upon the chapter which I was writing; and I was still writing away, with only half my mind, on the April day when the President read the fateful message which swung the Congress into war.

I had seen nothing of him, except in public, since we
arrived in Washington, and it was strange to think that
an old friend was in the White House, so preoccupied
with his burdens that I could not venture to call upon
him. He secluded himself from many other former intimates whose claims upon his attention were much greater
than mine. We were dining one evening with the Jus-
serands, shortly after the United States had entered the
War. After dinner the Ambassador talked with me for a
long time about his youthful enthusiasm for Browning,
and about a new book on Wordsworth. Carried away by
his ability to forget the War for a few hours, and to turn
for relief to books, I made a foolish suggestion. 'M.
Jusserand, why don't you stroll over to the White House
some evening, and talk Wordsworth with the President?
He is a veteran Wordsworthian, and it would do him
more good, just now, than anything I can think of.'
The Ambassador's face changed, sharply. *He doesn't
want to see any of us,* he remarked; and at that we joined
the ladies. It was true enough, and it was one factor in
the Wilson tragedy. Himself he could not save.

The year and a half of American participation in the
War seems to me now like a bad dream. Our oldest
daughter was married in June, 1917, in Washington, to
a young lawyer in government service, who expected any
day to be transferred to the army. Our son, like most of
his college mates at Williams, was drilling in training
camps, though he was not sent overseas. Mrs. Perry
and our daughter Margaret, who had been working dili-
gently for French and English soldiers ever since 1914,
now threw themselves into Red Cross and canteen activities for our own men; while I, a lifelong pacifist,

was busy with committees for War work, was deep in
Liberty Loan entanglements, taught depleted college
classes in the daytime, and in the evenings harangued
the enlisted men — many of whom could not speak English — in soldiers' and sailors' encampments. Theme:
'The aim of the War'!

And I believed everything I said, both then and at the
Memorial services at Williams and Harvard after the
fighting was over. I really thought that Germany had
left us no option, and that this was 'a war to end war.'
It seems to me now that we, like the other nations, were
caught in the fatal circle of fear, armaments, and then
battle; that we were doing evil in the hope that good
might come; and that our expectation of a world organized
for peace and good-will — as soon as the necessary machinery could be set up — was a gross underestimate of the
latent force of national suspicion and jealousy. As everyone knows, there is now more fear in the world than there
was in 1914, far heavier armaments, and a nationalistic
selfishness more stupid and arrogant than ever. The
truth is that war gets us nowhere and 'preparedness'
gets us nowhere but into war.

I have often quoted, to the applause of audiences,
the definition of civilization once framed by Lord Russell
of Killowen: 'Its true signs are thought for the poor
and suffering, chivalrous regard and respect for women,
the frank recognition of human brotherhood, irrespective
of race or color or nation or religion, the narrowing of the
domain of mere force as a governing factor in the world,
the love of ordered freedom, abhorrence of what is mean
and cruel and vile, ceaseless devotion to the claims of
justice.' If some Senator of the United States were to

quote those eloquent words tomorrow, he too would be applauded, for we are naturally a kindly and emotional people. But five minutes afterward the Senate would proceed to vote against a World Court or a League of Nations, and in favor of a bigger army and navy. There is still a long road ahead of us before we shall be willing to pay the price of civilization by abandoning the dream of an isolated nationalism and by taking our share of co-operation with an organized world. Yet I do not doubt that the road will be travelled in due time.

I saw Wilson but twice after the War was over. He addressed a great public meeting in Boston upon his first return from Paris in 1919. He was in high spirits that day, and made a confident speech about our entering the League. The platform was crowded with politicians who watched him keenly. He was not speaking their language, though he seemed at the moment to compel their assent. The next time I saw him was in his house on S Street in Washington, during Harding's administration and not long before Wilson's death. Physically he was broken. He sat at the right of the fireplace in his library, slumping a little in his chair, and holding a cane. His head, which he had always carried high, was bent, as if he had been bludgeoned. His voice was distinct, but low, slow, and without animation. His mind, however, seemed to me as clear as ever, though not so alert. We talked a little of the old days at Princeton, thirty years before, when we used to discuss Stevenson and Walter Bagehot. He spoke of the Peace Conference, saying that he thought that General Smuts had the best mind of any of the men whom he met in Paris. (Years afterward, when I heard General Smuts say precisely the same thing about Wilson, I could not help telling the South African what Wilson's opinion of him had been.) He asked me about the political situation in Massachusetts, and spoke grimly of Henry Cabot Lodge. No Scotch-Irish Presbyterian ever found it easy to forgive his enemies! And then, with a sudden flash of that indomitable religious faith which lay deeper than anything else in his nature, he assured me that a revival of moral idealism was bound to come to our American people. I took my leave then, fearing to weary him.

Only a little later I had occasion to write thus:[1]

'... If his career ended with his burial, as in some stormy Elizabethan play, it would be fitting to call Woodrow Wilson's life a tragedy. Take up the body and let "the soldiers' music and the rites of war speak loudly for him." But in the case of the true visionary, those trumpets of the sad fifth act and the fall of the tragic curtain are impertinences. Upon idealists such as he the curtain does not fall: the play evolves into the eternal drama that makes up the life of humanity. The illogical, impertinent bullet that pierced Lincoln's brain has now become a portion of his glory. "I meet him at every turn," said Thoreau of John Brown after he was hanged; "He is more alive than ever he was." Those who hated Wilson in his lifetime and those who loved him can agree at least in this: that his ultimate fame will depend upon the triumph of the political ideals which he clothed with fitting words. We make our guesses even now, but fifty years hence we shall begin to know something of the verdict of mankind.'

[1] In a commemorative tribute prepared for a meeting of the American Academy of Arts and Letters, 1924.

It is strange to think now how far away the Wilson epoch seems. I hope this is not due to the lassitude of the Superannuated. It may be the subtle influence of the Pond: the sense of detachment and of shelter which always comes with the shadow of the woods and the sound of falling water. The old agonies are lulled to rest. Instead of making the world safe for democracy, the important thing appears to be the discovery of something that will keep out the rain and let you slumber in peace: a tent, or a few strips of bark, or some hemlock boughs on the floor of an old camp, or simply a hollow in the dry sand under an upturned canoe. 'Warmth, food, sleep, and a book,' says Hazlitt; but I rarely take books into the woods — perhaps a worn pocket Virgil or a Latin version of the *New Testament and Psalms* bought long ago after infinite hunting in the bookshops of Rome. When the fish are rising, I do not read even these. It is enough to have the sense of shelter, beyond the reach of letters, telegrams, telephones, newspapers, and engagement calendars.

And I suppose that even at home I have had, more than most men, what would be considered a sheltered life. There has been no feverish anxiety about money, for there has always been a modest salary and no fear of losing the job; always a roof over our heads; always food and fire and libraries and friends, to say nothing of a household happiness so perfect that I cannot attempt to describe it here. My day's work, for more than half a century, has been with gentlemen. That fierce economic and class struggle which I read about in Marxian books has passed me by. I was brought up to believe that there are no 'classes' in the United States. Up till forty

I thought of myself as a Radical; then, for many years, as a Liberal; and when, the other day, one of my brothers described himself as 'an old-fashioned free trade gold standard Grover Cleveland Democrat,' I told him that I agreed with him, but that both of us were as obsolete as the Great Auk. However, having voted with the minority most of my life, on most questions, I do not mind being obsolete.

Perhaps the many summers passed in the old-fashioned State of Vermont have helped to create this feeling of sheltered permanence, of indifference to the passing show. The long holidays in Europe during a 'sabbatical leave' in 1927–'28, and again in 1933, have contributed something, likewise, to this feeling of detachment. London and Paris and Rome are indifferent to one stranger more. But I think that the sense of permanent human values comes more readily in the countryside than in the cities, and the months spent in Devon, Cornwall, and Sussex, in the French and Swiss Alps, in southern Italy and especially in Sicily, are the best antidote for American impatience. To fish in Ireland on that slow-moving Blackwater which Spenser loved, to saunter through long afternoons in Ashdown Forest dreaming of King Alfred and the Danes, to linger in the ruined temples and theatres of Paestum and Segesta and Taormina, is an elderly kind of happiness, perhaps, but it is surely happiness.

I discover also, in these years of increased leisure, that friendship, and even the memory of ancient friendships long since sealed by death, is a more significant part of the pattern than it once seemed. In the earlier period I naturally made friends more swiftly than now, but was

AN IRISH SALMON (1933)

too preoccupied by bread-winning to realize their full value. *Si jeunesse savait!* There is no excuse for a teacher who fails to keep his friendships in repair, for he has a better chance than most men both to make friends and to hold them. The ladies of my family sometimes rebuke me for neglecting academic persons and cultivating the conversation of brakemen, plumbers, carpenters, and especially those seductive souls described by a seventeenth-century Puritan as 'common fowlers, tobacco-takers, and other persons who can give no good account of how they spend their time.' The trouble is that I know more or less what the professors are going to say, while the other fellows are always taking me by surprise. The brakeman has been known to quote Gray's *Elegy*, and Walt Whitman was not the only carpenter who knew his Emerson. My Italian barber in Cambridge opens the drawer where he keeps his old razors, pulls out a canto of Dante translated by his brother, a priest in Philadelphia, and flatters me by asking my opinion of the translation. The assistant barber comes from Sorrento, Tasso's birthplace, and confides to me the dreadful news that he met in East Boston last Sunday a fellow Italian 'who never *heard* of Torquato Tasso! Think of *that*, Professor!' Why should I, with such privileges as these, have to depend upon my colleagues for literary conversation? Some of the colleagues talk well, too, but one may admire a man's learning without liking the man himself, and one may love many a person who has no book-learning at all.

'Sir, it is a great thing to dine with the Canons of Christ Church.' I have no doubt of it, but I wish that I could have introduced the mighty Doctor Johnson at one of the monthly dinners of 'The Club'[1] — so called because its members could never during sixty-six years agree upon any other name — and let him try his hand at brow-beating such seasoned disputants as Moorfield Storey, William James, Henry L. Higginson, Thomas Sergeant ('Tom') Perry, James Ford Rhodes, George F. Moore, and John T. Morse, Jr., who sat at the head of the table. We had a live Earl, also — something that would have pleased Johnson hugely, although our Earl was a Scot — George Duncan, Earl of Camperdown. He came into his title late in life, and it was delicious to hear the head waiter of the Algonquin Club, where we dined, change his habitual announcement of 'Mr. Duncan's carriage' into 'Your Lordship's carriage is waiting.'

By the time I joined The Club, Francis Parkman and John Fiske were dead, Henry Adams and Justice Holmes were living in Washington, Howells in New York and Henry James in London. But to represent science we had three doctors — Sturgis Bigelow, Henry P. Walcott, and Harvey Cushing — Theodore Richards the chemist and Raphael Pumpelly the explorer. John C. Gray and Storey and Morse knew law; Rhodes was writing his great *History of the United States*; and George F. Moore and 'Tom' Perry, our two most erudite members, could talk about anything — the latter's acquaintance with contemporary European literature, including Russian, being nothing less than amazing. Many of these men were also members of the Tavern and Saturday Clubs, but the circle of The Club was, in a way, even more intimate, and as

[1] Pleasant references to this Club, with a list of members, will be found in J. T. Morse, Jr.'s, *Thomas Sergeant Perry: A Memoir* (1929). See also *Letters of Thomas Sergeant Perry* (1929), selected by Edwin Arlington Robinson, and M. A. DeW. Howe's *Portrait of an Independent: Moorfield Storey* (1932).

there were rarely more than eight present at any dinner, we had 'general conversation' at its very best. No one seemed to want more members, and when the roll had become depleted by death, in 1928, The Club went out of existence. Mr. Morse, Dr. Harvey Cushing, and I are now the only survivors. But in such groups as The Club, the Saturday and Tavern Clubs, death does not really count. It is the young fellows who seem transient; the names marked with an asterisk are alive forever in one's memory.

There was one marked difference between these Boston and Cambridge men and the earlier friendships made in Williamstown and Princeton, some of which have happily lasted to this hour. The circle at The Club, for instance, was far more sophisticated. With but two exceptions they were all much older than myself, and during the years of the World War and for ten years thereafter they betrayed a mood of disillusion and despair. The world they had known, in America and Europe, was crumbling month by month, and they could not reconcile themselves to the new conditions. The published *Letters* of 'Tom' Perry are charming, like his talk, in their surface play of wit and humor, but if he ever discovered any real hope for mankind he failed to mention it. For a dozen years I was the only supporter of Wilson in The Club, and though no group could have been more courteous in refraining from direct comment upon my eccentric political opinions, I often felt ill at ease — much as a Jeffersonian must have felt, a century earlier, if admitted by accident into a group of Boston Federalists. I realized, rather late in the day, how idealistic and hopeful had been the talk of the groups of friends at Williamstown and Princeton, in my twenties and thirties, compared with the worldly-wise and often cynical tone of the Brahmins.

I saw more of Higginson and Rhodes (who was only an imported Bostonian) than any of the others. The dinners given by Mr. and Mrs. Rhodes when they were living on Beacon Street were, my wife and I thought, quite the most agreeable dinners to which we were invited. Sometimes there were lions there. I shall never forget Henry James the novelist explaining to John Morley how he strayed off the road when visiting his brother William in Chocorua: 'I had been *lost* had not a peasant emerged from the wood with a bundle of faggots upon his shoulder, and directed me to the Post.' (I am no Boswell, but I did write that sentence down!) Mr. Morley expressed his grave sympathy; evidently the novelist had had a very narrow escape.

This mention of Chocorua reminds me, perhaps illogically, of a predicament of William James, not in the woods, but in a place far more terrifying to a man of his temperament, a Banquet of the Universal Peace Congress in Boston. We were assigned seats together, as each of us had promised to make an after-dinner speech. 'There's Booker Washington!' exclaimed James as we took our places: 'let's get him over here with us.' But alas, Booker Washington was already placed at the high table with the foreign delegates. I have seen many men nervous at the prospect of making a speech, and I have been scared myself, but never so badly as William James on that occasion. 'What shall I do?' he whispered to me. 'I cannot remember one word of my address, and yet yesterday in Chocorua I recited it eleven times to my wife without a mistake!' 'Have you the manuscript?' I asked; and he pulled out of his pocket the sheets of yellow scribbling paper on which he had written every word in long hand. His fingers shook so that all the sheets dropped upon the floor. I picked them up, arranged them, and commanded him to read them when his turn came: the audience would be interested in his ideas, not in his capacity as a memorizer. Finally he pulled himself together and read beautifully the little address which was later printed in the *Atlantic* and in his *Memories and Studies*.

I never heard William James talk so brilliantly, however, as he did late one night when we had come out to Cambridge together, after a dinner of The Club. He had sat in one of his silent moods all through the dinner, and had scarcely spoken in the trolley-car. But as I was bidding him good-night in front of the Harvard 'Coop,' something turned on the current in that power-house of his brain. He began to characterize two of his colleagues, Münsterberg and Santayana. I do not know how long he talked, but he had all the time there was, and he painted such full-length portraits of those two philosophers as will never be painted again. Only once in my life, and that was in a monologue by another philosopher, Bergson, on the ultimate goal of Evolution — addressed to an astounded luncheon-table in Washington during the War — have I listened to such miraculous mastery of phrase.

More and more, during the post-War years and especially since my retirement, I have turned to books for reinforcement of my youthful faith in progress. The most durable foundations for hope for a better future for humanity seem to me to be found in history, literature,

and religion. I should of course add 'science' if I thought
that I had a really scientific mind. I read, like everyone
else, about the new physics, the new chemistry, the new
astronomy, but this reading does not transform the
world for me, as it does for many of my friends. When
my class at Williams held its fiftieth reunion in 1931, all
the other men, representing various professions, proclaimed their wonder and satisfaction in the advance of
the world since our graduation, particularly in the application of scientific discoveries to the conveniences and
comforts of life. There was the usual glorification of tele-
phone and radio and motor car and airplane and all that;
and even the stock market, just then, seemed to be picking up a little. I did not dissent openly, but I felt singularly isolated. I was almost the only representative of
literature at the table, and what competent critic would
assert that the literature produced in America, England,
and France during the previous half-century, has rivalled,
either in sheer power or in beauty, the books produced
during the fifty years between 1831 and 1881? I had
read, presumably, more contemporary prose and verse
than any of my classmates, since it was my professional
business to do so. I had no quarrel with the preceding
half-century except this: that in the one kind of activity
in which I was professionally interested, it had failed to
keep pace with the material advance which my classmates were celebrating. Literature's turn may come
again, of course. Some unknown American author may
publish tomorrow as good a book as *Moby Dick*, *The
Scarlet Letter*, Emerson's *Essays*, *Walden*, *Leaves of Grass*,
or *Huckleberry Finn*; but I have been waiting a long time
for it.

It may be that this preference for old books rather than new ones is one more sign of Superannuation. I am not wholly ignorant of the books of 1934 and 1935, but I am too near the Pond, perhaps, with its whisper of Timelessness. I gave the better part of ten years, once, to the discovery of 'timely' articles, and those articles sleep now in forgotten volumes of the *Atlantic*, while the pages of Burke, Wordsworth, Lincoln, and Emerson enchant me as they did sixty years ago. *Job* and *Don Quixote* and *Faust* are more timeless pages still. There are writers, it is true, who once tumbled the world upside down for me — Marlowe, Browning, Whitman, Tolstoi — whom I can no longer read with quite the same youthful transport. I could extend this list by adding the names of Victor Hugo, Balzac, Ruskin, Heine, Ibsen, and Rousseau. But in those evenings when I am too weary or too bored to read anything else — except perhaps a new detective story — I still find a serene refuge in Boswell's *Johnson*, Lockhart's *Scott*, Voltaire's prose, Byron's *Don Juan*, John Wesley's *Journal*, the *Letters* of Horace Walpole and the *Journal* of Thoreau.

I think I should never be bored on a desert island, and I have not cared much for lists of 'desert island books.' If I were to make a choice, however, I fear it would be Reactionary. Omitting books by living authors, I should certainly begin with the most fascinating book, or rather, library of books, ever put between covers: the Bible. I have read it in many translations, in many languages, but I vote — this time with the majority — for the English version of 1611. I should wish to take Plato's *Dialogues* and the *Antigone* and the *Prometheus*. There ought to be a *Divine Comedy* for certain moods, and a *Paradise Lost* when I was hungry for orchestral music; *Hamlet* and *Antony and Cleopatra* and a half-dozen other plays and a dozen sonnets by the same hand. I should take Chaucer if I could forget that I had ever been a professor obliged to reckon with 'sources' and 'influences' and etymologies. I should certainly want Swift and Fielding and Carlyle — though not all of any of them. I should pick Thackeray rather than Dickens, though the sense of Dickens's genius grows upon me year by year; Turgenev rather than Tolstoi, and George Borrow rather than the adorable Jane Austen. It would also be Wordsworth and Coleridge rather than Keats and Shelley — but why not take all four? There must be room for Hazlitt and Lamb and Montaigne and the *Colloquies* of Erasmus. And I would throw something else out to make place for *Barchester Towers*, *The Return of the Native*, and *The Testament of Beauty*.

Yet I suspect that I am not really a desert island man. I am childishly fond of escapes into the unbroken forest, where one can lie beside untravelled streams, and watch the water and meditate upon transiency and permanence. But I come back in a few weeks to the fireside; to wife and children, to the world of books and friendships and the small tasks that still remain to be done. 'A man's life is his whole life, and not the last glimmering snuff of the candle.' In these chapters which I am now concluding, I am aware that I have not portrayed a whole life, but only such aspects of a teacher's career as may conceivably prove interesting. I have said almost nothing about that transcendent relationship which we call 'religion,' for I think that religion is something to be lived and not to be talked about, except by the very few who are capable of making real the things that are invisible. If I had not been born a New England Congregationalist, in a family singularly indifferent to dogma, I would have preferred to be born into the Society of Friends; but I have worshipped in many widely differing churches, and am sure that men and women can worship without any 'steeple-house' — as George Fox called it — in spirit and in truth.

But into all that I will not enter now, nor into that other sanctuary which Dean Inge, with true English reticence, calls 'domestic happiness.' I think he will let me quote from his last book, *Vale*:

'What are the most precious gifts for which an old man, looking back on his life, ought to thank God? The Greeks put *health* first. I have never had a day's serious illness in my life.... But I have known so many men and women who have triumphantly overcome this handicap, that I could not rank health as the best thing in life. Some kind of recognition and encouragement is, I think, almost essential to happiness, except for a few proud or heroic natures. I have certainly had nothing to complain of under this head. But I have not the slightest doubt that domestic happiness is the greatest of all good gifts, next to that of "wisdom," for which Solomon prayed, and which, I suppose, may be defined as a right judgment of the relative value of things. The blessings which God has given me in my wife and children are in a different class from all other sources of happiness and pleasure that have come to me. At a time when many persons are not ashamed to assert that marriage is generally a failure, it is permissible to give this personal testimony.'

I am dedicating this book to my sister, in token of a

mutual affection which has been unbroken for nearly three-quarters of a century. She and my brothers, together with my wife and children, have urged me to write it, but only my wife will be able to read all that is written between the lines.

THE END

INDEX

INDEX

Academic freedom, 255

Actress, a Jewish, 93, 94

Adams, Brooks, 177

Adams, Charles Francis (the second), 158

Adams, John Quincy, 253

Æschylus, his *Prometheus Bound*, 293

Agassiz, Alexander, 233

Agassiz, Louis, 223, 270

'Alciphron,' 184

Alcott, A. Bronson, his Temple School, 231; his *Conversations with Children on the Gospels*, 231

Alden, Henry M., 141, 173; his *God in His World*, 141

Aldrich, Thomas Bailey, 68, 109, 158, 230, 254; office calls from, 168, 169; as editor of the *Atlantic*, 169; entertaining, 173; his last poem and his death, 196

Alexander, Francesca, 193

Alexander, Mrs. John, 193

Algonquin Club, 288

Allen, Rev. Dr. Alexander V. G., 166

Allen, Francis H., 186

Alsace and Lorraine, 104

Amadon, A. F., 71

American abroad, an intelligent, 110, 111

American Academy of Arts and Letters, 220, 272, 284 n.

American people, idealism of, 269

American thought and literature, European influence on, 210

Ames's stage, 28

Anderson, Mary, 78

Andover controversy, the, 62, 63

Andover Hill, 75

Andover Review, The, 76, 120

Andover Theological Seminary, 75

Angellier, Auguste, 88, 203, 204, 216; on Lanson, 216

Anglo-Saxon, studying, 82, 83, 95, 108; teaching, 119, 128

Antwerp, 106

Arles, 216

Armour, George, 154

Arms, W. D., 103, 106

Arnold, Matthew, 78, 79, 123

Ashfield, Mass., 86, 121

Athenæum, The, the Williams College journal, 58

Atkinson, Edward, 230

Atlantic Monthly, The, B. P.'s early contributions to, 109; the editorship of, 161–98; editorial policy as to controversial matter, 170, 171; rates of payment for contributions, 180; its fiftieth anniversary, 196, 197; its Diamond Jubilee in 1932, 197; taken over by the Atlantic Monthly Company, 197

Austen, Jane, 294

Austin, Mary H., 176; her *Isidro*, 175

Author's Club of New York, 140–42

Aviation, a speech on, 207

Avignon, 216

Avocation, struggle with Vocation, 266, 267

Babbitt, Prof. Irving, 253; at times intolerant, 55, 56

Bacon, Robert, 204, 218

Baden, Crown Prince of, 93

Pagehot, Walter, 156

Baker, Prof. George P., 135, 200, 204, 243

Baldensperger, F., 212, 214

Baldwin, Elbert, 82

Ballou, Aaron, 15

196, 223; conversations with, 224, 225; Robert Grant on, 224; on Theodore Roosevelt, 224; and the Saturday Club, 232

Noyes, A. D., 179

O'Connor, William Douglas, 189
Ogden, Rollo, his 'Letters to Literary Statesmen,' 184, 185
Olney, Richard, 158; and the Venezuela message, 146
Orange, 216
Ossian, 53

Packard, Prof. William A., 160
Page, Walter H., 172, 175, 179, 197; an aphorism of, 115; as editor of the *Atlantic*, 161, 164, 165, 167, 169, 170; founds *The World's Work* and joins F. N. Doubleday in Doubleday, Page & Co., 167; becomes Ambassador to Great Britain, 167; and *David Harum*, 168; his *Autobiography of a Southerner since the Civil War*, 175, 176; on literary criticism, 177, 178; as an expansionist, 182; his paper on 'The Writer and the University,' 196; his *Life and Letters*, 197 n.
Palmer, Prof. George H., 223
Paris, 107, 108; living and lecturing in, 202–18
Parker, William Belmont, 168, 174
Parkman, Francis, 271
Parsons, 'Turk,' 63
Pasteur, Louis, 206, 213
Patti, Adelina, 78
Patton, Pres. Francis L., 46, 123, 129, 143, 167; at faculty meetings, 130
Peabody, Elizabeth P., her *Record of a School*, 231
Peace movement, B. P.'s interest in, 183, 281–83
Pearl, The, 112
Peary, Robert E., 219
Pennland, S.S., 89, 90
Perkins, Rev. John C., 90, 93

Perry, Annie L. (Bliss), wife, 115–17, 166, 192, 193, 214, 215, 281, 296; collecting Harvard stories, 229; on the World War, 278, 279
Perry, Arthur, brother, 9, 16, 21, 29, 35, 42, 71, 74, 86, 117, 132
Perry, Arthur Latham, father, 3, 4, 8–10, 12–16, 20, 29, 31–34, 60, 63, 71, 72, 74, 75, 84, 85, 91, 120, 123, 132, 141; his son Carroll's picture of, 33, 188; and grammar, 41, 42; on college fraternities, 47, 48; as a teacher, 53–56; on Mark Hopkins, 61; on classroom discipline, 74; relations with President Carter, 80; on debt, 115; a conservative outvoted in the faculty, 117, 118; his *Principles of Political Economy, Origins in Williamstown*, and *Williamstown and Williams College*, 118, 152; his power of offhand phrase, 118; ill health and resignation of professorship, 121; old age and death, 188; eulogies, 188
Perry, Baxter, grandfather, 3, 4, 12, 75, 222
Perry, Baxter, uncle, 17
Perry, Bliss, ancestry, 3–8; parentage, 8, 9; birth, 9; childhood, 10–27; at school in Greylock Institute, 28–35; editing and writing for the school paper, 34; Williams College undergraduate, 35–69; editing the college paper *The Athenaeum*, 58; reading, 58–60; delivers two orations and reads the Class Poem at Commencement in 1881, 67–69; early travels, 70, 71; Instructor in Elocution and English at Williams, 72–78; studies public speaking under Prof. J. W. Churchill at Andover, 75–79; first visits to Boston (theaters and music) and Cambridge, 77–79; studies Anglo-Saxon, Gothic, and Old and Middle High German, 82, 83; recreations, tramping, and fishing, 84–86; gives public lectures on Browning, 86;